Early Language Learning in Context

EARLY LANGUAGE LEARNING IN SCHOOL CONTEXTS

Series Editor: **Janet Enever**, *Umeå University, Sweden*

The early learning of languages in instructed contexts has become an increasingly common global phenomenon during the past 30 years, yet there remains much work to be done to establish the field as a distinctive area for interdisciplinary investigation. This international research series covers children learning second, foreign and additional languages in educational contexts between the ages of approximately 3 and 12 years. The series will take a global perspective and encourage the sharing of theoretical discussion and empirical evidence on transnational issues. It will provide a platform to address questions raised by teachers, teacher educators and policy makers who are seeking understanding of theoretical issues and empirical evidence with which to underpin policy development, implementation and classroom procedures for this young age group. Themes of particular interest for the series include: teacher models and teacher development, models of early language learning, policy implementation, motivation, approaches to teaching and learning, language progress and outcomes, assessment, intercultural learning, sustainability in provision, comparative and transnational perspectives, cross-phase transfer issues, curriculum integration – additional suggestions for themes are also most welcome.

All books in this series are externally peer-reviewed.

Full details of all the books in this series and of all our other publications can be found on http://www.multilingual-matters.com, or by writing to Multilingual Matters, St Nicholas House, 31–34 High Street, Bristol, BS1 2AW, UK.

EARLY LANGUAGE LEARNING IN SCHOOL CONTEXTS: 7

Early Language Learning in Context

A Critical Socioeducational Perspective

David Hayes

MULTILINGUAL MATTERS
Bristol • Jackson

DOI https://doi.org/10.21832/HAYES5843
Library of Congress Cataloging in Publication Data
A catalog record for this book is available from the Library of Congress.
Names: Hayes, David, author.
Title: Early Language Learning in Context: A Critical Socioeducational
   Perspective/David Hayes.
Description: Jackson [Tennessee]: Multilingual Matters, [2022] |
   Series: Early Language Learning in School Contexts: 7 | Includes bibliographical
   references and index. | Summary: "This book critically analyzes early
   school foreign language teaching policy and practice across six
   geographical contexts. Criticizing the worldwide trend for a focus on
   English, it argues for a broader perspective that values multilingualism
   and knowledge of regional and indigenous languages alongside a more
   diverse range of foreign languages"—Provided by publisher.
Identifiers: LCCN 2022016331 (print) | LCCN 2022016332 (ebook) |
   ISBN 9781800415843 (hardback) | ISBN 9781800415836 (paperback) |
   ISBN 9781800415850 (pdf) | ISBN 9781800415867 (epub)
Subjects: LCSH: Native language and education. | Language and
   languages—Study and teaching. | English language—Study and
   teaching—Foreign speakers.
Classification: LCC LC201.5 .H39 2022 (print) | LCC LC201.5 (ebook) |
   DDC 370.117/5—dc23/eng/20220609
LC record available at https://lccn.loc.gov/2022016331
LC ebook record available at https://lccn.loc.gov/2022016332

British Library Cataloguing in Publication Data
A catalogue entry for this book is available from the British Library.

ISBN-13: 978-1-80041-584-3 (hbk)
ISBN-13: 978-1-80041-583-6 (pbk)

Multilingual Matters
UK: St Nicholas House, 31–34 High Street, Bristol, BS1 2AW, UK.
USA: Ingram, Jackson, TN, USA.

Website: www.multilingual-matters.com
Twitter: Multi_Ling_Mat
Facebook: https://www.facebook.com/multilingualmatters
Blog: www.channelviewpublications.wordpress.com

Copyright © 2022 David Hayes.

All rights reserved. No part of this work may be reproduced in any form or by any means without permission in writing from the publisher.

The policy of Multilingual Matters/Channel View Publications is to use papers that are natural, renewable and recyclable products, made from wood grown in sustainable forests. In the manufacturing process of our books, and to further support our policy, preference is given to printers that have FSC and PEFC Chain of Custody certification. The FSC and/or PEFC logos will appear on those books where full certification has been granted to the printer concerned.

Typeset by Nova Techset Private Limited, Bengaluru and Chennai, India.
Printed and bound in the UK by the CPI Books Group Ltd.

For

Toye Chanpen Hayes

with endless gratitude for her love, patience and understanding

สำหรับ
ต้อย จันทร์เพ็ญ เฮย์ส
ขอบคุณเหลือเกิน สำหรับความรัก ความอดทน และความเข้าใจ
ที่เธอมีให้ตลอดเวลา

Contents

Acknowledgements		xi
1	Rationales for Early Language Learning in State Sector Education Systems	1
	Introduction	1
	The Value of Learning Additional Languages in Primary Schools (and Beyond)	2
	Policy Rationales for Prioritising Learning English in Primary Schools	3
	The Impact of Learning English on Children in School	15
	(English) Language Learning in Primary Schools in State Educational Systems	17
2	Thailand: An Educational Paradox	22
	Introduction	22
	The Thai Context: Languages, National Economic Development and the Quality of the Education System	24
	Basic Education in Thailand, the Curriculum and the Place of Foreign Languages	30
	In the Classroom	34
	Teachers' Subject Knowledge: English Language Levels	38
	Teachers, Curriculum and Training	40
	Reflections: Resolving the Educational Paradox in English Language Teaching and Learning in Thai Primary Schools	42
3	South Korea: A Severe Case of 'English Fever'	44
	Introduction	44
	Languages, the Economy and Education	46
	Teaching, the Curriculum and English	48
	Initial Teacher Training, Homeroom Teachers and English Specialists in Schools	54
	'Native Speaker' Teacher Programmes	57
	Private Tuition and its Impact	59
	Social Stratification in Korea, Education and English	62

Reflections: Future Directions for English Language Teaching and Learning in South Korean Primary Schools ... 63

4 Sri Lanka: Language Education and Peace-Building in Primary Schools ... 67
   Introduction ... 67
   The Sociopolitical Framework for Primary School Language Education in Sri Lanka ... 69
   Language Education and 'Positive Peace' ... 72
   The Education System ... 74
   Second National Language Learning and Interethnic Attitudes in the Primary School ... 78
   The Status, Teaching and Learning of English, the 'Link' Language ... 80
   Reflections: Languages in Primary Schools and Social Cohesion ... 88

5 Equity and Multilingual Diversity in Primary School Language Teaching and Learning in Malaysia ... 91
   Introduction ... 91
   The Linguistic Landscape of Malaysia, National Language Policies and Educational Language Policies ... 92
   The Primary Curriculum and the Teaching of English ... 98
   Curriculum Change, Teachers and Context ... 100
   Teacher's English Language Proficiency, Pedagogical Skills and Continuing Professional Development (CPD) ... 103
   CPD and the Implementation of KBSR and KSSR ... 107
   Reflections: Socioeconomic Disparities in English Language Learning, Vernacular Language Endangerment and Multilingualism ... 109

6 Early Language Teaching and Learning in Ontario, Canada and Finland: Experiences of Bilingualism and Multilingualism ... 113
   Introduction ... 113
   Canada: Languages, Language Policies and Language Practices ... 114
   Elementary Schooling, Languages and Language Education Policy in Ontario ... 118
   Multilingualism, Language Diversity and FSL ... 123
   Finland: Languages, Language Policies and Languages in Education ... 125
   Finnish Education and International Comparisons ... 127
   English and Foreign Language Diversity in Basic Education ... 132
   The Ecology of Schooling in Finland ... 135

	Reflections: Contrasting Experiences of Bilingualism and Multilingualism	137
7	Rethinking Early Language Learning in State Sector Education Systems	141
	Early Language Learning, Education and United Nations Goals	141
	Revisiting the Economic Rationale: Languages, National Economies and Education	143
	Revisiting Issues of Curriculum, Policy and Practice	152
	Educational Ecosystems and Early Language Learning	161
	Concluding Thoughts	163
	References	165
	Index	185

Acknowledgements

It has been a great pleasure to work with the team at Multilingual Matters on this book, all of whom are models of professionalism and support. I feel, however, that I should single out for special thanks Janet Enever, the series editor, who helped to sustain my motivation over the time it took to get the manuscript completed and who offered consistently helpful feedback; also Laura Longworth who was understanding and encouraging in equal measure as the book was being written; and Rosie McEwan who efficiently shepherded the manuscript to its final form. I would also like to thank the external reviewer for insightful comments and suggestions to improve the manuscript. Last, but very far from least, I owe a considerable debt of gratitude to the numerous colleagues in the schools, colleges, universities and Ministries of Education in all the countries in which I have worked over the years and from whom I have learnt – and continue to learn – so much.

The author and publisher are grateful to the following for permission to reproduce copyright material: John Benjamins Publishing Company Amsterdam/Philadelphia for Table 2.3 from page 248 of 'Language education policy and practice in state education systems: Promoting effective practice in foreign language education for young learners' by David Hayes, in *Language Teaching for Young Learners* 2 (2), 2020, https://doi.org.10.1075/lytl/19017.hay; the Commissioner General, Educational Publications Department, Ministry of Education, Sri Lanka for Figure 4.1 from page 81 of *Let's Learn English, Pupil's Book, Grade 3*; the Finnish Education Evaluation Centre for Figure 6.2 from page 22 of *Outcomes of Language Learning at the End of Basic Education in 2013* by R. Hildén, M. Härmälä, J. Rautopuro, M. Huhtanen, M. Puukko and C. Silverström. Every reasonable effort has been made to locate, contact and acknowledge copyright owners. Any errors will be rectified in future editions.

1 Rationales for Early Language Learning in State Sector Education Systems

Introduction

This book is concerned with early foreign language teaching and learning in state sector education systems in four Asian countries – Thailand, Sri Lanka, South Korea and Malaysia – with which I have had extended experience at various times in my professional career. By 'early' I mean in the primary school grades, although the discussion may at times extend into lower secondary grades in some contexts to cover the entirety of 'basic education'. The age range is, then, from five or six to 13 or 14 years. The language in focus is primarily English, as this is the first choice of foreign language in these countries and, increasingly, in other education systems throughout the world. In one of the countries, Sri Lanka, as well as English I also explore the teaching and learning of the second national language, Sinhala, for students in Tamil-medium schools and Tamil for students in Sinhala-medium schools, which is central to Sri Lanka's vision of a trilingual nation and 'social harmony' following the end of a 26-year civil war in 2009. To provide a comparison with the experience of teaching and learning English in the four Asian countries, I also examine the teaching and learning of a foreign language in another geographical area, the Canadian province of Ontario, where I currently work. The language here is what is known as 'core' French, that is, French as a school subject rather than French as a medium of instruction in immersion programmes. In addition, in the same chapter, I also review early language learning in Finland, which appears to be successful in developing more widespread and higher levels of competence in English, attempting to identify factors within and beyond the educational system that contribute to this success. In all cases, I contend that reflection on contextual factors that support successful school language learning is a necessity for educational policymakers before they attempt to transfer policies and practices from what they believe to be a 'more successful' or 'higher achieving' system in one country to their own. The book concludes by arguing for a reimagining of early language learning in state sector education systems. The current predominant focus worldwide is on learning English for instrumental purposes, but I would argue that there is a case for a greater focus on a diverse range of languages as well as on learning languages for intercultural understanding. Whatever the goals of early language learning, it is also important to consider whether there is equitable provision of language learning opportunities in particular contexts or whether opportunities for high-quality language education are restricted to higher socio-economic groups. Unless there is equitable provision, I contend that the possibility that language learning, particularly of English, will ever contribute to economic and social advancement for most children later in their lives, as policymakers so often claim, is chimerical.

The Value of Learning Additional Languages in Primary Schools (and Beyond)

As a language teacher educator, I take as a starting point that – all other things being equal – learning additional languages in primary school (and beyond) can be of great benefit to students. The advantages of knowing more than one language have been documented in many spheres. For students who become bilingual, bilinguals 'outperform monolinguals on the combined measures of metalinguistic and metacognitive awareness [...] and on measures of abstract and symbolic representation, attentional control, and problem solving' (Adesope *et al.*, 2010: 229). Also, although this is obviously not of immediate concern to school children, bilinguals tend to earn more than their monolingual counterparts, 'Even after controlling for cognitive ability, educational attainment and parental socio-economic status' (Agirdag, 2014: 449). Later in life, bilingualism may even help delay the onset of dementia (Alladi *et al.*, 2013). Even if bilingualism is not the goal, research indicates that learning a foreign language as a subject in primary school can have a positive impact on educational achievement generally. For example, an American study (Taylor & Lafayette, 2010) comparing Grade 4 students learning a foreign language (FL) with those who were not, showed that 'FL students significantly outperformed their non-FL peers on every test (English language arts, mathematics, science, and social studies) of the Grade 4 LEAP [Louisiana Educational Assessment Program]' (Taylor & Lafayette, 2010: 40). In addition to all of these benefits, learning another language at any age provides an opportunity to explore other cultures and through this to better understand one's own. In this connection, the development of intercultural competence for students 'to acquire and use [...] in their relationships with others in their immediate community, in their national community, or at the international level' (Byram & Wagner, 2018: 147) is regarded as increasingly important in a 'globalised' world and can be promoted to varying degrees in all types of educational programmes, whether the language is the medium of instruction in an immersion programme or taught as a school subject.

Of course, 'all other things being equal' implies that there are a number of factors that influence whether the teaching and learning of languages in primary schools does provide the benefits that research has shown have been achieved in some contexts. These factors encompass the availability of appropriately trained teachers of the language for primary schools (including teachers' own language proficiency), the resources available to support learning and the place of the language in the environment beyond the school, all of which I shall discuss in later chapters. Other non-school variables may be important too. Bialystok (2018) noted in her review of bilingual programmes for young children in American contexts that insufficient attention has been paid to the impact of variables such as 'home literacy, parental education, children's levels of language proficiency, ability of parents to support children's education in that language, and numerous other factors' (Bialystok, 2018: 676). Butler (2015: 329) also identified these variables as an 'emergent topic in research in East Asia', and noted that parents' interest in their children learning English meant that 'the means by which children learn English and the outcomes they achieve largely depend on their parents' SES [socioeconomic status] or class'. There is, then, a danger that the learning of English as a foreign language in particular in primary schools becomes another way in which the children of higher SES gain a competitive advantage in schooling over those of lower SES. Or, to put it another way, given that education is a form of social capital, an important question that needs to be asked is whether the focus on English in primary schools in so many countries is simply 'another obstacle to educational achievement for the world's poor' (Hayes, 2011: 337).

Policy Rationales for Prioritising Learning English in Primary Schools

As the arguments about the value of learning another language in school are not contingent on a particular language being chosen for the curriculum, it is also important to understand why governments around the world have placed so much emphasis on school children learning English rather than other languages. And, even if the need for English is accepted, a related question is: why do policymakers believe it is necessary to begin learning English in primary schools rather than at other stages of schooling? Answers to these questions may be found in official discourse in many countries which centres on the economic value of learning English to the country as a whole, as well as to individuals, and which is associated with an 'earlier is better' rationale for introducing it in primary schools. Increasingly, English is taught in schools from Grade 1 and there is a growing trend to introduce English-medium education too, yet the general educational value of

4 Early Language Learning in Context

language learning is rarely mentioned, let alone the benefits of becoming bilingual. I will examine the economic and 'the younger the better' rationales in turn before exploring other reasons for the spread of English as the first foreign language in education systems worldwide.

The economic rationale

Illustrating the economic rationale, some years ago the then President of South Korea, Myung-Bak Lee, claimed that 'English ability is the competitive power of individuals and states' (Lee *et al.*, 2010: 337), which was clearly associated with 'a belief that English proficiency would strengthen South Korea's international competitiveness' (Lee *et al.*, 2010: 339). This type of economic argument has become widespread. In Malaysia, a leading businessman asserted that a 'Good grasp of English among the Malaysian populace will definitely be the X-factor that improves the country's competitiveness as we can communicate with the rest of the world easily' (Kana, 2017), and a newspaper article began, 'A strong command of English enhances employability. It's a fact the Education Ministry knows only too well' (Lee, 2019). In Thailand, the need for Thais to improve their English skills in order to compete with their Association of South-East Asian Nations (ASEAN) neighbours features regularly in the English-language press: 'Thais' poor English to hurt job prospects in Asean community', as a *Bangkok Post* headline put it (Thanthong-Knight, 2015). There appears to be a clear connection in the minds of policymakers between economic competitiveness in a globalised world and the ability of a nation's citizens to communicate in English, although direct evidence to support this connection is noticeably absent from public discourse. Proficiency in other languages for economic competitiveness does not appear to be an issue of concern, even if a country's trading partners are not all English speaking.

National economic development and proficiency in English

If the connection between English and economic competitiveness has a grounding in economic reality rather than just the beliefs of policymakers, one would then expect close links between indices of national economic development and measures of English proficiency. This does not, however, appear to be the case. Arcand and Grin's (2013: 262) econometric analysis found that 'widespread competence in a dominant language such as English is in no manner associated with a higher level of economic development, when the latter is measured by its most common incarnation of GDP per capita'. Taking Korea as an example, official statistics reveal a healthy growth rate as measured by increases in GDP over a considerable period of time, averaging 7.35% from 1961 until 2019.[1] On the 2018 statistical update of the 2017 UN Human Development Index (HDI), which ranks the quality of life for a country's citizens based on life expectancy, education and per capita income, South Korea scored 0.903 (out of 1.00), among the highest in the world. South Korea's HDI score 'put the country in the very high human development category – positioning it at 22 out of 189 countries and territories' (UNDP, 2018: 2), and has been increasing consistently from 1990 to 2017.

Meanwhile, Korea's position on international English-language proficiency scales such as the English First 'English Proficiency Index' (EPI) has remained in the 'moderate proficiency' band since the inception of the scale in 2011, with a score that changes little from year to year. In the 2020 rankings, Korea was placed 32nd out of 100 countries (EF, 2020). It is easy to dismiss these rankings on methodological grounds – most obviously, the sample is self-selected rather than representative and there is no information on its demographic make-up – but their publication routinely prompts soul searching in national media about the country's English language standards, particularly if other countries in the region are said to have 'improved'. Korea's lack of progress in earlier rankings provoked the *Korea Herald* to complain that 'Despite huge investment and educational zeal, the English language skills of Korea's adults have not improved and have remained at a moderate level over the past six years' (Kyu-wook, 2013). The complaints have continued over the years. In 2021, a member of the National Assembly Education Committee gave the country's decline in EPI ranking as a rationale for lowering the starting grade for English from Grade 3 to Grade 1 (Ji-hye, 2021).

Similarly, in Thailand, Mala (2018) noted that 'Thailand has dropped 11 spots in the [EPI] proficiency rankings for non-native English speaking countries' and 'has the worst English proficiency except for Cambodia and Myanmar' in East Asia. In 2020, Thailand's ranking was 89th (EF, 2020), a further drop from 74th in 2019, although more countries were included in the index in these years than in 2018. Yet if we examine Thailand's economic performance over the years, again as measured by GDP, growth has been strong, averaging 3.73% from 1994 until 2019,[2] which includes the negative impact of the 1997 Asian financial crisis and the 2008 global financial crisis, as well as periods of chronic domestic political instability. For example, after mass protests by supporters of rival political groupings which paralysed large parts of Bangkok in 2013–2014 and ultimately led to a military coup in 2014, there was a decline in growth rates from 6.5% in 2012 to 0.8% in 2014, followed by a recovery to 2.9% in 2015.[3] Thailand's GDP for 2018 reached 4.1% (ADB, 2019). The correlation between national instability and decline in GDP in Thailand seems to be clear, but the country's GDP rates appear to be unconnected to its position in the EF EPI rankings.

Proficiency in English, education and employability

While the link between national levels of English proficiency (setting aside the problems with how this is measured) and national economic growth rates is implausible, there is micro-level evidence that proficiency in English has an impact on employability and remuneration for individuals in contexts where English is a foreign language. A report prepared by Euromonitor International (2012) found a pay gap of as much as 30% between employees proficient in English and those who were not across eight countries in the Middle East and North Africa. However, the database for the study was limited, with only a high of 23 companies being involved in the study in Jordan and a low of six in Algeria. The report also noted that 'multinationals are the primary driver for demand in English speakers, irrespective of the sector in which they specialise' (Euromonitor International, 2012: 10), and the positions requiring English were in middle and senior management. We should note that the numbers employed in middle and senior management in multinationals anywhere will inevitably be a small percentage of a country's total labour force and the ability to communicate in English will not be the only skill required for employment in this sector. Elsewhere, the returns to English language proficiency in India were examined by Rassool (2013: 61), who cites labour market research by Azam *et al.* (2010: 21) which found that 'For recent entrants [to the Indian labour market], English skills help increase wages only when coupled with high education; those who have not completed their secondary schooling would not see wage increases due to acquisition of English-language skills'. The basic criterion for employability is, then, the completion of secondary education, and English language proficiency is of value only when allied to that.

At the individual level, we would do well to heed Seargeant and Erling's (2011: 256) conclusion that 'a simplistic formula which equates English competence with economic mobility can be perniciously misleading in terms of the false assumptions it promotes'. This is echoed by Ricento (2018), looking at the role of English in terms of political economy, who noted that 'the role and utility of English worldwide is a vehicle for some people, in some economic sectors, mainly the knowledge economy, but is generally not connected to socioeconomic mobility for the vast majority of the global workforce' (Ricento, 2018: 221).

English, global structures and global events

Arguments questioning the functional value of English to national economies are supported by an analysis of the relationship between English as the first foreign language in schools and whether or not English is the language of a country's primary export partner, conducted by Cha and Ham (2008). This analysis indicates that the relationship was statistically significant for both the primary and secondary school levels in the 1945–1969 period but has been diminishing since then, a period that coincides with the ascendancy of English. They explain the change through a focus on English in terms of institutional theory, commenting that 'In this line of thought, the school curriculum is understood as largely influenced by the institutional dynamics of a world-cultural system' (Cha & Ham, 2008: 321), which 'implies that the legitimacy of a specific school subject keenly reflects changes in global structure and shifts in world discourse which might be quite extraneous to a given country' (Cha & Ham, 2008: 323).

Thus, factors other than the purely economic have become increasingly important in deciding which foreign language to teach in national educational systems. If we examine foreign language choice in schools over an extended period, a correlation with major world events becomes apparent. Cha and Ham (2008) researched the percentage of countries teaching English, French, German, Spanish and Russian as the first foreign language in schools at both primary and secondary levels from 1850 to 2005. No foreign languages were taught in primary schools until the 1900–1919 period, when English and French were both taught in 5% of 40 countries. From 1920 to 1944, English was taught in 12.3% of 65 countries, German was taught in 3.1% and the proportion teaching French fell to 1.3%. Foreign languages were thus taught in a minority of countries' primary schools until the 1945–1969 period when, for the first time, the percentage of countries teaching foreign languages rose above 50%. The proportion choosing English as the first foreign language doubled from 32.8% of 134 countries in 1945–1969 to 67.5% of 151 countries in the 1990–2005 period.

As we can see, it was only after the end of WWII that English began to assume a dominant position, coinciding with the onset of the United States as the pre-eminent world power. In secondary schools, German was the preferred foreign language until the end of the 19th century (44.4% of only 18 countries), superseded by French up to 1919 (45.9% of 37 countries) and French (35.2%) and English (33.3% of 54 countries) until 1944. Russian has had a limited place only since 1945, largely in those countries that formed the Soviet Bloc in ideological opposition to the USA after WWII. However, since the end of the Cold War and the collapse of the Soviet Union, the teaching of Russian has been in decline in both primary and secondary schools, at 3.3% and 3.2%, respectively, in the 1990–2005 period (Cha & Ham, 2008). As with primary schools, English has become increasingly dominant in secondary schools, rising from 35.4% of 48 countries in the 1920–1944 period (second to French with 39.6%) to 64.3% of 112 countries in the 1945–1969 period and to 84.3% of 127 countries in the 1990–2005 period (Cha & Ham, 2008). Again, there is a correlation with the increase in economic and political power of the United States during this period.

English-speaking countries and 'language ignorance'

Turning the economic argument around, with English dominant as the first foreign language of choice in both primary and secondary schools worldwide and as the language of international business, it would be logical to expect that English-speaking countries would not suffer economically through lack of proficiency in other languages. However, an analysis of bilateral national trade for the UK revealed significant costs due to 'language ignorance', that is, not being able to communicate in the language of the country to which businesses hoped to export. Foreman-Peck and Wang (2014) reported a negative effect of an estimated 3.5% of national income in 2006 terms, equivalent to £48 billion. Language barriers for UK businesses were global, as Foreman-Peck and Wang (2014) explained:

> language barriers are shown to hinder the UK's participation in the potential trade growth of the fast-emerging economies like BRIC [Brazil, Russia, India and China], as well as to developed countries like France, Germany and Japan. Non-European languages in which there is likely to be the least investment include Chinese, Japanese and Russian. These countries' markets have huge potential. (Foreman-Peck & Wang, 2014: 35)

From this brief review, the economic arguments for teaching English as a foreign language in schools are not supported. Indeed, an exclusive focus on English seems, at best, short-sighted in economic terms for both English-speaking and non-English speaking countries.

General education and economic development

In contrast to the specific impact of English, the importance of improving the quality of education as a whole is amply supported by studies of the relationship between education and economic development. Summarising the research, Grant (2017: 13) found that 'for every US$1 spent on education, US$10 to US$15 can be generated in economic growth' and

> investment in education and human capital development are crucial to growth for middle income countries. As the returns to physical capital accumulation diminish, the rate of productivity improvement and technological innovations depend largely on the presence of highly skilled human capital. (Grant, 2017: 17)

Relating this to specific countries, the World Bank (2015) saw improving the quality of education as a whole in Thailand as a priority if the country was to raise itself out of the 'middle income trap' and 'move up the value-added ladder to a more knowledge-based economy' (World Bank, 2015: 8). In Sri Lanka, an education sector assessment raised similar concerns about the quality of education, concluding that 'there are major deficiencies in Sri Lanka's delivery of education and training that affect its goal of inclusive growth' (Dundar et al., 2017: 26), and that notwithstanding 'its wide access and high completion rates in general education, learning achievements are modest' (Dundar et al., 2017: 28). Hence, the economic evidence indicates that, although there is a benefit to increasing participation rates in schooling, greater attention needs to be paid to what happens in schools as 'there is strong evidence that the cognitive skills of the population – rather than mere school attainment – are powerfully related to long-run economic growth' (Grant, 2017: 3). It is, then, a highly educated and skilled labour force that is generally accepted as being a key driver of economic growth. Proficiency in English has value only when it is part of a larger skillset, not on its own, and the value of proficiency in other languages is grossly underestimated.

'The younger the better' rationale

Turning to the 'younger the better' rationale, there exists a widespread perception that because young children (or, to be more accurate, all those without developmental difficulties) learn their first language easily, they can also learn a foreign language with similar ease if only they are exposed to it as early as possible in their educational experience. This belief, in common with those pertaining to the necessity of learning English for national economic well-being, permeates policy discourses worldwide. In a self-reinforcing cycle, it influences parents who demand that their children be taught English as early as possible which motivates policymakers to respond so they can then take credit for acceding to parents' wishes (Baldauf *et al.*, 2011). We can see this pressure in practice in a study of the introduction of English into primary schools in Vietnam, where a survey of parents about the best starting ages found that the majority (62%) wanted instruction to begin in Grade 1, 36% thought it should be in Grade 3 and only 2% thought introduction should be delayed until Grade 6, the beginning of lower secondary school (Hayes, 2008b). In the same study, head teachers of primary schools reported 'immense parental pressure to provide English in their schools, and commented that they would like to introduce the language at Grade 1' (Hayes, 2008b: 17). Although the study identified a number of critical factors militating against the effective introduction of English into primary schools – the complete lack of pre-service training for primary English teachers at the time being the most notable – a decision was nonetheless made to introduce English as a compulsory subject from Grade 3 and as an elective subject in Grades 1–2. Not surprisingly, the policy has given rise to inequity in provision between rural and urban areas (Nguyen *et al.*, 2014), an issue in many countries to which we shall return in later chapters.

The Critical Period Hypothesis and young language learners

The 'younger the better' belief has its theoretical foundation in the Critical Period Hypothesis (CPH) first formulated by Lenneberg (1967), according to which there is a cut-off point, generally held to be at puberty, in the ability to learn a second language to the same degree as speakers who acquire it as a first language. This hypothesis is often linked to an innatist conception of language acquisition in the Chomskyan tradition whereby older learners lack access to the Universal Grammar available for first language acquisition, hence their lack of success in learning a second language to so-called 'native-like' standards. The existence of a critical period is, however, disputed and many researchers prefer to think of any age-related phenomenon as a 'sensitive period' encompassing a more gradual decline in capacity to learn (Long, 1990). The notion of a sensitive period is supported by theories of lifespan cognition wherein adults get progressively poorer at all kinds of cognitive operations after maturity, not just language acquisition (Staudinger, 2001). More important for our purposes in discussions of the CPH is the lack of critical attention paid to the context of learning. Findings from research in naturalistic contexts, such as differences in the second language development of adult and child immigrants, are inappropriately generalised to instructional contexts where the target language is not a language of the environment outside the classroom. This approach was criticised many years ago by Marinova-Todd *et al.* (2000), who argued that there is misinterpretation, misattribution and misemphasis of the research on age and language learning: misinterpretation as research reveals younger learners do not learn as effortlessly as is claimed; misattribution of conclusions about language proficiency to brain functioning; and misemphasis on cases of failure among older learners rather than learning from cases of successful learning. Misinterpretation also exists with respect to extension of research on immigrant children in naturalistic settings to children in instructional settings. Children in naturalistic settings invariably – over the long term – learn the language of the new country better than adult family members, while children in instructional settings, where the target language is not spoken outside the schools and who do not have the same exposure to the language, typically do not learn a second language to the same level. Conditions of learning, rather than age, are crucial determinants. As Marinova-Todd *et al.* (2000: 9) concluded, 'age differences reflect differences in the situation of learning rather than a capacity to learn. They do not demonstrate any constraint on the possibility that adults can become highly proficient, even native-like, speakers of L2s'.

Like the economic rationale, the 'younger the better' rationale for teaching a foreign language in primary schools is not adequately supported by research. Moreover, there is criticism of much of the research on age and acquisition itself. DeKeyser (2013: 61) comments that 'There is little research on age effects that meets very high methodological standards … and almost no evidence that is clearly of educational relevance'. One study that does have education relevance is a longitudinal study conducted by Muñoz and her colleagues (Muñoz, 2006a) in what is known as the Barcelona Age Factor (BAF) project. BAF was one of the most comprehensive investigations of age and foreign language learning at different ages, and its findings established that there were no proficiency gains in beginning instruction in schools at earlier ages. Thanks to rapid, successive changes in the starting age at which foreign languages were introduced into schools, Muñoz (2006b) was able to compare learners who started at ages 8, 11, 14 and 18+ and after 200, 416 and 726 hours of instruction. Her conclusion was that, with the same amount of instruction, learners who started later were faster and more efficient learners on all four skills tested (Muñoz, 2006b). Further, there did not seem to be any prospect of younger learners outperforming older learners in the long run: 'On the contrary, if the older learners' advantage is mainly due to their superior cognitive development, no differences in proficiency are to be expected when differences in cognitive development also disappear with age' (Muñoz, 2006b: 34).

Age and environmental factors in learning

The inappropriateness of comparing children immersed in a naturalistic second language environment with children learning a foreign language in an instructional environment cannot be overstated. Environmental factors have a profound influence on language acquisition. Even from first language acquisition research it is clear that adequate input is not the only factor in successful acquisition of a language. Children need to be in an environment where the language makes sense and within which they have access to ways of working out the language. Mitchell *et al.* (2013: 261) note the importance of this 'language socialization perspective [which] predicts there will be a structured strategic relationship between language development and "culturally organized situations of use"'. We then need to reflect on whether these structures and situations of use either exist or are replicable in the typical primary school foreign language classroom where children may learn the language for an hour a day or even less and rarely encounter it outside the classroom. If they are neither present nor replicable in the environment, more classes of a language in school are not likely to lead to more learning. In Thailand, a former Minister of Education expressed his concern about the length of time spent learning and poor outcomes in English among Thai students, saying: 'Each Thai student studies English for at least 12 years at primary and secondary school, but most remain unable to communicate in English' (Mala, 2018). The Ministry of Education has progressively lowered the starting age for the introduction of English in an effort to enhance learning but it would seem that 'the younger the better' is not working. Linking poor outcomes in school to the economic rationale, the Minister went on to claim, 'This is the main obstacle to global competition' (Mala, 2018) but, again, without adducing evidence to support the claim. If policymakers require children in schools to study English as a foreign language for 12 years or more, in Thailand and elsewhere, and yet remain concerned about poor outcomes, it would seem sensible for them to re-examine both the rationale for emphasising the teaching of a single foreign language, English, for so long and research the reasons why it appears at present to produce such poor outcomes.

Beyond 'the younger the better': English-medium education

It should be more than clear that, by itself, the provision of more English in schools will not necessarily lead to enhanced learning. Nonetheless, in response to the perceived lack of success in teaching English in primary schools in many countries (Nunan, 2003), even after many years of formal education, there has arisen in some contexts a demand for English-medium (EM) education from the earliest grades of schooling. This is particularly noticeable in post-colonial South Asian countries – India, Nepal and Pakistan, for example – but is also evident in other countries, such as Thailand, which have never been colonised by English-speaking powers. The pace of this expansion is such that Dearden (2014: 2) labelled it 'a rapidly growing global phenomenon', and it continues irrespective of evidence that shows that 'using these languages [English and other former colonial languages] as the medium of instruction has a positive relationship with inequality' (Coyne, 2015: 630). Trudell *et al.* (2015: 136) debunk the 'common sense' belief 'That the most effective way to build fluency in a language the learner does not speak is to maximise the time spent using that language as the medium of instruction, without building fluency in that language first and without using the learner's first language as a resource', and note that 'This is one of the most pernicious myths in the entire field of language and education, even though it is solidly refuted by research on language and learning'. The research evidence demonstrates quite clearly that if children are taught in a language in which they are not fluent prior to entering formal schooling, their learning of both the language itself as well as other subjects will be severely compromised. In contrast, children taught through their mother tongue and who learn English as a subject outperform children taught through EM on all measures. For example, in research comparing teaching in 29 local languages with EM teaching in Cameroon, Trudell (2005) found that use of the mother tongue 'makes instructional time more efficient, as well as allowing more students to successfully learn the subject matter'; moreover, in mother-tongue classrooms 'students outperform their [EM] peers in reading and writing – in English as well as in the mother tongue' (Trudell, 2005: 244). The quality of instruction is also enhanced in mother-tongue classrooms as 'two-way communication between teacher and pupil is the norm, even as early as grade 1; pupil questions and ancillary comments are common. This compares favorably with the English-only classroom, in which pupils tend to speak only when questioned by the teacher and do not typically initiate communication' (Trudell, 2005: 244).

Similar results to Trudell (2005) have been found elsewhere. Mohanty (2017) reviews a range of studies with children of various ethnicities in India enrolled in both mother-tongue and EM schools and comes to the conclusion that 'when the quality of schooling and the socio-economic status of the parents are controlled, mother tongue medium children perform better than their EM counterparts in measures of academic achievement, understanding of the science and maths concepts and skills in language use' (Trudell, 2005: 274). Not only do they perform better in other school subjects, but their learning of English is also not hampered in the long run: 'when children learn through their MT [mother tongue] and then learn English later, they learn English at a faster rate and, in about four years, achieve the same level of competence in English as the English medium children. Early development of mother tongue proficiency in schools comes at no cost to effective learning of English and other languages at a later point in schools' (Trudell, 2005: 274).

It is unfortunate that all the research evidence that demonstrates that children are best educated in their first language, the language of the home, rather than a language that is alien to their environment, does not seem to have had widespread influence on – perhaps does not even reach – policymakers and parents who seek a competitive advantage for their children through English. Here, it is taken as a given. Although the issue of the spread of EM education is undeniably important, there are still many more children in schools learning English as a subject and it is this that will remain the principal focus in ensuing chapters of this book, rather than EM education.

Beyond economics and age: English, power and inequality

English and globalisation

The actual economic value of English is debatable but it is an undeniable reality that some languages are *perceived* to be of greater value than others both culturally and economically, which then influences whether or not they are taught in schools. Within this reality, the current position of English as the most powerful international language is unchallenged and has a significant impact on children's educational experiences with foreign language learning around the world. As was noted earlier, there was little teaching of foreign languages in primary schools until the 1945–1969 period, but since then English has been on an upward trajectory and has also displaced French as the first foreign language at the secondary level. These changes in foreign language choice in schools have coincided with the rise to dominance of the United States as the world's largest economy and military superpower, at the same time reflecting the acceptance of English as the language of economic 'globalisation' and globalisation itself as a new norm. The word 'globalisation' has connotations with universality, but the fact that globalisation itself serves particular rather than universal interests has been recognised by many critics, among whom Bourdieu (2001) has been frequently quoted. He explains:

> 'Globalization' serves as a password, a watchword while in effect it is the legitimatory mask of a policy aiming to universalize particular interests, and the particular tradition of the economically and politically dominant powers, above all the United States, and to extend to the entire world the

economic and cultural model that favours these powers most, while simultaneously presenting it as a norm, a requirement. (Bourdieu, 2001: 84, cited in Phillipson, 2009: 60)

The success of the policy to legitimise the interests of the 'economically and politically dominant powers' is amply demonstrated by the widespread acceptance of globalisation as the new economic norm with insufficient scrutiny of whom it benefits. Alongside the economic policy, English is widely presented and accepted as being the language through which access to the benefits of that model is gained. The reality, however, is that 'the degree of our social attention to English education often exceeds the functional requirements of individual national societies' (Cha & Ham, 2008: 323) and English, rather than being a useful tool for a restricted number of people in international commerce, has instead become a form of symbolic capital reflecting the power of those who possess it. Park (2011) explains the connections between language and power:

> English (or any other language) does not exist in some neutral social space, but in regimes of language organized by relations of power and inequality. Thus, while it is true that learning English will bring some material and social benefits to some people or communities in some contexts, the rosy picture of English as a liberating language of social and economic advancement is an overly simplistic and facile assumption, and more importantly, one that works to obscure the historical, material, and political basis that gave rise to the myth of such a promise in the first place. (Park, 2011: 443–444)

Thus, foreign language educational policies as enacted in school systems at present reflect the economic dominance of the United States and reinforce a linguistic hierarchy which has English at its apex. The use of English by the powerful as an element in the maintenance of their power in societies where it is a foreign language is not new, particularly in countries that are former colonies of the UK or the US. In Hayes' (2010) study, a teacher recalls how, growing up in Sri Lanka as the child of a farmer, he realised that, coming from a rural background, 'I think in me there would have been this feeling that I'm denied opportunities, I'm not like others, because I don't have my English or English background, so I thought I should learn it' (Hayes, 2010: 523). Another Sri Lankan teacher said simply of other people, 'they think you're educated if you know English' (Hayes, 2013: 78). Languages, then,

> are associated with power and hierarchy; some languages enable greater access to privileges and social opportunities and others lead to deprivation and discrimination. Under such conditions, use of languages becomes the basis for freedom, opportunities and capability development or for discrimination, denial of opportunities and constraints in realisation of capability. (Mohanty, 2017: 262)

English and educational opportunity

When considering whether or not to teach English in schools, it is incumbent on policymakers to consider whether to do so is to provide educational opportunity for all children in the system or simply to further the interests of the already privileged. Most education systems declare that they are determined to offer the same quality of education to all children as a means to promote social justice, by which is commonly meant adherence to 'three basic principles of justice: fairness as defined by treating individuals according to merit, by treating them according to need and by treating everyone equally' (Smith, 2018: 1). To illustrate, in Sri Lanka the second of the longstanding Sri Lankan national goals for education, originally articulated in 1992, was 'the establishment of a pervasive pattern of Social Justice and active elimination of inequalities' (NEC, 1992).[4] We will return to the implementation of the Sri Lankan goals later (and the changes made since 1992) but, using an example from India, a recognition that for at least some educational policymakers possession of English may be associated with discrimination and denial of opportunities can be seen in the introduction to the State Curriculum Framework for English from the state of Madhya Pradesh, which declares that 'It is our primary objective to teach English to every child of the State and to ensure that the child gains a sufficiently high level of proficiency in it and does not suffer discrimination for lack of it' (RSK, 2007: 2). Although the goal of universal access to English is laudable, there is an implicit admission in the objective that children will 'not suffer discrimination for lack of' English, that for some 'a high level of proficiency' will not be achieved and that discrimination does indeed exist. If education is one of the ways in which a society attempts to ensure that all of its young people have equal access to opportunities for self-fulfilment and meaningful lives, the question of whether the teaching of English functions as a means to reduce inequality, is complicit in maintaining inequality or acts as an instrument of inequality in itself needs to be addressed by everyone concerned with education in contexts where it is deemed to be an essential subject in the school curriculum.

The Impact of Learning English on Children in School

What impact do all these pressures to learn English have on children in schools? There is evidence that students at higher levels of education retain a belief in the instrumental value of English, that it is a necessity for their future economic well-being (see Hayes, 2017b, for evidence from Thailand; Young, 2006, for Macao, China; Bradford, 2007, for Indonesia) but this does not necessarily relate to high levels of proficiency or enjoyment in learning. Evidence from other levels of schooling indicates that attitudes towards learning may shift from earlier to later grades in a negative direction. Arda and Doyran (2017), for example, in a cross-sectional study in Turkey, found that a class of Grade 3 children had very positive attitudes towards learning English but a class of Grade 7 children had much more negative attitudes. In this case the shift in attitudes seems to have been the result of the more formal type of instruction children experienced in the later grades, perhaps combining with physiological changes in the children themselves as they matured. Some longitudinal studies have also found a decline in attitudes towards foreign language learning over time, e.g. Heinzmann's (2013) study of 9–12-year-old Swiss learners of English and French. Fenyvesi (2020) compared changes in attitudes of Danish learners beginning to learn English in Grade 1 with those beginning in Grade 3 over the course of a school year and found that, while children's attitudes to beginning learning in Grade 1 were initially higher, 'positive attitudes toward the learning situation decreased significantly within one year in both age groups, which means children who started learning English in the first grade did not retain their more positive attitudes toward English compared with those who started in the third grade' (Fenyvesi, 2020: 708).

Negative attitudes were also found in a qualitative study of students' attitudes to learning English in Seoul, Korea (Moon, 2013). She asked Grade 6 students to complete the sentence 'English is ...', and received responses such as:

- 'English is something that takes my freedom away'
- 'English is a prison for life'
- 'English is something that should never exist'
- 'English is hell'

In total, 65% of the students had negative attitudes towards English. As other research shows that learning languages has many positive effects, ranging from cognitive to educational, socioeconomic, cultural and social-psychological (Adesope *et al.*, 2010; Bialystok, 2011, 2018), these reactions are surprising in their vehemence. They also seem anomalous when set against the backdrop of a society in which educational success is given enormous importance, including in English which is tested in the high-stakes national university entrance examinations every year. The potential general educational value of learning another language, in terms of higher achievement in other subjects, did not seem to be reflected in the views of these Grade 6 students in Seoul, nor did the importance attributed to English in high-stakes tests equate with positive attitudes to learning the language. These views may not, of course, be representative, but when combined with the national soul-searching about 'poor' standards of English they indicate – at the very least – a need to reflect critically on the focus on English in the Korean school curriculum and the emphasis given to it in national policy discourses. This will be examined further in the case study of Korea later, as well as the other countries studied here, and the same degree of critical reflection to the rationale for and purposes of language teaching and learning in primary schools would, I contend, be productive in many other contexts worldwide.

(English) Language Learning in Primary Schools in State Educational Systems

Key questions for the introduction of foreign languages in primary schools

Whether the teaching of foreign languages in primary schools, most particularly English, contributes to the socioeducational capital of *all* children in a school system is a major concern of this book. Education is, as I have pointed out earlier, a potential resource for achieving social justice in a society. However, it is not just what happens inside a school that provides children with opportunities for achievement: social networks outside school are also key determinants of success. Within the education system itself, the importance of examining whether the necessary enabling conditions exist for any educational policy to be implemented equitably across the system is critical for the achievement of social justice. Thus, a number of interrelated questions ought to be addressed by policymakers when English (or any other foreign language) is introduced into the primary school curriculum, viz.:

(1) What is the place of the foreign language in the national context? Where is it used, by whom, and for what purposes?
(2) What is the status accorded to the foreign language in economic and social terms in the context?
(3) To what extent does the possession of the foreign language act as a gatekeeper to educational opportunity and higher level employment (irrespective of its actual use in those areas)?
(4) Are the necessary resources available in the system, both human and material, for effective teaching of the foreign language at the primary level?
(5) What are the goals of the curriculum at the primary level?
(6) Are the curriculum goals appropriate to the socioeducational context?
(7) Are the curriculum goals likely to be achievable in the context?
(8) Is there equal access to human and material resources in all schools nationwide?
(9) What is being done or can be done to make the teaching of the foreign language at primary level a positive experience for children?

And finally, returning to the theme of social justice in education:

(10) Does the teaching of the foreign language function to minimise or exacerbate inequality in the education system and in the wider society?

These questions beget others. For example, the issues of resources and curriculum are very wide ranging and policymakers would need to consider whether there are adequate material and financial resources available to implement teaching the language at the primary level, asking:

(1) Are there adequate numbers of teachers with sufficient competence in the foreign language to teach it at the primary level?
(2) Have these teachers been appropriately trained for the task in their pre-service courses?
(3) Is sufficient instructional time available to achieve curriculum goals in the teaching of the subject?
(4) Are curriculum materials and teaching-learning approaches appropriate to the age group?
(5) Are appropriate and timely continuing professional development (CPD) opportunities available to support teachers in teaching the subject at the primary level?
(6) Is adequate in-school advisory support available to support teachers as they implement the curriculum?
(7) Are appropriate procedures in place to evaluate the effectiveness of teaching and learning the language at the primary level?

Even then, policymakers need to recognise that teaching a foreign language at the primary level, just as with any subject, is not carried out in isolation but is integrated with teaching at subsequent grades at the secondary level. There should, therefore, be a logical and harmonious progression between levels, and secondary-level teachers should be aware of the knowledge and skills that individual students will bring with them as they transition from the primary level. Perhaps most important is to acknowledge that the teaching of a foreign language does not exist in isolation from the rest of the school curriculum, nor is it disconnected from the administrative and sociocultural structures of the school system and the wider society but is embedded within these structures.

Language teaching methods, learner-centred education and context

The teaching of English as a foreign language in particular is also peculiarly subject to influences from beyond the context in which it is taught. It is not just a question of recognising that the language itself is far from value neutral, given its associations with political and economic imperialism, but also of acknowledging the power of Western influences on the way in which the language is taught. Although the appropriacy of the worldwide export of English language teaching methodologies such as Communicative Language Teaching (CLT) and its later variant, Task-Based Language Teaching (TBLT), from Western countries has been questioned for more than a quarter of a century (see, for example,

Holliday, 1994), these methodologies continue to dominate official curricula in Asia and beyond. This appears to be part of a wider trend for the export of learner-centred education (LCE) into curricula as a whole worldwide, not just for English as a foreign language. The export of LCE has not been met with the success its advocates expected and its relevance continues to be questioned. As Schweisfurth (2011) notes:

> the history of the implementation of LCE in different contexts is riddled with stories of failures grand and small. [...] Furthermore, a culturally nuanced perspective raises questions about how teaching and learning are understood in different contexts, and about whether LCE is ultimately a 'western' construct inappropriate for application in all societies and classrooms. (Schweisfurth, 2011: 425)

In an effort to take account of local understandings of teaching and learning English, which are equally applicable to the teaching and learning of other languages, a number of researchers have sought to identify ways in which teachers might adapt CLT and TBLT in contextually appropriate ways, urging teachers 'to trust their own voice and develop a pedagogy suited to their own specific situations' (Littlewood, 2007: 248). Yet recommendations such as this tend to propose a methodological 'global product in different local flavours', to use Cameron's (2002: 70) description of the concept of language as a set of Western-oriented communication skills. They often also go against the mandates of official curricula which may constrain teachers' actions in the classroom and do not seem to take account of whether the institutional parameters of schools would provide support for teachers as they develop their own pedagogies nor whether they have acquired sufficient expertise from their own teacher preparation courses to be able to do so. It is essential, therefore, to investigate the teaching and learning of English and other foreign languages from a wide-ranging perspective that encompasses a focus not only on the implementation of a curriculum and its associated methodology but also that attempts to come to an understanding of what the language means to the teachers who teach it and the children who are required to study it. What place does it have in their lives? Why are they required to teach and study it? What value does it have for them? Is it of equal value to all learners? Is the same quality of teaching and the same level of resourcing equally accessible to all learners? Is the educational experience that learners and teachers have as beneficial as possible in the context?

School language learning and plurilingualism

Answering the questions at the end of the earlier section, particularly those that relate to the place languages have in learners' and teachers' lives, leads us to the consideration of policies designed to promote appreciation of linguistic diversity rather than linguistic exclusion, the teaching and learning of many other languages rather than just one held to be more important than others. A plurilingual perspective on language learning in primary schools is emerging in some contexts, notably the European Union. The European Centre for Modern Languages of the Council of Europe (n.d.) states that education in the member states should recognise[5]:

- Europe's linguistic diversity
- The mobility of Europe's citizens
- Social cohesion
- Access to quality education for all

In so doing, the Council of Europe views bi/plurilingualism as a norm and something that is achievable by everyone. However, the focus is not on high levels of achievement on the Common European Framework of Reference (CEFR) language scales but, instead, developing learners' partial competencies in a variety of languages within which there is 'complementarity and interplay'. For young learners, the teaching approach is termed an 'Awakening to languages', one that raises 'awareness of the diversity of languages in their homes, schools and societies [and where] several languages are introduced in order to encourage thinking about language and to give value to the different languages in the school' (Council of Europe, n.d.).[6] While this approach may be more urgent in those European countries that have been experiencing considerable migration flows from other parts of the world and, hence, would benefit from demonstrating appreciation of migrants' home languages for purposes of social integration, it also holds great promise for other bi/plurilingual contexts which, we should remember, are common worldwide. That said, we should also recognise that plurilingual language policies are affected by answers to the 'key questions for the introduction of foreign languages in primary schools' that we asked earlier, as much as any other language policies. If there are insufficient material and human resources for the teaching of the languages, and equitable access to resources across the system is lacking, then any policy will suffer in its implementation.

Coda

In the case study chapters in this book, framing the teaching and learning of English as the primary foreign language and, occasionally, other languages within the sociocultural and educational contexts in which they are situated is a major concern. Also important is the discussion of the place of other languages, whether foreign or indigenous, in the contexts discussed. Based on the analyses in the case studies, in the final chapter I reflect on other ways in which young children may encounter new languages in primary schools, ways that may make the experience more productive and more able to provide a foundation for successful language learning in later years.

Notes

(1) Source: https://tradingeconomics.com/south-korea/gdp-growth-annual. I have not included figures for 2020–2021 as these will have been affected by the global Covid-19 pandemic and are not representative of normal economic performance.
(2) Source: https://tradingeconomics.com/thailand/gdp-growth-annual
(3) Source: Asian Development Bank Basic Statistics Series, available at https://www.adb.org/publications/series/basic-statistics
(4) See Annex A of *Action Oriented Strategy Towards a National Education Policy*, available at http://nec.gov.lk/wp-content/uploads/2014/04/National_Policy.pdf
(5) See https://www.ecml.at/Thematicareas/PlurilingualEducation/tabid/1631/language/en-GB/Default.aspx
(6) See https://www.ecml.at/Thematicareas/PlurilingualEducation/tabid/1631/language/en-GB/Default.aspx

2 Thailand: An Educational Paradox

Introduction

This chapter explores the teaching and learning of English as the compulsory first foreign language in the Thai basic education system. Although the principal focus is on young learners, given the argument that one can only understand what happens in the primary sector if it is situated in the wider education system, and that the education system itself needs to be understood as part of Thai society, the chapter inevitably goes beyond just the teaching of English. Hence, it begins with consideration of the national language context and the general educational context and reference to national economic development before examining key issues in the system that impact the teaching and learning of English. These include a number of persistent quality issues that affect education as a whole, not just outcomes in English. The most important of these is equity, with an OECD/UNESCO report arguing that the education system 'tends to reinforce disparities rather than help to overcome them' (OECD/UNESCO, 2016: 43). Educational outcomes in subjects across the curriculum and at all levels of schooling are widely acknowledged to be poor and have been a source of both public and academic concern for many years (Bangkok Post, 2016, 2019; Lathapipat & Sondergand, 2016; Singhadechakul, 2015).

English, as the first foreign language taught in primary schools, suffers from the same poor outcomes as other subjects. This is exemplified by the results of O-NET, the Ordinary National Educational Tests, including English language proficiency, which have been a source of much soul-searching each year when results are published. The most recent results for Grade 6 students, taken at the end of the primary cycle, show that only in Thai did the score exceed 50%, while scores for English and other subjects were below 40% (see Table 2.1).

Although there have been criticisms of the nature of the tests, and they were discontinued for Grade 6 and Grade 9 students in 2020 because of the Covid-19 global pandemic, these results are indicative of poor outcomes throughout the system. A number of causes of this lack of

Table 2.1 Comparison of O-NET scores for Grade 6 students in 2018 and 2019, all subjects

Subject/Scores (max 100)	2018	2019
Thai	46.58	54.4
English	36.34	34.4
Mathematics	37.12	32.9
General sciences	39.12	35.6

Source: Scores collated from *The Nation*, 27 March 2018, https://www.nationthailand.com/in-focus/30341839 and *Bangkok Post*, 2 January 2019, https://www.bangkokpost.com/thailand/general/2044427/long-overdue-end-of-o-net-exams

achievement have been identified in the research, both pedagogic and organisational. Chief among the pedagogic causes is the lack of congruence between a curriculum that is student centred and teaching-learning methods that continue to be teacher centred and predominantly reliant on rote learning. Studies of the impact of learner-centred educational reform initiated by the 1999 National Education Act reveal 'a lack of deep penetration of the reforms in a large percentage of schools' and 'the pattern of implementation as variable across teachers, and partial or surface in the nature of impact' (Hallinger & Lee, 2011: 154). We will return to these issues later.

Of course, poor results in O-NET (or any other test) do not tell the whole story and should be set against the numerous success stories of primary school children regularly excelling in international competitions in maths and science. For example, 'Thai students won the 12th International Mathematics and Science Olympiad for Primary Schools 2015 with a total of 48 medals', according to the *Bangkok Post* (Mala, 2015) and, similarly, 'Thai pupils have bagged a total of 36 medals at a maths competition for primary schools in India' (Mala, 2016). Also, in school visits I conducted as part of a recent evaluation of an in-service teacher development programme, some students from primary classes were able to talk about their language classes in high levels of English. However, my school visits were arranged through the Office of the Basic Education Commission, Ministry of Education, and it would not be unusual if schools received instructions to present the best possible front. Indeed, in the larger, well-resourced provincial schools, some of the students selected to participate in focus group interviews were studying in the primary school 'English Program', where English, mathematics, science and physical education are taught through English. As in any education system, where children are taught in well-resourced classrooms by highly skilled teachers they are likely to perform well, but the wider picture in Thailand remains one of under-achievement across the system. This chapter thus argues that the solution to raising standards in English, which has been a longstanding aim of all Thai governments since the mid-1990s, lies

The Thai Context: Languages, National Economic Development and the Quality of the Education System

Languages in Thailand

Thailand is a multilingual, ethnically diverse country with 51 Indigenous languages spoken, including what some consider to be dialects of standard Thai such as Thai Lao in the northeast, often referred to as 'Isaan', and 22 non-Indigenous languages.[1] Standard Thai is estimated to be the first language of 50% of the population, but Kosonen (2008: 175) estimates that 'If the four related major Thai languages are considered as dialects of the national language, the total population speaking a variety of Thai is above 86% of the total'. (This view is, however, contested, with some linguists maintaining that 'Isaan' is a minority language [Draper, 2015]). The remaining languages are officially marginalised and/or marginal, some with large numbers of speakers such as Patani Malay (1,700,000 speakers) and others with fewer, such as Lahu (32,000 speakers), while 25 are listed by UNESCO as endangered, such as Bisu (2740 speakers). Despite this abundance of ethnicities and languages, Thailand has presented itself as a monolingual country since the early 20th century, with standard Thai, based on the dialect of the central plains, as the sole national language. Standard Thai is used in government administration, education and the media as a means to promote national unity and a sense of 'Thai-ness' (Huebner, 2019). This ideological policy of creating a nation-state through language was first encapsulated in the 'Twelve Cultural Mandates' issued by the government between 1939 and 1942, with Mandate 9 focused on language policy:

> (1) Thai people must extol, honour and respect the Thai language, and must feel honoured to speak it; (2) Thai people must consider it the duty of a good citizen to study the national language, and must at least be able to read and write; Thai people must also consider it their important duty to assist and support citizens who do not speak Thai or cannot read Thai to learn it. (Cabinet Secretariat, 1940: 78, cited in Draper, 2019: 233)

The policy endures in the education system today through the 2008 Basic Education Core Curriculum which aims to inculcate 'Knowledge, skills and culture in [Thai] language application for communication; delight in and appreciation of Thai wisdom; and pride in national language' (MOE, 2008: 10). Its outcomes by the end of formal schooling can be seen in, for example, the attitudes of the majority of a group of 167 university students in a northern city sampled by Hayes (2016), whose perceptions of the Thai language included views such as 'I am very proud of being Thai and using the Thai language' and 'It is an important identity marker of

Thailand' (Hayes, 2016: 86). Policies introduced by the recent military government (2014–2019) reinforced the emphasis on 12 'core values', including upholding the three pillars of nation, religion and monarchy, as well as 'treasuring cherished Thai traditions',[2] which all students are expected to recite at the beginning of the school day. As the government which took office in 2019 is led by the former military prime minister, this emphasis on core values, with the Thai language as the symbol of nationhood, is likely to continue for the foreseeable future.

For many decades, the lack of official acknowledgement of language diversity or of any benefits deriving from multilingualism has had negative implications for learning at the primary school level in those areas of the country where central Thai is not the first language for school children but a second language. The scale of the problem is reflected in figures from the *UNESCO 2017/18 Global Education Monitoring Report*, which indicated that 50% of school children in Thailand are not taught in the language spoken at home (UNESCO, 2017). Only relatively recently have initiatives to introduce bilingual education been authorised by the Ministry of Education (MoE), with projects funded by UNESCO and developed by the Research Institute for Languages and Cultures of Asia of Mahidol University.[3] Research throughout eight years of a pilot project which introduced Patani-Malay as a medium of instruction into 16 schools in the south of the country has revealed outcomes similar to those of mother-tongue based primary education projects in other countries (see, for example, Trudell, 2005); that is, students who learn through their first language and are then gradually introduced to a national language or language of wider communication, in this case Thai, not only perform better in the learning of content subjects such as maths and science but also learn Thai more effectively than students who are taught only in Thai from the start of their schooling (UNICEF, 2018). Trudell's (2005) research also showed that children who speak a minority language and who do not receive instruction in their first language in the early years of schooling find the learning of a third language, English, even more problematic. In Thailand the challenge is now to scale up from pilot projects with small numbers of schools to all schools that have large numbers of minority language students.

I now turn to the role of foreign languages and education as a whole in economic development.

National economic development, language and education

As we saw in the previous chapter, the Thai government, like many others, considers proficiency in the English language to be an important factor in human resource development and, hence, national economic development, a notion that has been prevalent in discussions of language education policy in Thailand since the 1990s (Hayes, 1995). This perspective has strengthened in recent years, particularly since the establishment in 2015 of the ASEAN Economic Community for which English is the working language. Concomitantly, Thailand's acknowledged poor standards in English relative to its ASEAN neighbours are a source of continuing concern and are thought to hamper the country's ability to compete in the regional and global economy (Franco & Roach, 2018; Kaur *et al.*, 2016). The booming tourist industry in the country, for which English is the most common international language, is often cited as a counter-example of successful language learning but, in this case, as Kaur *et al.* (2016: 352) note, 'the ability to conduct limited English conversation, while highly important for those working with tourist[s], is not equivalent to genuine proficiency in the language'. High levels of proficiency are restricted to the elite, who often receive some of their education in English-speaking countries, and are a marker of social status, while 'Thais in general do not use English for intranational communication among themselves' (Trakulkasemsuk, 2018: 100). Apart from limited English for tourism, the need for English proficiency among the wider workforce is not based on hard evidence of direct links between such proficiency and economic success (Hayes, 2017b), nor on research into actual language use in the workplace. Indeed, reporting on a conference panel on 'Thailand's English language readiness and action plans for ASEAN 2015', an attendee had a 'sense of puzzlement [which] comes from a near absence of research reports on the actual language needs in Thailand's employment sectors' (Takahashi, 2012: np), further commenting:

> This strikes me as odd, particularly since the current push for English has a strong employment basis [...]. At the conference, little was offered as to what level of proficiency – and in what languages – is needed or valued for what kinds of positions in what industries. The lack of such research, and the single-minded focus on English, also seems to blind us from multilingual resources that already exist and have worked well in industries such as tourism, and that could be expanded to strengthen Thailand's competitiveness. (Takahashi, 2012: np)

We also noted in the previous chapter that there is a direct association between improving the general quality of education and national economic development, which does not exist for improvements in proficiency in English alone. Thailand's education system has been repeatedly criticised for under-performing both domestically (see, for example, Tangkitvanich & Sasiwuttiwat, 2012) and internationally. The OECD concluded that 'improving the quality of human capital', through educating the workforce, is 'an urgent matter for Thailand' (OECD, 2016: 313), although without placing any specific emphasis on English. Weakness in education generally is also evident in the 2019 Global Innovation Index, where Thailand's overall ranking of 43 is not matched by its component ranking for education of 81 out of 129 countries (Cornell University *et al.*, 2019).

Thailand long ago succeeded in taking the first step towards improving educational quality through expanding access to education. Enrolment at the primary level is now almost universal and 99% of students complete the primary grades. Participation has also increased at the lower secondary level up to Grade 9, although only 80% of the poorest complete this level compared to 100% of the richest (UNESCO, 2017). However, enrolment remains comparatively low at the upper secondary level (65% in 2014), as well as at the tertiary level where a significant issue is the large disparity in enrolment rates between children from the wealthiest quartile in the country and the poorest quartile: this gap actually grew from 39% to 80% between 1986 and 2014 (Lathapipat, 2018).

Expanded access to schooling, although a necessary precondition, is insufficient by itself to raise general levels of achievement across the system. Equally important is enhancing the quality of education that is offered, particularly to children from the poorest sectors of society in order to enable them to compete with their richer peers. In Thailand there are considerable disparities in access to quality education based on the level of schools' resources and the socioeconomic status of the communities in which they are situated. Location is especially significant, as Lathapipat (2018) notes:

> In terms of location, the disadvantaged and poorer performing students are clearly concentrated in rural village schools [and] the performance gap between students in village schools and those in large city schools has also expanded over the 2003–2012 period. The difference in the average learning outcome between the two groups in 2012 is estimated to be around 1.8 years of formal schooling. (Lathapipat, 2018: 351)

More worrying is that 32% of Thai 15-year-olds are functionally illiterate in their first language according to PISA (Project for International Student Assessment) benchmarks and 'The greatest concentration is found in villages, where 47 percent of their 15-year-old students are functionally illiterate' (World Bank, 2015: 15). Disparities between outcomes in high-performing schools in large urban areas and low-performing small village schools have widened in recent years, damaging both prospects for better life chances for the students concerned and the development of the economy as a whole, as the Word Bank (2015) explains:

> Improving educational outcomes amongst these poorer-performing students can have major impacts at the individual level and for Thailand's economic growth prospects. For individuals, being equipped with the necessary skills and competencies to obtain productive employment can help them secure a better future and, for those who are poor, help them break out of the cycle of poverty. Looking at the bigger picture, having a workforce with stronger analytical reasoning and problem solving skills – skills that extend well beyond simply being functionally literate – can help Thailand move up the value-added ladder to a more knowledge-based economy. (World Bank, 2015: 3)

Government spending on education is not an issue. Thailand spends 7.6% of its GDP or around 25% of its annual budget on education, more than any of its ASEAN competitors (Khoman, 2018). Fry and Bi (2013) have spoken of 'the Thai educational paradox' which, put simply, is that the large sums of money invested in education do not provide an adequate return in terms of educational outcomes for its students. Hence, any solution to the problem of improving outcomes in schools would seem to lie more in the distribution of resources than in their overall levels. Thailand operates a practice of equal per-student budget allocation which does not take account of local conditions and is not adjusted for school location, school size or area poverty levels. The result is 'inequity among regions and schools and means that big schools have many more resources and small schools, where more resources are needed to ensure educational quality, have barely sufficient means to function' (Shaeffer, 2018: 110–111). The number of small schools, defined by the Office of the Basic Education Commission (OBEC) as those with fewer than 120 students, is 13,830, providing education to a total of 47% of all primary school students (Shaeffer, 2018). These small schools have insufficient teachers and high turnover of the teachers they do have.

This is a considerable problem when the system as a whole has widespread resource quality issues, with an OECD/UNESCO (2016) report noting that 'The average quality of educational resources in Thai schools is among the lowest of any country participating in the Programme for International School Assessment (PISA), and the uneven distribution of educational resources across schools poses equity challenges' (OECD/UNESCO, 2016: 70). Figure 2.1 shows the rural–urban disparities for material resources in Thailand in comparison with the OECD average,

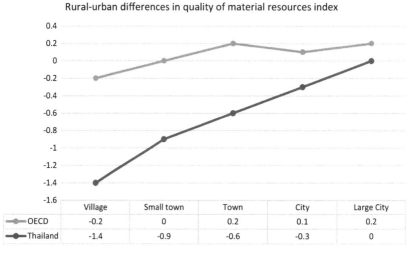

Figure 2.1 Quality of material resources index by school location
Source: World Bank (2015: 28).

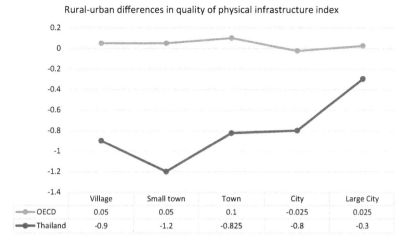

Figure 2.2 Quality of physical infrastructure index by school location
Source: World Bank (2015: 28).

and Figure 2.2 shows the disparities for physical infrastructure based on PISA 2012 data (World Bank, 2015).

The problem of educational quality is exacerbated by the existence of a large centralised educational bureaucracy of some 30,000 civil servants in the MoE which consumes significant expenditure but does not contribute directly to educational quality: in comparison, China, a much larger country, has only 1000 employees in its central educational ministry (Fry, 2018). There is also too much emphasis on spending on buildings 'rather than on the enhancement of learning and teaching' (Fry & Bi, 2013: 307). The overall impact is that the country's educational potential is not realised and disparities in access to quality education are acute, 'with the disadvantaged being primarily those who are economically poor and/or in remote rural areas, particularly the northeast and deep south' (Fry, 2018: 690).

The need to improve the general quality of education and to reduce inequality are both issues of which the government is well aware, with the first two development strategies of the *Twelfth National Development Plan (2017–2021)* (ONESCD, 2017: ii) being:

Strategy 1: Strategy for Strengthening and Realizing the Potential of Human Capital
Strategy 2: Strategy for Creating a Just Society and Reducing Inequality

Education is referred to frequently in the plan – there are 147 mentions as opposed to just four for English – and the objectives for human resource development include:

5) Educational excellence should be promoted at all levels by improving the management of primary education quality in small schools, reforming teaching and learning methods, and developing the quality of teachers within the whole system. (ONESCD, 2017: 19)

Education also features repeatedly in Section 2.2.4 of the plan, 'Creating a Just Society and Reducing Inequality', where Objective 3 is to 'Enhance the more equal distribution of quality public services including education' (ONESCD, 2017: 20). Time will tell whether these objectives will be translated into concrete actions but, since the publication of the plan, there has been little sign of significant progress. The reform that the National Development Plan calls for is hardly helped by frequent ministerial changes, with the 22nd minister of education since 1999 taking office in March 2021. New ministers come with new priorities and policies, tending to focus on their own initiatives rather than continuing the policies of their predecessors. The 20th minister instigated a large-scale in-service teacher development programme to improve teachers' English proficiency and teaching skills at both primary and secondary levels, but whether this will be capitalised on by the new minister remains to be seen. What is certain, unfortunately, is that the end result of these frequent changes at the ministerial level will be a lack of the policy continuity that is essential for improving the quality of education in general and that of foreign language learning in particular.

Within this wider framework of the Thai 'educational paradox', then, it is not surprising that there are numerous challenges confronting teachers and learners in primary schools as they try to make sense of the teaching and learning of English as a foreign language. It is to these challenges – as well as prospects for success – that we now turn.

Basic Education in Thailand, the Curriculum and the Place of Foreign Languages

Thai children are required to begin formal schooling by the time they are seven years old and compulsory education extends for nine years, comprising six years of primary school (Prathom 1–6) and three years of lower secondary school (Mathayom 1–3). Government statistics for 2016, the most recent available, indicate that there were 3,759,586 (78%) students enrolled in the primary grades of government schools and 1,067,184 (22%) in private schools (MOE, 2017). While the vast majority of children are educated in government schools nationwide, in the Bangkok metropolis the ratio is 53% in government schools and 47% in private schools (MOE, 2017). The higher number of children attending private schools in the Bangkok metropolis is likely to be a reflection of the economic strength of the capital region and the higher levels of discretionary spending available to its wealthier residents, who seek a competitive advantage for their children through private education.

The desire for a competitive advantage may begin even prior to starting primary school. Pre-primary education was made free in 2009 and, although it is not compulsory, UNICEF statistics showed a 93% net enrolment ratio in 2012 with a high gender parity index of 0.98 (cited in Shaeffer, 2018) and almost a quarter (23%) of kindergarten students enrolled in private institutions. Students in private institutions have the advantage of access to three years of pre-primary education while government schools offer only two years (MOE, 2017), and Shaeffer (2018: 98) also reports that 'There is severe competition to enter some of the prestigious private preschools which can facilitate access to elite basic education'. Thus, the disparities in quality that affect the system can be found at even the earliest stages of education and mean that not all children enter primary school with the same background in early childhood education.

The curriculum for primary education is based on the provisions of the National Education Act (NEA) of B.E. 2542 (1999), which stipulated as a 'major task':

> 1. **Learning reform** which will follow the guideline and spirit of the provisions in the Act by attaching **highest importance to learners**. The ONEC [Office of the National Education Commission] has conducted research and development on learner-centred teaching-learning process allowing learners to develop at their own pace and in accord with their potential. (ONEC, 1999: 26, emphasis in original)

Section 21 of the Act specified that 'In organizing the learning process, educational institutions and agencies concerned shall: (1) provide substance and arrange activities inline with the learners' interests and aptitudes, bearing in mind individual differences' (ONEC, 1999: 11), while Section 28 stated that the curriculum 'shall aim at human development with desirable balance regarding knowledge, critical thinking, capability, virtue and social responsibility' (ONEC, 1999: 12). The focus on individualised, learner-centred teaching was a reaction against the longstanding 'traditional' focus on teacher-centred rote learning which was widely criticised following social upheaval in the early 1990s and the 1997 financial crisis for producing students without the skills necessary to participate in an increasingly globalised economy.

The curriculum for English is detailed in the Basic Education Core Curriculum (MOE, 2008). Although the subject area is 'foreign languages', content is only prescribed for English while content for other languages is left to individual schools to decide. In reality, very few primary schools offer languages other than English. The curriculum specifies the overall objectives for foreign language teaching in this way:

> The learning area for foreign languages is aimed at enabling learners to acquire a favourable attitude towards foreign languages, the ability to use foreign languages for communicating in various situations, seeking knowledge, engaging in a livelihood and pursuing further education at higher levels. (MOE, 2008: 252)

The curriculum outlines four strands for 'What is learned in foreign languages' (MOE, 2008: 252–253):

- Language for Communication
- Language and Culture

- Language and Relationship with Other Learning Areas
- Language and Relationship with Community and the World

It also specifies the 'Learners' Quality' that is expected by the end of Grades 3, 6, 9 and 12, which focuses on the achievement of various communicative functions in speaking and writing. For example, Grade 6 graduates (at the end of their primary schooling) should, *inter alia*, be able to:

> Speak/write in an exchange in interpersonal communication; use orders and requests and give instructions; speak/write to express needs; ask for help; accept and refuse to give help in simple situations; speak and write to ask for and give data about themselves, friends, families and matters around them; speak/write to express their feelings about various matters and activities around them, as well as provide brief justifications

> Speak/write to give data about themselves, friends and the surrounding environment; draw pictures, plans, charts and tables to show the various data that they have heard and read; speak/write to show opinions about various matters around them

> Use words, tone of voice, gestures and manners politely and appropriately by observing social manners and culture of native speakers; give data about the festivals/important days/celebrations/lifestyles of native speakers; participate in language and cultural activities in accordance with their interests. (MOE, 2008: 254–255)

The curriculum reflects the prevailing methodological paradigm worldwide of Communicative Language Teaching (CLT), which prioritises the ability to communicate meaningfully through the target language. The ultimate objective in Thailand is, as Punthumasen (2007: 8) puts it, 'to build the capacity of Thai people to communicate in English language in order that they will be able to seek new knowledge by themselves and benefit their profession as well as international competitiveness'. The target model of English is not specified, but in practice 'native speaker' (NS) American and British English are regarded as valid, although this is inherently difficult for Thai teachers of English to model if they have not had exposure to it themselves. The acceptability of an English as a lingua franca (ELF) model or local or regional varieties rather than an idealised NS model does not feature at the policy level (Trakulkasemsuk, 2018).

The curriculum allocates 40 hours per year for foreign languages in Grades 1–3 and 80 hours in Grades 4–6 from a maximum of 1000 instructional hours per year for all subjects in each of the primary grades. This translates to one hour per week in Grades 1–3 and two hours per week in Grades 4–6 for a total of 360 hours by the end of primary school. The curriculum goals appear to be very ambitious for this limited amount of instructional time, even if it were all well used. Perhaps on the basis that more instructional time would solve the problem of under-achievement, in 2016 the then Deputy Minister of Education announced plans to increase teaching in Grades 1–3 to five hours per week and for students to learn five new words a day (which would give a student a vocabulary of 3000 words by the end of Grade 3). These announcements were greeted with scepticism in an editorial in the English language newspaper, the *Bangkok Post* (2016: np).

> […] while the plans look good on paper, there is, as always, a huge gap between design and achievement. The truth is that we have not only been here before, but it's beginning to look like the movie Groundhog Day. For years, every government and new minister of education has touted plans for improvements.

The editorial went on to criticise the habit of top-down decision making and the vocabulary learning objective as one that would be achieved by rote learning, saying there were two major problems:

> First, is the attitude within the ministry that all instruction must come from the very top and apply to the very bottom, where the student struggles to learn. The second problem is the unfathomable faith in the 18th century's rote-learning procedures. Every successful education system has thrown off this antiquated and actually harmful classroom tool. [The Deputy Minister's] instruction to teach five words per day will encourage more of it. (Bangkok Post, 2016: np)

This editorial not only highlights the issue of new initiatives by successive ministers of education failing to generate meaningful reform (indeed, this initiative failed to be implemented because of the lack of qualified teachers), but also widespread criticisms of education as remaining teacher-centred and focused on rote learning in spite of the intentions of the NEA. The underlying reasons for education remaining rooted in teacher-centred pedagogy are, unfortunately, not explored in the editorial, although the criticism of top-down initiatives indicates clearly that those who are supposed to implement classroom changes – teachers – are not involved in their formulation. This perspective is supported by Methitham (2009: 37), who described the curriculum as being 'entirely initiated from above' with the effect that it serves to 'disempower [teachers'] instructional judgements and devalue their teaching experience'.

At a philosophical level, the NEA's focus on learner-centred education as the key to the transformation of Thai education has seen it labelled as 'progressive' (Fry, 2018), a label that is often equated with 'Western'. Indeed, Kulsiri's (2006) analysis of the NEA and the ensuing 2001 curriculum makes clear their Western origins. Kulsiri (2006: 223) also indicates that many basic concepts in the 2001 curriculum such as 'critical thinking' were inadequately explained, leaving them open to multiple interpretations in practice and ultimately leading to 'confusion rather than positive change'. The same is true of the current Basic Education Core Curriculum, designed to remedy problems in 'application process and results' (MOE, 2008: i) of the 2001 curriculum while still conforming to the NEA of 1999. For example, the second of the 'Learners' Key Competencies' which the curriculum aims to inculcate is:

1. Thinking Capacity
Capacity for analytical, synthetic, constructive, critical and systematic thinking, leading to creation of bodies of knowledge or information for judicious decision-making regarding oneself and society. (MOE, 2008: 6)

But whether this key competency should be thought of in a 'weak' sense as akin to a technical skill or in a 'strong' sense as a form of emancipatory social practice is not specified. Different interpretations of this competency (and others) will result in different classroom practices and, ultimately, different behaviours beyond the classroom.

With such a lack of clarity surrounding key concepts and with its origins in Western conceptions of learner-centred education, the relevance of the curriculum to the Thai context must be questioned. While writers such as Fry (2018) believe that Thailand's majority Buddhist epistemology and 'philosophy of learning and thinking is totally consistent with the progressive student-centred learning philosophy emphasized in the 1999 NEA' (Fry, 2018: 678) – which would also hold for CLT – the consistency would seem to hold true only at the philosophical level rather than at the classroom level where teacher-centred pedagogy still holds sway. Another Thai educational paradox thus exists here: if student-centred learning is compatible with the Buddhist philosophy of learning and thinking, why does classroom teaching remain largely teacher-centred? An examination of classroom practice is thus warranted.

In the Classroom

I think the teaching styles of Thai teachers make the lessons more complicated. For instance, when Thais, no matter how old they are, live abroad, they are able to speak the language because they have a chance to listen to it and speak. The Thai way of teaching English focuses on the course book, practicing listening and speaking is limited. (Thai student, Chiang Mai)

It is a common observation that many, perhaps most, Thai teachers of English rely on a course book to guide their teaching. The majority of books approved for use in schools by the MoE are repackaged series from major Western publishers such as Cambridge University Press and Oxford University Press, although locally produced series such as 'Projects: Play and Learn'[4] are also approved for use in primary schools. Whichever book is used, the style of teaching seems to differ little from school to school. Not surprisingly, how English is taught in the primary classroom has similarities with how Thai is taught, as Shaeffer (2018) explains:

The approach to teaching language and literacy in early grades is a special problem. A focus on spelling and deciphering words, rather than expressing concepts and ideas, prevents students from learning to be creative and analytical. This affects both non-Thai-speaking and Thai- speaking students. The same approach is used for teaching English as a second language and may explain why Thailand fares badly in English. (Shaeffer, 2018: 115)

This observation accords with my own experience. During the course of an evaluation of a national in-service teacher-training project that ran from 2017 to 2019, I conducted a number of classroom observations in different parts of the country to gauge the degree to which teachers demonstrated classroom behaviours consistent with those recommended in the training they had received and which were consistent with the expectations of the curriculum. Common patterns of behaviour could be observed across many lessons which were then related to the training course and curriculum expectations as: (a) 'Indicators of development', or positive indicators of change; (b) 'In need of further development', or areas where there was little evidence of change; and (c) 'Contextual factors', those factors impacting teachers' classroom behaviours over which they had no control. Findings in each of these three areas relevant to primary school classroom behaviours were:

(a) Indicators of development

(1) Some teachers are implementing more activity-based, communicatively oriented lessons as a result of input received on the course. This was observed in terms of activities that were taken directly from the course and used appropriately in classrooms at varying levels. Progressing from simply using what had been learnt on the course, some teachers were genuinely innovative and generated their own activities, demonstrating a genuine enthusiasm for teaching and a commitment to helping their students learn English.

(2) Many teachers were using English for significant amounts of time in their lessons. This is clearly important as students will not have the confidence to use the language if their own teachers do not provide models of confident second language users.

(3) In a number of schools it was clear that students were used to working in groups and were able to form these when asked. The students also demonstrated enthusiasm for the activities teachers used from the training.

(4) Generally, teachers have good relationships with their students, and are respected by them. These relationships provide fertile ground for teachers to change their teaching styles, knowing that they are likely to have their students' support if they do so.

(5) Many teachers continue to use Thai in the classroom alongside English, but this is often for a purpose appropriate to the lesson and thus an intelligent use of the students' mother tongue to support learning.

(6) Many teachers prepare supplementary written practice materials to support their students' learning and are aware that textbooks alone do not meet their students' needs. They are attempting to provide differentiated learning materials to cope with the different skill levels in the same class (but could do with more support here).

(b) In need of further development

(1) Teachers do not connect lesson stages well to each other, or link target language for a lesson back to previously learned language. As the time for English language learning is relatively short and students have few (if any) practice opportunities outside the classroom, continued linking of language learning points within a lesson as well as recycling across lessons to reinforce learning is necessary.

(2) The influence of the grammar-translation method remains, especially in small rural schools where the students have no exposure to English outside the classroom. Although this is understandable to a certain extent as a reaction to the context, students are then denied any opportunity to see English as a means of communication rather than an object of study.

(3) Teachers' classroom management skills are in need of further development, particularly basics such as ensuring they have all the students' attention before, for example, they give instructions, check understanding or elicit answers to questions. Gaining the students' attention is particularly important in large classes with greater potential for distraction: all students must be able to hear what the teacher is saying in order to be able to participate fully in the lesson.

(4) Checking of students' understanding is not always conducted effectively. There remains a tendency among some teachers to ask 'Do you understand? Yes or no?' when checking understanding.

(c) Contextual factors

(1) Class sizes in the larger schools are not conducive to the use of group and pair work. The largest class observed in a primary school was 53, in a room where the teacher could barely get between the rows of desks to monitor children as they worked (although she tried valiantly).

This picture of partial implementation of more student-centred teaching and learning approaches is consistent with the conclusions of other research. (It is worth noting too that the observations themselves were arranged beforehand by the MoE and teachers may have been chosen to present a positive picture of the impact of the training and, of course, the teachers would be more likely to use what they had learnt on their course when an observer was scheduled to observe a lesson.) Hallinger and Lee (2011: 151) found that as far as teaching-learning reforms initiated by the NEA were concerned, only 17.5% of teachers were at the 'routine use' stage and 15.7% at the 'early use' stage, while others remained at the 'information' (29.1%), 'interest' (18.8%) and 'preparation' (18.9%) stages. Hallinger and Lee (2011) attribute this in part to the complexity of the reforms themselves and the concomitant scale of the demands on teachers.

With respect to English, the change from a teacher-centred grammar-translation approach to a student-centred CLT approach requires not simply a new methodological skill-set but also, and perhaps even more importantly, a fundamental shift in the conception of the roles of teachers and students in the classroom. This shift is sociocultural, with the reforms promoting new forms of teacher and student behaviours which are at odds with cultural norms. Thai students are taught from primary school onwards to respect teachers (indeed, all adults) and not to do anything that could disrupt the harmony which is highly prized in society. Thai society is very hierarchical and this is reflected in how schools operate, as Hallinger (2004) explains:

> Principals naturally expect their orders to be followed with relatively little discussion, few questions from staff, and no overt dissent. This would be the same in terms of relationships between principals and their superordinates, as well as between teachers and their students. (Hallinger, 2004: 68)

Translated into classroom behaviours, teachers possess knowledge which is a gift they pass on to their students and, in return, students honour their teachers by, for example, not causing them to 'lose face' by posing questions to which they might not know the answer. With a teacher-centred, grammar-translation approach, teachers remain in control of the knowledge base and do not have to risk using the language themselves, or providing language to students, in ways that cannot be predicted and that may cause them to make mistakes – also entailing 'losing face'.

From a sociocultural perspective, the persistence of teacher-centred methods is readily understandable and represents what Pomson (2002: 24, citing MacIntyre, 1985: 221) calls 'a not-yet-completed narrative'. In this view, the 'persistence of inherited traditions of teaching' (Pomson, 2002: 23) occurs because the methods continue to be useful to teachers in their particular contexts whatever the prescriptions of the official curriculum. Although teachers have little autonomy in whether or not they accept an officially mandated curriculum at the level of theory, at the level of practice they nonetheless retain *de facto* control over the degree to which the official curriculum is actually implemented in the classroom. The learner-centred curriculum instantiated in CLT conflicts with the cultural norms of teacher and student behaviours in the classroom. Not only that, but CLT has expectations of English language use that are difficult to realise in the Thai context. As one teacher I interviewed put it, using English is:

> *not real, because in our society we don't really use English and the students know I can speak Thai. I always try to speak English with my students and they always reply in Thai because they know I can understand Thai. That's the problem for me. [...] All teachers, I think, are willing to speak English but the society doesn't ... like, we use Thai.*

Teachers' Subject Knowledge: English Language Levels

When even using English is 'not real', the challenge to implement learner-centred communicative teaching is exacerbated by Thai teachers' own English language levels which are generally below agreed standards for teachers of a foreign language in primary schools. Research contradicts the commonplace view that 'primary English teachers do not need much English as they only have to teach beginners'. Assessing teachers' proficiency needs on the widely used CEFR, Enever (2011) concluded that:

> Observation evidence from the ELLiE [Early Language Learning in Europe] study indicates that a minimum entry level of B1 [on the CEFR] is needed, with a desirable level of C1 for a teacher to be fully functional in the informal and incidental language regularly required in the primary classroom. (Enever, 2011: 26)

B1 on the CEFR indicates an 'independent user' at an intermediate level, while C1 indicates a 'proficient user' at an advanced level. Fuller descriptors for these levels are given in Table 2.2. The language levels of all teachers on the in-service training programme I referred to earlier were assessed by the MoE prior to the start of the programme, using an online standardised instrument, and results for the participating teachers are given in Table 2.3.

The English language level of many of these teachers was low, with 9.3% at A1 and 50.6% at A2 level (A1 & A2 = basic users) on the CEFR, which has been adopted by the MoE to assess teachers' proficiency. Descriptors for A1 and A2 levels are given in Table 2.4. Almost one-third of teachers (32%) were at B1, Enever's (2011) 'minimum entry level', with 7.6% at B2 (B1 & B2 = independent users), while just 72 (0.6%) of the 12,236 teachers were at the 'desirable' C1 level and only one at C2 (proficient users).

Table 2.2 CEFR descriptors for B1 and C1 levels

CEFR level	Global descriptors
B1 (intermediate)	Can understand the main points of clear standard input on familiar matters regularly encountered in work, school, leisure, etc. Can deal with most situations likely to arise while travelling in an area where the language is spoken. Can produce simple connected text on topics which are familiar or of personal interest. Can describe experiences and events, dreams, hopes & ambitions and briefly give reasons and explanations for opinions and plans.
C1 (advanced)	Can understand a wide range of demanding, longer texts, and recognise implicit meaning. Can express him/herself fluently and spontaneously without much obvious searching for expressions. Can use language flexibly and effectively for social, academic and professional purposes. Can produce clear, well-structured, detailed text on complex subjects, showing controlled use of organisational patterns, connectors and cohesive devices.

Source: https://www.coe.int/en/web/common-european-framework-reference-languages/table-1-cefr-3.3-common-reference-levels-global-scale

Table 2.3 CEFR levels of teachers on an in-service teacher development programme

CEFR level	No. of teachers	%
A1	1133	9.3
A2	6194	50.6
B1	3910	32.0
B2	926	7.6
C1	72	0.6
C2	1	0.0
Total	12,236	100.0

Source: Hayes (2020: 248).

Table 2.4 CEFR descriptors for A1 and A2 levels

CEFR level	Global descriptors
A1 (beginner)	Can understand and use familiar everyday expressions and very basic phrases aimed at the satisfaction of needs of a concrete type. Can introduce him/herself and others and can ask and answer questions about personal details such as where he/she lives, people he/she knows and things he/she has. Can interact in a simple way provided the other person talks slowly and clearly and is prepared to help.
A2 (elementary)	Can understand sentences and frequently used expressions related to areas of most immediate relevance (e.g. very basic personal and family information, shopping, local geography, employment). Can communicate in simple and routine tasks requiring a simple and direct exchange of information on familiar and routine matters. Can describe in simple terms aspects of his/her background, immediate environment and matters in areas of immediate need.

Source: https://www.coe.int/en/web/common-european-framework-reference-languages/table-1-cefr-3.3-common-reference-levels-global-scale.

Whatever the merits of using this scale to benchmark teachers' performance, the preponderance of scores at the lower levels is clearly concerning in light of curriculum expectations as it indicates that many participants had poor skill levels in the language they were required to teach. However, 'A2 is normal' was the comment by a teacher on a colleague's CEFR result as reported by Franz and Teo (2017: 323), which both underscores the quantitative finding of 50.6% of teachers being at this level and indicates that these teachers did not seem to be unduly concerned by such a result. The MoE is aware of the problem, however, and the Deputy Minister announced in late 2018 that all graduates from the major teacher-training universities, the Rajabhat Universities, would in future be required to achieve B2 (upper intermediate) on the CEFR and those who wished to teach English would have to reach C1 or 'proficient user' level (Saengpassa, 2018). There have been no further details made publicly available of how this ambitious target is to be achieved and the change of government (and ministers) in July 2019 inevitably calls it into question, for the reasons discussed previously.

Teachers, Curriculum and Training

From a practical perspective, the CEFR results in Table 2.3 indicate that the education system does not at present possess the human resources necessary to implement the curriculum through a methodology that emphasises communicative English language use. Even if the English language requirements for new teacher graduates are realised, it will be many years before they have an impact across the country. It is hardly surprising, then, that research finds a gap between curriculum policy and classroom practice (Fitzpatrick, 2011; Prapaisit de Segovia & Hardison, 2009). Unfortunately, this is often explained by blaming teachers for their deficiencies instead of rethinking the curriculum in line with existing teachers' capabilities and the contextual realities of English language use in Thailand and then using this as the basis from which to develop long-term plans which could – if given adequate resourcing and support – eventually lead to the higher achievement levels the MoE has as a goal. A failure to confront the realities of English teaching in primary classrooms and English language use outside the classroom is not new, however. Successive curriculum changes have included prescriptions for CLT, but research continually shows it has not been widely adopted due to:

(1) Lack of communication about and clarity of the educational philosophy underlying the curriculum
(2) Lack of training provision for in-service teachers
(3) Negative exam washback
(4) Environment not being conducive to learning English (Franz & Teo, 2017: 324)

Viewed in historical perspective, the issue of under-achievement in learning English as a foreign language in primary schools is longstanding, as are many of its causes. Sukamolson (1998) analysed successive phases of English education in schools prior to the NEA of 1999, identifying levels of success and systemic problems. From the 1931–1960 period, labelled as the 'Early Dawn of Democracy', one of the most consistent problems identified has been a lack of qualified teachers, and all of the phases from 1931 to 1995 have been categorised as 'failure', irrespective of the teaching methods supposed to have been adopted, the starting grade or the number of hours of instruction. In the most recent period covered by Sukamolson (1998), i.e. 1996 onwards, the assessment changes to 'sceptical' rather than 'failure', which may be as much a reflection of the short time since the period began as the actual success of English language instruction during this period. However, 'insufficient qualified teachers' remained a problem, now joined by 'students' low motivation & interests' (Sukamolson, 1998: 85).

The issue of sufficient *qualified* teachers is one that persists today. Given that teachers have a powerful influence on students, accounting for as much as 30% of variance in student achievement (Hattie, 2003), teacher quality is paramount in any education system. Moreover, teacher quality is an educational variable that is alterable through initial teacher training and continuing professional development (CPD) throughout a teacher's career and so potential for improvement in quality is ever present. The caveat, of course, is that both initial teacher training and CPD need themselves to be of high quality, capable of developing teachers with the skills and qualities needed to make the learning of English meaningful to all children in all schools across the country. At present, the quality of Thai teachers is intended to be assured by having a five-year Bachelor of Education degree – comprising four years of coursework, in which students specialise in teaching a particular level, and one year of practice teaching – as the standard academic prerequisite for entry to the profession.[5] Since 2003 there has also been a formal licensing system with qualifications accredited by the Teachers' Council of Thailand. Whether these requirements assure adequately qualified teachers to implement the mandated curriculum as expected is open to question, most obviously in terms of English teachers' language proficiency but also in terms of pedagogic skills. Another factor, just as important as their quality, is the distribution of teachers across the country. Not surprisingly, the achievement gap between urban and rural schools is reflected in 'the existence of a similar "human resource gap" when comparing urban and rural school leaders and teachers' (Piyaman *et al.*, 2017: 717). Particularly worrying is the dearth of teachers qualified to teach English (as well as mathematics and science) in rural primary schools, according to the chair of the Education Deans Council of Thailand (Mala, 2017).

These are significant challenges for educational policymakers to overcome but, at present, it seems that there is little understanding of processes of change at the upper echelons of policymaking, where top-down decision-making results in well-meaning policies that are generally unrealisable in the context. Change is not an 'event' that can be mandated but a process that takes time and resources to achieve. Hallinger and Bryant (2013: 415) comment:

> The tendency of policy-makers to treat change as an event leads to incomplete strategies, distorted time frames for assessing success and a lack of commitment to persist over the long term.

The constant changes at the ministerial level discussed earlier only worsen prospects of commitment to long-term processes of change at the system level. Meanwhile, teachers bear the brunt of public criticism for failures which are not of their own making and are left to cope as best they can with insufficient support in implementing multiple top-down mandates designed to 'improve' their performance. It is telling that the 'Southeast Asia Teachers Competency Framework', which claims to have been 'designed for Southeast Asian teachers by Southeast Asian teachers' (SEAMEO *et al.*, 2018: 1) was in fact developed 'by key high officials from the eleven Ministries of Education as well as experts in teacher education from the 11 countries' (SEAMEO *et al.*, 2018: 1), while classroom teachers are simply told: 'As a teacher, you may find it useful in keeping yourself informed of the competencies that you need to successfully perform your role' (SEAMEO *et al.*, 2018: 3). This does not augur well for the framework to achieve its intended aim of acting 'as a guide for Southeast Asian teachers to improve their performance to bring about the quality education for all students in Southeast Asia' (SEAMEO *et al.*, 2018: 1).

Reflections: Resolving the Educational Paradox in English Language Teaching and Learning in Thai Primary Schools

Any realistic account of English language teaching in primary schools in Thailand sounds, unfortunately, like a litany of failure. As is all too common worldwide, teachers receive much of the blame for not implementing policies that ministries enact to 'improve' standards. Another way to look at the situation, however, is to see a failure of language education policy specifically and of educational planning generally. The problem of under-achievement in English in primary schools (and, indeed, at other educational levels too) in Thailand is intimately bound up with problems of general educational quality and inequality and is unlikely to be solved outside the wider context of solutions to these systemic problems. To return to the OECD/UNESCO report cited at the beginning of this chapter, it remains deeply concerning that 'inequalities are reproduced in the education system, which [...] tends to reinforce disparities rather than help to overcome them' (OECD/UNESCO, 2016: 43). English teaching and learning are part of the ecology of primary school education, not separate from it. More of the same, for example in terms of policies which increase the number of hours of instruction in English that students receive in primary school from one hour per week in Grades 1–3 and two hours per week in Grades 4–6 to five hours per week for all grades, are unlikely to have any impact other than to exacerbate the existing rural–urban divide. If small rural schools do not have the resources to teach one hour of English a week effectively, how can they be expected to teach English for five hours?

As a means to enhance the educational prospects of children in all primary schools in all areas of the country, a different approach to the learning of English and other foreign languages could be more productive. The following suggestions derive from this chapter's analysis. To begin with, in implementing any educational reforms, a more realistic approach to the timescales and resources required to implement them, taking account of the capacity of the system (in human and material terms) to absorb change would be beneficial. This would recognise that change is a complex process which often takes a considerable amount of time to achieve, that change cannot simply be mandated by Ministry officials and that, to maximise the chances of success, policymakers would do well to involve teachers more actively in the development of educational reforms. There is also potential in having a language education policy which emphasises the value of learning other regional languages as co-equal to the focus on English as an international language. A reformulated language education policy should also consider the role of mother-tongue based multilingual education in the primary school for children for whom Thai is not a first language, as research indicates that learning in the first language in primary school offers children a higher chance of success (Trudell *et al.*, 2015). Of course, the implementation of any reform requires quality teachers, and there seems to be an urgent need for improved teacher training, both initial and CPD (which presupposes effective development for teacher educators), focusing on both language skills and language pedagogy for the primary classroom. These teachers also need a contextually appropriate foreign language curriculum to work with, one that takes account of the realities of English and other languages in young learners' lives.

Thai students rank highly in well-being (the so-called 'PISA Happiness Index') – scoring 7.71 on a scale of 0–10 against the OECD average of 7.31[6] – irrespective of the educational achievement and quality issues that they experience in primary schools. It is to be hoped that in the future all children in primary schools nationwide will be able to match high levels of happiness with higher levels of achievement in English and other languages in classes taught by more highly skilled teachers using a contextually appropriate curriculum. I will return to discussion of suggestions for a more productive and child-centred approach to foreign language learning in primary schools in Thailand and in other countries in the final chapter of this book.

Notes

(1) See http://www.ethnologue.com/country/TH
(2) See http://122.155.92.12/nnt_en/Core_Values/
(3) See https://uil.unesco.org/case-study/effective-practices-database-litbase-0/patani-ma lay-thai-bilingual-multilingual-education
(4) For details, see www.dekthai.net/Flipbook/eng_info.pdf
(5) A reduction in the length of the degree programme from five to four years beginning with the 2019 intake was announced in 2018, but few details are publicly available of this policy change.
(6) See http://gpseducation.oecd.org/CountryProfile?primaryCountry=THA&treshold =10&topic=PI

3 South Korea: A Severe Case of 'English Fever'

Introduction

Consistent with the emphasis of the preceding chapter on the Thai education system, this chapter examines the teaching and learning of the main foreign language in South Korean schools, English, with a principal focus on the primary sector. Placing language learning in primary schools in its wider socioeducational context of necessity includes a discussion of factors *beyond schools* which influence what happens *inside schools*, most notably here the place of English in South Korea[1] and its functions in society, both overt and covert. Or, as B.-R. Kim (2015: 188) puts it:

> Ultimately, the problem of English education is that of 'constructed reality' into which the success psychology of each Korean is condensed; therefore, it must be viewed from the historical, structural, institutional, hierarchical, and cultural perspectives of Korean society. (Kim, 2015: 188)

As a starting point for this discussion, any review of the South Korean education system will reveal that it is regarded as high performing according to commonly cited international metrics. For example, in the Project for International Student Assessment (PISA) rankings of performance among 15-year-old students, South Korea has consistently been near the top of the country rankings in every iteration. The strong performance in the PISA tests, as well as success in other international measures such as the Trends in International Mathematics and Science Study (TIMSS) for Grade 4 and Grade 8 students, is generally adduced as evidence that the Korean education system provides its students with a strong foundation in compulsory basic education, from the primary level to the end of lower secondary school. In the 2018 PISA results, the relative proportion of top performers in all three subject areas assessed – mathematics, science and reading – was higher than the OECD average, and the relative proportion of low-performing students was lower than the OECD average (OECD, 2019). However, once we go beyond the headline indicators, other aspects of the 2018 PISA results reveal a system with some contradictions. On the one hand, albeit to a lesser degree than the OECD average, success is tied to socioeconomic status which is 'a strong predictor of performance in mathematics and science', explaining '11% of the variation in mathematics performance in PISA 2018 in Korea (compared to 14% on average across OECD countries), and 8% of the variation in science performance (compared to the OECD average of 13% of the variation)' (OECD, 2019: 4). On the other hand, in spite of this correlation between socioeconomic status and educational achievement, some 13% of disadvantaged students in Korea scored in the top quarter for reading which, for the OECD, indicates that 'disadvantage is not destiny' (OECD, 2019: 4). Even so, an issue of significant concern in the 2018 results is a continued widening of the performance gap between the highest-achieving and lowest-achieving students across all subjects, with the scores of the lowest 10% declining 'by more than 7 points, on average, per 3-year period [between PISA assessments], or more than 20 points per decade' (OECD, 2019: 3). We will return to the impact of socioeconomic status on education and achievement in English specifically later in this chapter.

The high overall level of educational performance in Korea as reflected in PISA and TIMMs results is one of the major outcomes of centralised planning to restore the country's social infrastructure following the devastation caused by the 1950–1953 Korean War. In a country with sparse natural resources, successive post-war governments perceived education to be the foundation for economic growth, and a series of national educational development plans were designed to rebuild the education system, focusing first on the primary sector in the 1960s, then on the secondary sector in the 1970s and finally on the tertiary sector in the 1980s. With the implementation of these plans, the transition rate from primary to middle school increased from 54.3% in 1965 to 99.9% by 1995, and from middle school to high school from 69.1% in 1965 to 98.5% in 1995 and 99.5% by 2000.[2] The government philosophy was that:

> Education raised people's competence, which brought about economic, political, social and cultural growth in Korea, and the resulting enhanced national competence brought about educational growth. Within this virtuous cycle, education and national growth created a synergy effect. (KMOE, 2017: 7)

Support for the economic impact of government planning is provided by other research with, for example, Hultberg *et al.* (2017: 5) explaining in their analysis of education and human capital accumulation in Korea that 'expenditures on education are an investment that produces future economic and social benefits. Education in general is also associated with greater productivity, higher wages and increased Gross Domestic Product (GPD)'. Per capita annual GDP growth, rising from $94 in 1961 to $11,948 in 2000 and to $31,363 in 2018,[3] bears witness to the success of government educational policies in helping to provide the foundation for economic development as Korea transformed from a largely agrarian economy in the 1950s to the major industrial power that it has become in the 21st century.

Also prominent in the task of rebuilding the education system was an 'egalitarian ideal', an emphasis on equal opportunity for all (G.-J. Kim, 2002), one outcome of which may be the lower than average proportion of low-achieving students in the system today. Another important contributory factor in rebuilding was the longstanding 'zeal for education' (G.-J. Kim, 2002) in Korean society at large, with parents making financial sacrifices for their children's education and being actively involved in their schooling. The zeal for education persists to this day and is reflected in many parents seeking a competitive educational advantage for their children from increasingly young ages. Typically, this is manifested through children's participation in supplementary private tuition across a range of subjects. This has boomed for English, in particular, since 1995 when it was announced that English would be taught in elementary schools from 1997 onwards. The extent of private tuition is a response to the intensely competitive nature of the education system, although whether private educational institutes contribute to the aforementioned 'egalitarian ideal' is a matter of debate (again, the issue will be discussed later in this chapter). However, a brief account of the context of language(s) in Korean society is first required.

Languages, the Economy and Education

South Korea is a linguistically homogeneous country, one where there is an exceptionally high 'degree of congruity of speech community and nation' (Coulmas, 1999: 408, cited in Song, 2012: 10), i.e. 'Korean nationals speak Korean, and most speakers of Korean are [...] Korean nationals' (Song, 2012: 10). The 2018 census showed that there were 49.98 million South Korean nationals in the country and 1.65 million foreign nationals (3.2% of the total population). Of the foreign nationals living in Korea, the largest group was Chinese nationals (including Taiwanese) at 45.2% of the total, followed by Vietnamese at 10.2% and Thais at 9.1%, while Americans comprised 4%. Nationals from other English-speaking countries were not individually listed but would presumably be in the category of 'others', comprising 31.4% of the total of foreign nationals.[4] With its homogeneous linguistic make-up, it is unsurprising that there should be just one official language in South Korea, Korean. This has been the case since the inception of the Republic of Korea in 1948, following a period of colonial rule by Japan (1910–1945) during which Japanese was promoted in all areas of life to the detriment of Korean. Although the assimilationist policy of the Japanese engendered bilingualism among those Koreans who received Japanese-medium schooling, post-war stigmatisation of the Japanese language and 'cultural imports' until the late 1990s has meant that 'Korean-Japanese bilingual South Koreans are no longer common or, more accurately, they constitute a dying breed' (Song, 2012: 23).

The position of Korean as the sole national and official language remained unchallenged until the later 1990s when an 'Official English' movement emerged. Given the congruity between the Korean speech community and nation, and also in light of the failure of attempts at assimilation by the Japanese during the period of colonisation, this is, at first sight, a 'bizarre phenomenon' (Song, 2011: 35). The movement, which continued to garner attention through the first decade of the 21st century, arose following the 1997 Asian financial crisis, when stock markets plummeted and currencies lost up to 70% of their value across Korea, Malaysia, Thailand and other Asian countries. The crisis in Korea was associated with the perception that foreign investment was limited because of communication difficulties in an international language and hence the economy was particularly vulnerable to external market forces. The argument ran that, as the lingua franca of global business, English was needed 'to ensure that South Korea will play an active and important role in world political and economic activities' and that 'Rather than wait for speakers of other languages to learn Korean, the government wants its people prepared to communicate in English with those who do not speak their language' (Li, 1998: 681). This argument later gave rise to former president Myung-Bak Lee's 2008 proposal for an 'English Immersion education' policy for high schools, a proposal withdrawn over public concerns, although the president continued to affirm that English was a 'tool needed for competing in the twenty-first century' (Lee *et al.*, 2010: 338).

While the proposals for English as an official language and English immersion education were rejected, belief in English as a national economic necessity endures to the present day among most Korean policymakers, as well as in society at large. The 'English as an economic necessity' argument tends to be treated as an act of faith, however, rather than being subjected to critical analysis. Much of the literature on English language education in the country also subscribes to this argument. For example, Jo (2008: 376) states: 'Learning English is an essential skill that enables Koreans to be more competitive in the global market'. Primary school teachers themselves also subscribe to the instrumental value of English. In a randomised survey which produced responses from 828 primary school teachers, Chang *et al.* (2006: np) found that the two most common reasons cited for teaching English in primary schools were 'international exchange' and 'future career'. This was true whether the responding teachers were English specialists or generalist homeroom teachers.

However, in reality, just as we have seen in Thailand, it is general education rather than proficiency in a specific foreign language that is important to national economic competitiveness (Hultberg *et al.*, 2017); investigations of language use in the workplace reveal a different motivation for the emphasis on English. Cho (2014: 8), for example, comments that 'even though most companies rarely use English while they work, job applicants have to achieve high scores in [...] standardized English tests to be qualified to apply for a job'. Moreover, even before they enter the workforce, all students who go on to tertiary education are assessed in English in the high-stakes College Scholastic Ability Test (CSAT), which determines the university to which students are admitted, upon which so much depends for them. The test is 'considered a national event, with working hours at public offices delayed by an hour to 10 a.m. to prevent traffic congestion for applicants going to test venues. The local stock and currency markets also open an hour later than usual' (Korea Times, 2019: np). The English tests have a particular impact as 'Flight schedules will also be affected for 35 minutes from 1:05 p.m. to 1:40 p.m., when English listening tests will take place' (2019: np). Although strongest and most immediate at the secondary level, the prospect of the CSAT is not simply of concern at that stage but also impacts parents' commitment to their children's education from the earliest grades through significant expenditure on private tuition. This occurs even though standardised national tests, the National Assessment of Educational Achievement (NAEA), are not administered until Grade 9.

It seems, then, that English functions more as a gatekeeping requirement than an employment-related skill. Nevertheless, irrespective of its actual function in society at large, English is a mandatory subject throughout the education system with teaching officially beginning in Grade 3 of primary schools.

Teaching, the Curriculum and English

In general, teaching in Korea is a prestigious profession, as teachers are part of the civil service with good working terms and conditions which provides social status. It is this status and security of employment that prompts many parents to urge their children, particularly daughters, to become teachers and, as in many other countries, teaching at the kindergarten and primary levels is a gendered profession (Hayes, 2008a; Linse, 2005). In 2013 the percentage of female teachers in Korean kindergartens was 98.4% and in primary schools 76.6% (Kim *et al.*, 2015: 28). The government controls the supply and demand of primary teachers, resulting in most prospective teachers being hired, and only students in the top 5% of high school graduates are admitted to teacher-training programmes at universities (S. Park, 2010).

Children are required to attend school from the age of six until 15. In common with the first country case study, Thailand, English is the first foreign language in Korean schools. This is unsurprising given such strong and longstanding commitment to English as an economic necessity at the highest policy levels. It was first introduced into primary schools as a compulsory subject in 1997, although as previously indicated the decision to do so was made in 1995 prior to the Asian financial crisis. It is currently taught for one hour per week in Grades 3 and 4 and two hours per week in Grades 5 and 6 (although private tuition outside school can begin much earlier). The primary school curriculum is governed by the 2015 Revised

National Curriculum, the main goal of which is to transform education from a reliance on standardised knowledge and rote learning, long acknowledged to permeate teaching and learning in classrooms, and instead advance a 'new vision [which] seeks to promote flexibility and creativity on how the students address the new challenges of the 21st century', as well as to 'cultivate a "creative and integrative learner"' (Cho & Huh, 2017: np). For students in Grade 1 of primary schools, the revised curriculum encompasses general social formation subjects called 'wise living', 'pleasant living' and 'we are first grade' alongside Korean language arts, mathematics and ethics. The time allocated to 'we are first grade' is distributed among the other subjects in Grade 2. 'Wise living' and 'pleasant living' are also dropped in Grade 3 when English and other subjects such as science and social studies are introduced.[5] With respect to English, the revised curriculum emphasises communicative language use for 'real life', and this is reinforced in approved textbooks, as the Ministry of Education (MoE) website proclaims:

> Textbooks provide contents that connect students' everyday situations, and systematically provide participatory learning activities for acquiring English expressions so they can use what they have learned in real life. (KMOE, 2018a)

The focus on communicative language use itself is not new but has been a feature of English teaching and learning for many years, since the introduction of the 7th national curriculum in 1997 which emphasised learner-centred education across the curriculum. It has been reinforced by revisions from 2007 onwards, including the most recent changes in 2015 emphasising competency-based learning over knowledge-based learning.

The degree to which teachers in schools actually adopt the mandated communicative approach is variable and differs across educational levels, with a higher degree of implementation at the primary level. Moodie and Nam (2016: 78) note that 'the communicative methods more prevalent in primary schools lose their place to the grammar-translation approach as the students move to the higher levels of school', when the need to do well in the CSAT overrides the need to develop communicative English proficiency. But even at the primary level, Garton (2014) found that the 125 teachers in her survey were adopting a weak form of the communicative approach and that there was little evidence of unstructured, creative activities being used in the classroom, which she attributed to their time-consuming nature in a system which has insufficient time for activities beyond those prescribed. The degree of centralised control of the curriculum can be illustrated by prescription of not just the number of words to be learnt per grade, which is common in many educational systems, but even the number of words to be used in a sentence which textbook writers have to adhere to: in the Revised 7th Curriculum of 2008 this was seven for Grades 3 and 4 and nine for Grades 5 and 6 (H.D. Kang, 2012).

Unsurprisingly, Garton (2014: 213) concludes that 'the strictly prescribed curriculum and materials [...] may prove a barrier to the full implementation of methods policy', a conclusion echoed by So and Kang (2014) who characterise the curriculum as 'teacher-proof', observing that:

> teachers must follow detailed prescriptions, and they have little authority to determine the learning contents for their classes. In addition, all teachers are provided with textbooks published in accordance with the national curriculum guidelines. Hence, most teachers believe that implementing the national curriculum is equivalent to teaching the textbook [...]. (So & Kang, 2014: 798)

The difficulties encountered in the implementation of communicative methods in primary schools are the focus of Choi's (2015) examination of the policy of 'Teaching English through English' (TETE).[6] Introduced in 2001 as a response to the perceived failure of previous methods relying heavily on the use of Korean as the medium of instruction, the expectation was that if teachers would only speak English for most of the lesson time, children would become more competent speakers of English (Lee, 2014). In the context, TETE meant using English for 80% or more of instruction in the lesson (Choi, 2015). Surveys of teacher take-up of the policy revealed it to be slow to be adopted, however, and by 2007 only 34% of teachers reported that they taught English in English (Choi, 2015). This proportion is similar to that in a survey administered by the Korea Institute for Curriculum and Evaluation, in which only 39% of primary school teachers responded that they were certified to teach English in English, while 61% were not (H.D. Kang, 2012). The TETE policy was criticised for its negative impact on teachers, increasing levels of stress and failing to provide them with guidance on exactly how it should be implemented (Johnson *et al.*, 2017). There was even confusion about the amount of English teachers were expected to use. Although the official policy was to use English for 80% of instructional time, notices for training for the official certification scheme introduced in 2009 'refer to the ability to be measured as conducting lessons exclusively in English' and training manuals 'asked teachers to use English exclusively during the training and assessment procedure' (Choi, 2015: 207). Once implemented, the impact of the policy was even perceived differently by parents and teachers. In a 2011 study in the Seoul metropolitan area, 40% of parents believed the policy had had an impact on improving students' English proficiency, while just 22% of teachers shared this perception (Choi, 2015).

Irrespective of how it was implemented, the policy and its associated training seemed to place greater emphasis on English language *proficiency* than language *pedagogy*: 'speak more English and all will be well' appeared to be the message. However, in a curriculum framework where the prescribed communicative teaching methods emphasised less teacher-talking time and more opportunities for children to talk, teachers were left not knowing exactly when and for what purposes to use the language. Even those teachers who did use a significant amount of English in their lessons continued to use Korean, principally to sustain children's motivation to participate in class, to scaffold students' learning and for classroom management, as Rabbidge and Chappell (2014) found in a study of primary school teachers in Gwangju. This is to be expected in a monolingual environment where teachers are also judged on their ability to help their students to pass exams, whatever the curriculum might say about using language for communication, and where this requires them to keep students committed to learning. Washback from the high-stakes examination culture in secondary schools results in parental pressure on teachers even in primary schools. Hence, in their classes, if students fail to understand when they use English, teachers inevitably resort to Korean to communicate lesson content. For many teachers, as in Rabbidge and Chappell's (2014) study, it seems that 'the need to maintain student motivation in the subject overrides the need to comply with the government's TETE policy' (Rabbidge & Chappell, 2014: 12).

No matter the language mix in the classroom, the challenge of sustaining student motivation to learn English is a significant issue. One might expect motivation to taper off in the higher years of schooling, but even among younger learners demotivation exists. In a survey of 6301 primary school students between Grade 3 and Grade 6, T.-Y. Kim (2011) found that 'There was a statistically significant and consistent decrease in the students' satisfaction with their English learning experience; expectation of ultimate success in English; and intrinsic/extrinsic motivation and integrative/instrumental motivation' (Kim, 2011: 2). Thus, in spite of the emphasis given to it by parents, students themselves were less interested in English and perceived it to be less important as they advanced from Grade 3 to Grade 6 (Kim, 2011). This finding is not confined to English but is echoed in other studies which reveal that, in general, levels of interest in learning are low, in spite of high scores on international tests such as PISA and TIMMS (Choe *et al.*, 2013).

Student motivation also interacts with classroom discipline in the later stages of primary school (Garton, 2014). One teacher in Garton's (2014: 214) survey reported that a major challenge was '*Dealing with the older children who sometimes do not want to be learning anything*'. The complexity of factors affecting student's motivation is summed up in Kim and Seo's (2012, cited in Butler, 2015: 319) study, in which 'teachers attributed their students' demotivation for learning English to negative influences from teachers' practices and attitudes, excessive societal pressures and widening achievement gaps among students'. With respect to teachers' practices, one issue may be a mismatch between students' developmental levels in the later stages of primary school and the activities that are common in English classes which 'often create the notion among students that "English class has lots of games but is not serious business" (a Korean 6th grade teacher), and that this can eventually demotivate students' (Butler, 2005: 436). After several years of studying English, it is also likely that 'Some students appear to grow frustrated with what they can do in English versus what is possible in their native language' (Butler, 2005: 436). Hence, the question of whether the English language curriculum is sufficiently developmentally sensitive across the primary age range, which was raised by teachers in Butler's (2005) study, needs to be addressed.

Whatever the causes, the decline in student motivation contrasts with the dominant national discourse of the economic value of English and the increasing educational emphasis placed on the need to succeed in the language, ultimately for the CSAT, which, as noted, has a far-reaching washback effect. However, the two factors combined (student demotivation and the strong washback effect of the CSAT) help us to understand Moon's (2014: 207) assertion that by the time they get to university and after 'years of arduous toil [...] English falls among students' most loathed subjects'. In other research, T.-Y. Kim (2011: 9) maintained that his own study 'provides solid evidence that the key to maintaining increasing EFL motivation is not the prevailing discourse on English as an international language and the expenditure on private English education but each learner's personal senses of the importance and meaning of English learning'. Unfortunately, any need for personal meaning seems currently to be lost among the emphasis on extrinsic, instrumental sources of motivation in society and the education system.

Learners' own families contribute to extrinsic, instrumental motivation over any intrinsic desire to learn English by sending their children to private English tuition classes to ensure they receive a head start in a subject perceived as difficult. While this may be understandable from the parents' viewpoint, private tuition impacts classroom teaching in government schools in two important ways. First, teachers are confronted with varying language levels among their students, largely corresponding to the degree to which students receive private tuition, to which – ideally at least – they would tailor their lessons in order to meet each group's needs. However, this approach is difficult to implement with a curriculum which does not cater for such divergent levels. As one teacher put it, there is '*too big [a] gap between fast learners and slow learners caused by private education*' (Copland *et al.*, 2014: 753). Second, students' private tuition may even affect teachers' self-confidence in their own language abilities: as another teacher commented, '*Since Korean students' English proficiency is getting higher, I feel some burden about my own English proficiency*' (Copland *et al.*, 2014: 753). Garton (2014: 211) confirms that 'Lack of English proficiency is a matter of real concern for the Korean teachers': in her survey of 125 primary school teachers, 'nearly half the respondents report their level to be intermediate or lower' (Garton, 2014: 211). Teachers are also subject to regular criticism from their peers, parents and even students which produces 'everyday feelings of anxiety and shame' and results in the 'closing off any possibility to view themselves as legitimate English teachers' (Lee, 2014: 127). Because teachers equate their teaching competence with language competence, they fear that lack of proficiency sees them marked as poor teachers (Hiver, 2013), further adding to the stresses that they experience. Teachers' perceptions of themselves as inadequate models of English because of their divergence from native-speaker models is a longstanding issue (Lee, 2009) and appears to be exacerbated by the presence of native-speaker teaching assistants in schools, which we will discuss later.

Concern about teachers' language competence has also been evident at the policy level for some time, with Chang *et al.*'s (2006: 114) study of primary English concluding that 'a continuing challenge for the government is the language level of teachers'. One of the outcomes of this government concern was a large-scale, six-month in-service programme – the Intensive English Teacher Training Programme (IETTP) – which had a heavy emphasis on improving teachers' language proficiency. The medium of instruction for these courses was English, trainers were predominantly 'native speakers' of English from other countries, training centres included an 'English Only Zone' and up to two months was spent in an English-speaking country. The courses included a methodology component for young learners, but the primacy of language improvement was clear in the means of assessment of the two components. The pedagogy component was assessed by means of a self-assessment checklist whereas teachers' English language proficiency was measured by standardised pre- and post-course tests and improvement calculated statistically (Hayes, 2012). Assessing language skills with standardised tests while teaching skills are measured through self-assessment implies that priority has to be given to language, even though, as Chang *et al.* (2006: 114) acknowledge, 'language alone is not the sole determinant of success in teaching English at the primary level' and 'Just as important is age-specific pedagogy'. How teachers are trained in language pedagogy for young learners has varied, however, roughly corresponding to teachers' experience in the system. Those teachers who qualified to teach before English became a compulsory subject in primary schools in 1997 received only in-service training, which was somehow expected to be sufficient to enable them to teach the language, even though the language content was criticised for being focused on general English communicative ability and disconnected from the primary school English curriculum. Since 1997, newly trained teachers have had English courses as part of their initial teacher training, whether or not they decided to become English specialists. In practice, this has had an impact on the experience of novice teachers in their early years of teaching.

Initial Teacher Training, Homeroom Teachers and English Specialists in Schools

Initial teacher training for primary school teachers is conducted by the 11 National Universities of Education, the Korea National University of Education and the private Ehwa Women's University. Entry into these programmes is very competitive, with successful candidates being in the 95th percentile of high school graduates (Moodie & Nam, 2016). Prospective teachers study elementary education which includes at least two courses in teaching English; hence all teachers are potentially teachers of English. There is also an option to specialise in English. There have been criticisms of both generalist primary teachers teaching English and the provision of English specialists in primary schools. On the one hand, primary teachers are 'models for the children who use the Korean language [which is] the basis of learning and social life for them', for whom 'mastering English is, in a sense, a burden' (Shiga, 2008: 388). On the other hand, the increase in specialist English teachers which represents an 'inclination to English' (Shiga, 2008: 388) is said to diminish the symbolic importance of generalist primary teachers.

Whatever route they take, after their training courses all graduates must take a competitive exam to become public school teachers. This is often problematic for generalist primary teachers as it includes interviews and teaching demonstrations both in the first language and in English. Many teachers feel they are inadequately prepared for the English component of the exam during their training. In a survey of 868 pre-service teachers, Jung and Choi (2011, cited in Moodie & Nam, 2016) found that while some 75% were able to observe English lessons, only around 50% were able to teach English during their practicum. Not only does this discriminate in favour of those who are able to afford private tuition to enhance their English language abilities, but it also deprives the education system of those graduates who may have the potential to be effective in the classroom but who, without English proficiency, cannot pass the employment exams (Moodie & Nam, 2016). If they do pass the exams and secure a post, teachers then have guaranteed tenure until they reach the mandatory retirement age of 62, although they will not be able to remain for the long term in any one school. All teachers are required to transfer to a new school every four to five years, a system designed to ensure that more advantaged schools do not hold on to the 'best' teachers and that expertise is more evenly spread throughout the system.

Newly qualified teachers are subject to multiple pressures when they enter their first schools. As there is no official policy requiring teachers who teach English to have had specialised training, in many schools it is the younger teachers who are often assigned to teach the language, based on the simple assumption that they will be better at English than older teachers who had no mandatory English when they were themselves training (Lee, 2009; Moodie & Feryok, 2015). Because newly appointed teachers feel a need to be perceived as cooperative and respectful of the wishes of school administrators and their more senior peers, maintaining social harmony in the workplace, they are reluctant to demur if asked to teach English, even if they would prefer to be homeroom (i.e. class) teachers. Indeed, there appears to be a general preference for homeroom teaching over English subject teaching among many teachers as there are significant differences in the way that children respond to homeroom teachers and English subject teachers. Moodie and Feryok (2015) found numerous challenges for English teachers, viz.:

- There was a general lack of respect for subject teachers, giving rise to serious discipline problems (although these also seemed to occur in Grade 6 homeroom classes)
- There were problems meeting the needs of mixed-level classes, ranging from beginners to high proficiency in the same class
- The mixed level classes exacerbated behavioural problems among students
- English teachers were routinely assigned more administrative duties than homeroom teachers (Moodie & Feryok, 2015: 463–464)

From Moodie and Feryok's (2015) study, we can see that the differentiation between generalist primary school teachers and subject specialists has had a significant impact on the experiences of teachers in schools. The discipline issues they identify may arise from traditional perceptions of the role of the homeroom teachers acting as moral guides *in loco parentis* while children are at school, which extends even into secondary schools (Shin, 2007). Homeroom teachers are with the students for most of the day, teach multiple subjects and act as the first point of contact for parents in discussion of their children's behaviour and performance at school, and hence they are seen as more important than subject-only teachers. Children are more inclined to be respectful of their homeroom teachers and cooperative in the classroom, particularly in the early grades.

Classroom behaviour may also be linked to student achievement levels. In a case study of two primary school teachers, D.-M. Kang (2013) found that:

> While high-level students cooperated with the teacher's disciplinary calls, low-level students did not considerably modify their behavior. Additionally, while the high-level students were in agreement with the teacher's emphasis on the prioritization of order maintenance, the low-level students seemed to be disinterested in it. (Kang, 2013: 158)

Interestingly, a low-level student's viewpoint reported in D.-M. Kang (2013) indicates that at the root of the problem is the students' feeling that they are not being helped to learn rather than any desire to be disruptive, as this student's own words make clear.

> *I am not that interested in English learning because I'm poor at it, so I talk a lot to my friends or move around during class. And when my English teacher scolds me in Korean, I don't sit still and quiet. You see, what she teaches is hard to understand and boring. Also, what she says during her scolding is much harsher than what other teachers say in math or science classes. Her harsh words turn me off, and I don't actively participate in the activities. Funny, she doesn't try to help us poor achievers learn English better. My friends and I would talk and move around a lot less, if she helped us first.* (Kang, 2013: 159)

Such behavioural challenges are not unusual among poor achievers. Education systems prioritise conformity to norms of behaviour, and expect teaching of standardised content and attainment of standardised levels of achievement in each subject. Teachers are under continual pressure to ensure that children score highly on tests whatever their background or interest in a particular subject. School quality – and, thereby, teacher effectiveness – is determined by high student test scores. If test scores fall, teachers invariably receive the blame for their 'poor' teaching (Kumashiro, 2012). This appears to be true irrespective of the fact that the curriculum, in Korea as in so many other countries, is avowedly learner-centred and that curriculum revisions in 2009 promoted 'differentiated instruction to meet [students'] particular needs and to maximize the effect of teaching' (Chang, 2015: 73), also implying a recognition that any student's achievement levels might differ from subject to subject.

Although ostensibly designed to improve teaching and learning across the curriculum, in practice the plethora of centralised education reforms in Korea since 1995 have been criticised for 'increasing [teachers'] workload, while reducing their role to that of a mere technician, rendering teachers powerless in their efforts to overcome standardized teaching' (J.-W. Kim, 2004: 127). The policy overload has also led to high levels of stress and burnout among teachers (Chung & Choi, 2016). This intensification of teaching has become commonplace worldwide under neoliberal reform programmes, for example, in Australia (Fitzgerald *et al.*, 2019), England (Braun, 2017) and Japan (Katsuno, 2012). One aspect of intensification is the increase in administrative tasks that teachers are required to perform, often as a part of accountability compliance. Teachers routinely complain about the burden of these administrative tasks and the impact on their teaching. K.-N. Kim's (2019: 31) research demonstrates that 'teachers' administrative workload carries an opportunity cost of instructional activities. Teachers with greater administrative workloads are less likely to spend time on instructional preparation and providing feedback on students' assignment'. Whether this affects students' achievement, attitudes or classroom behaviour would need further research as it is already widely recognised that what happens in classrooms is very complex. Student behaviour, both acceptable and not acceptable in the system, does not occur in a vacuum but as a response to factors in schools – such as the teachers' capacity to deliver stimulating lessons which engage students' interest and motivate them to learn, alongside teachers possessing empathy for all students and treating them fairly – and beyond (such as family expectations of high achievement which is, in turn, affected by its valorisation in the wider society). There is a symbiotic relationship between 'good' behaviour and 'good' lessons and, to achieve both of these, it is the responsibility of the education system to establish the conditions under which teachers can create lessons that are stimulating for their students and that they can enjoy teaching with minimal stress.

'Native Speaker'[7] Teacher Programmes

A complicating factor for Korean teachers of English as they prepare and teach their lessons is the presence of 'native speakers' in many classrooms under the nationwide 'English Programme in Korea' (EPIK) or other programmes at the local Office of Education level.[8] Eligibility requirements state that 'EPIK teachers <u>must</u> be citizens of one of the following countries: Australia, Canada, Ireland, New Zealand, United Kingdom, United States, or South Africa' and that 'Indian citizens are eligible for positions if they meet all other requirements and hold a teacher's license in English'.[9] The restricted number of approved countries, the recent addition of qualified Indian teachers notwithstanding, reveals the societal association of English as being primarily with Western native speakers, a preference reinforced by the criterion that even ethnic Koreans domiciled in the listed countries are not eligible unless they have received education in English from junior high school level (Heo, 2013). The minimum educational requirement for applicants is a Bachelor's degree: an initial teacher-training qualification is not mandatory, although successful applicants are paid more if they do have one (Shiga, 2008). Although the programme began in 1995, it was not until 2005 that the objective was to place a native-speaker conversational assistant in every primary school under the 'Five Year Plan for English Education Revitalization' (Heo, 2013). EPIK typically places over 1000 teachers in every academic year, with 1324 placed in schools at all levels in 2018 (the breakdown by school level is not given).[10]

EPIK native-English speaking teachers (NETs) are required to undergo a 10-day orientation course which aims to provide an introduction to 'Korean culture, life, and language, to share useful teaching methods, resources, and classroom management ideas, to examine Korean curriculum and Korean school textbooks and find the most effective ways to teach, and to improve teaching skills through lesson planning or presentation' (Heo, 2013: 21). This is an ambitious range of topics to cover in a

10-day orientation course and, indeed, Heo's (2013) analysis of EPIK reveals that participants felt there was inadequate orientation for newcomers to the Korean context, coupled with an over-intensive introduction to teaching English as a foreign language for those who have not received any initial language teacher training. Jeon (2020) also found that, once they began their teaching in schools, host Korean teachers felt that the lack of adequate training and teaching experience of EPIK teachers was problematic for both groups.

> The local [i.e. Korean] teachers of English highlighted in their interviews that the lack of proper training for EPIK teachers without teaching experience and a teaching certificate created much conflict between local teachers and native-English speaking teachers, since the expectations of local teachers were not met while the native-English speaking teachers struggle in doing their job. (Jeon, 2020: 9)

While team teaching has potential advantages if it is conducted effectively and in a true partnership (Carless & Walker, 2006), collaboration works best when it is voluntary rather than imposed by an administrative directive as with EPIK. There also needs to be mutual professional respect between the groups based on recognition of each other's qualifications and experience. Where there is success in the Korean context, however, it seems to depend more on interpersonal relationships between the two teachers, which are inevitably variable, rather than appropriate training and structured institutional support for each teacher in their individual and collaborative roles.

An overriding disadvantage of models such as EPIK is that there are inherent power differentials in the roles of the Korean and foreign teachers. The NETs are seen as the providers of authentic linguistic input (for both students and teachers), while the regular teachers set the framework for learning because of their knowledge of the local curriculum and also support the students if they have difficulties with English, making productive use of a shared first language where necessary. Although on the surface this seems to offer shared responsibility in the classroom, with the NET being the English language expert and the Korean teacher the educational expert in the context (Heo, 2013), it nonetheless reinforces an underlying inequity and prioritises one type of expert over the other. As the subject content of the lesson is the English language, the NET 'linguistic expert' is inevitably accorded preference as a model for the language because of their 'nativeness', reflecting the widespread preference in Korean society for native speakers to teach English (J.S.-Y. Park, 2009). English thus continues to be seen as the preserve of the 'native speaker' who provides an 'authentic', valid representation of the language, while Korean teachers of English, who are deemed to provide less than authentic models, are not provided with opportunities to present themselves as successful second language learners. Hence, if their regular teachers are regarded as inferior to NETs, English is unlikely to be seen as a language that Korean students can themselves master: it will always be something in which only 'native speakers' can be truly proficient. Korean children are exposed to the ideological preference for native speakers at a very early age whether they learn English only at school or in the increasingly important private tuition classes, to which we now turn.

Private Tuition and its Impact

Competition begins at a very early age for Korean children and, for the majority of students, the route to an advantage is for parents to enrol their children in private classes after regular schooling. B.-R. Kim (2015) reports that participation rates in after-school tuition for primary school children increased from 38.1% in 2008 to 58.2% in 2013, that 'most of the expenditure goes into general subjects such as English and Math', and that 'many parents and students rely on private education for English learning because they feel that they do not receive good enough education from school' (Kim, 2015: 96). Expenditure on private education is extremely high. In 2021, total expenditure on private tuition for English was 7.14 trillion South Korean won (US$5.74 billion), followed by 6.74 trillion won (US$5.42 billion) for mathematics, with sport a distant third at 2.22 trillion won (US$1.77 billion) (Yoon, 2022a). By school level, total expenditure on all subjects in 2021 for the elementary level was 10.53 trillion won (US$ 8.46 billion), for middle school 6.35 trillion won (US$5.1 billion) and for high school 6.54 trillion won (US$5.25 billion) (Yoon, 2022b).[11] Relative expenditure on English in comparison with other subjects may indicate the difficulty that students have with the language as a subject alongside its importance in the CSAT, while the high levels of expenditure on private tuition at the primary level are an indicator that parents feel the necessity to give their children a good foundation for later examinations. Taken to an extreme, this results in children of wealthy parents, the most privileged few, being taken to English-speaking countries for their early years education so that they receive a head start with the language. Usually the children are accompanied by their mothers while the fathers stay at work in Korea so that they can financially support them, a phenomenon known as 'kirogi' or 'wild geese' families, as 'wild geese are traditionally celebrated among Koreans for their lifetime commitment to one partner and are believed to migrate over long distances to bring back food for their offspring' (Chang, 2016: 210).

The financial outlay of 'wild geese' families is far beyond the means of most households, however, who have to rely on private tuition in Korea itself. Associated with the high in-country expenditure, the amount of time children spend in additional classes has been a source of official concern for some time. There have been failed attempts both to reduce the hours children spend in these classes and to ban private tuition altogether.

Perhaps realising they could have little impact on the private sector after these failed attempts, the MoE turned its attention to after-school classes in English which, paradoxically, were the only way in which children from poorer families could even begin to compete with the more affluent. In March 2018 the Ministry banned government schools from offering after-school classes in English for Grade 1 and Grade 2 students as they were particularly concerned about the negative effect of private tuition in the early school grades. However, somewhat illogically, in October of the same year it then announced that it would permit English in kindergartens for one hour a day as long as it was 'play-based', acknowledging 'a considerable demand for English education in early childhood and [as] most parents agreed with the educational purpose of play-based early childhood English lessons' (KMOE, 2018b). The mismatch with policy in Grades 1 and 2 was recognised and at the same time the MOE announced that 'given the quite extensive demand in English education, it is necessary that the restriction on after-school English classes [in Grades 1 and 2] is reviewed' (KMOE, 2018b). It seems likely that the restriction will be lifted, although at the time of writing no announcement had yet been made. This is a telling illustration of the strength of the 'parentocracy' (Enever, 2018) in South Korea and is intimately connected to social inequality. Although standardised tests such as PISA indicate that the system is generally equitable, wealthier parents (even if not wealthy enough to become 'wild geese' families), irrespective of government policy, can afford to send their children to private tuition with socially valorised native-speaker English teachers while the less wealthy can only afford schools with Korean teachers of English. The poorest parents cannot, of course, afford private tuition of any kind and are reliant on government after-school programmes such as the one for English suspended in 2018. There is thus a conundrum. The official policy recognises the value of children becoming literate in their first language before embarking on the study of English, but if the after-school programmes in English do not run in Grades 1 and 2, children in the poorest socioeconomic groups risk being at a disadvantage when formal instruction begins in Grade 3. The impact at the school level is, as we have seen, that often children with very different language levels are in the same grade, causing difficulties for teachers who have to cope with the varying proficiency levels in their classes.

There are other potentially widespread and harmful impacts of private tuition on the national education system. Kim and Lee (2010) argue that the value attached to private tuition, the time devoted to it and its duplication of what is taught in the national curriculum may devalue education in government schools.

> If more duplicative instructions are provided through private tutoring, the desire and energy for teaching and learning at schools may diminish. Students may find schools irrelevant and teachers find students

unmotivated and exhausted. If the key party develops low expectations for the other, the formal school system may become ineffective and marginalized. (Kim & Lee, 2010: 290)

Kim and Lee (2010) also contend that the prevalence of private tuition is a response by society at large to stringent government regulations governing education, including in private schools, which are designed to promote educational equity across the system through controlling 'inputs'. In response, parents who have the financial resources to do so simply go outside the system for the additional support which they believe will, in the long term, secure a competitive advantage for their children in the CSAT with the goal of increasing their chances of admission to one of the elite universities (from more than 100). Significant benefits derive from attendance at elite universities. Song (2011) explains that

> universities are strictly ranked, employers know whom to hire by referring to which university applicants graduated from, and parents know whom to endorse as prospective sons or daughters-in-law by referring to their educational or university background. (Song, 2011: 43)

There is also substantial financial benefit to graduates of the five highest ranked universities in the country, with Kim and Lee (2010) referring to

> empirical evidence of a pronounced wage premium of about 42% for graduates from the top five universities over graduates from universities ranked below 30. [Further] the quality premium depreciates very quickly after the top five schools. For the next top five universities, the premium decreases to less than 10%. (Kim & Lee, 2010: 269–270)

Hence, since admission to a prestigious university, subsequent employment with a good company and associated financial success are all dependent on success in the CSAT, it is little wonder that many parents decide to invest heavily in private tuition from the earliest grades. Peer pressure among parents also has a role to play in the decisions. Parents fear both being themselves stigmatised as irresponsible parents and of their children missing out on a possible advantage that others may enjoy in an educational 'arms-race' (Ryu & Kang, 2013). The emphasis on private tuition then has consequences not only for the aforementioned efficacy of teaching and learning English in government schools but also the well-being of children themselves. So and Kang (2014: 797) note:

> A low index of happiness amongst Korean students has nevertheless become a more serious problem than their low levels of interest in learning. Korean students feel unsatisfied with their overall lives as well as their learning. According to a survey conducted by the Organization for Economic Co-operation and Development (OECD), when asked to rate their general satisfaction with life on a scale from 0 to 10, Korean students who had only completed primary education reported a 4.5 level, which was much lower than the OECD average of 6.2. (OECD 2011)

Since the OECD 2011 survey, student unhappiness has not diminished. Students' well-being was surveyed in PISA 2015 (OECD, 2017: 1), with the following results:

> 75% of Korean students reported that they worry about getting poor grades at school (OECD average: 66%); 69% often worry that a test will be difficult (OECD average: 59%); and 42% get very tense when they study (OECD average: 37%).

The curriculum reforms in 2015 were in part designed to redress the high levels of student unhappiness documented in surveys such as these, epitomised by the Ministry's 2016 policy plans being headed 'Happy Education for All' alongside 'Creative Talent Shapes the Future', aimed at fostering less of a focus in schools on reproducing standardised knowledge (KMOE, 2016). The policy plans also included a section on reducing the economic burden on parents and students, particularly reducing private education expenditure, although it was not clear how the promised monitoring of the operation of private education institutes would achieve this. The effect of stress on students is also sadly evident in the need for plans to 'prevent student suicide' (KMOE, 2016), which has been rising among teenagers.

Social Stratification in Korea, Education and English

The teaching of English in primary schools is not, of course, solely responsible for children's lower than average levels of happiness, but the heavy emphasis on the importance of English for success and the extent of private tuition for English is clearly implicated in the problem, just as it is implicated in reinforcing rather than diminishing inequality. The primacy of the economic argument for English obscures the reality that English functions as 'a mechanism of elimination [...] whereby the privileged classes can conserve the established class structure to the disadvantage, if not detriment, of the other classes' (Song, 2012: 17). Regardless of government pronouncements about its value to the economy, English has very limited use in Korean society for the majority of people but immense importance as a gatekeeper to prestigious universities and employment with the most high-status employers. Even though the education system aims to be meritocratic, it cannot entirely compensate for the comparative advantages and disadvantages that certain socioeconomic groups have. The OECD (2005: 2) notes from the research on student learning that:

> The first and most solidly based finding is that the largest source of variation in student learning is attributable to differences in what students bring to school – their abilities and attitudes, and family and community background. (OECD, 2005: 2)

The odds are thus against students drawn from lower socioeconomic groups, even if they have comparable ability to students from more affluent backgrounds. This is borne out by statistics from, for example, the 2018 PISA results which we referred to at the beginning of this chapter. There has also been, as we noted, a widening of the performance gap between the highest-achieving and lowest-achieving students across all subjects over the last decade, with the scores of the lowest 10% declining by 20 points. The fact that 13% of disadvantaged students in Korea scored in the top quarter for reading, while a welcome achievement, does not negate the fact that it is the children of the privileged who primarily benefit from the opportunities afforded by entry to the highest-status universities and employment in the best white-collar jobs. As Song (2011) notes:

> The privileged classes have the means to enable their children to excel academically; the socio-economically deprived lack the financial resources to do likewise; and the socio-economically challenged (or the middle classes) struggle to keep up with the privileged classes. (Song, 2011: 441)

But, although they may have the advantage in securing opportunities to enter the highest-ranked universities and thus jobs with the most prestigious employers, even the privileged classes are not immune from what So and Kang (2014) call the 'dark side' of Korean education. They comment:

> Beneath Korea's academic success lies the dark side of its education system, namely students' declining interest in learning due to excessive studying, increasing amounts of stress and unhappiness resulting from a test-driven education system, and a loss of skills among teachers associated with a prescriptive national curriculum. (So & Kang, 2014: 798)

It remains to be seen whether the revisions to the curriculum and the annual education plans do anything to redress these effects.

Reflections: Future Directions for English Language Teaching and Learning in South Korean Primary Schools

'English fever', as it has been called (J.-K. Park, 2009), is a manifestation of the wider, longstanding 'education fever' which pervades South Korean society and through which an improved life for one's children is sought. 'English fever' permeates the entire education system and its effects are felt even before children begin primary school: the groundwork for the development of the 'dark side' of education is laid early. In light of the high levels of stress and student unhappiness children experience by the end of their basic education, a question that needs deeper consideration in discussion of primary English teaching in South Korea is whether the current approach is best for the children – and the teachers – who have to experience it. Moreover, on a practical level, if the goal of English in primary schools is, as the MoE puts it, to 'systematically provide participatory learning activities for acquiring English expressions so they can use what they have learned in real life' (KMOE, 2018a), it seems to be on a path to failure as soon as it begins. H.D. Kang (2012) remarks:

> the number of English class hours for four years [at primary school] is not enough to make students express themselves in English in their daily lives successfully as the intended goal of primary English education [...] it seems that there is not nearly enough learning hours to enable Korean children to become fluent in English. (Kang, 2012: 68–69)

In reality, rather than fluency in the language *per se*, the intense pressure on South Korean students to do well in English in school and the time spent on English in private tuition outside school seems to be focused on exam success in the CSAT. It is this that appears to be the priority for parents – and thus their children. The CSAT has a powerful washback effect extending to the earliest years of schooling, as is evidenced by the huge expenditure on private tuition at the primary level and for English more than any other subject. The goal of fluency in English for all students has even been questioned by a former president, Park Gyeun-hye, who said, 'not every student has to learn English beyond the basic level, except for those who want to make careers requiring professional English proficiency' (Korea Times, 2014: np). Indeed, there is little evidence to support the widely expressed rationale for teaching English that all Koreans need to be adept in the language because of the globalisation of the economy. Rather, the need to learn English appears to be a 'constructed reality' which is the result of historical and structural forces as much as economic. Most important among these forces are the US military government in Korea (1945–1948) following post-WWII liberation from Japan and the continued presence of US forces in the country, both as important as the much-cited economic globalisation, and which give English its special status (B.-R. Kim, 2015).

If it is the case that not all students need to learn more than basic English, it would seem to be time to rethink the teaching of the language in South Korean schools. As in Thailand, there is a case for an approach to teaching English more firmly grounded in contextual realities, starting with a reconsideration of the curriculum to capitalise upon teachers' capabilities and strengths while responding to actual English language needs and use in South Korea. The comments made some time ago by Y.-H. Choi (2006) offer a useful basis for consideration:

> English language education in Korea can be influenced by linguistic theories or psychological theories. But whether or not they have any impact on English education in Korea depends on Korea's situational, structural, cultural and environmental factors. These factors can have an impact individually or collectively. (Choi, 2006: 5)

And:

> Until now most of the approaches and learning contents in the national curriculum have been adopted from other countries, particularly English-speaking countries (an example of environmental factors), with no consideration of Korean situations and cultures. [...] In order to design a model for Korean education, a long-term plan and research is much needed. (Choi, 2006: 22)

Any long-term plan for teaching English in primary schools (and beyond) in South Korea would benefit from reflection on the key factors identified in this chapter which influence the language learning experience for children and their teachers, both in the classroom and outside in the wider society. As Y.-H. Choi (2006) intimates, a more locally appropriate curriculum with less reliance on outside influences would be a good starting point; that is, subscribing to Western conceptions of 'communicative language teaching' need to be reconsidered. Teaching and learning would also benefit from having more emphasis on children's well-being rather than just their projected language competence by the end of primary school. The one initiative that would most improve children's well-being would be the removal of English as an examination subject in the CSAT, because of its immensely powerful washback effect on all levels of learning. Unfortunately, this would also likely be the one initiative most likely to create a storm of objections, founded on the perception that English is essential in a globalised economy rather than on a purely educational rationale.

To overcome objections to removing English from the CSAT as well as to place language education policy on a firmer foundation, research into current and projected English language needs and use in Korea – a language audit – is urgently needed. This language audit would likely indicate that a variety of languages – if a utilitarian perspective is adopted – is useful to Korean society and the economy. If this is the case, several languages could be offered in schools for children to choose from, depending on the availability of teachers, rather than one language being mandatory. Teaching Mandarin as a foreign language immediately springs to mind as a possible option, given that expansion of trade volumes between Korea and China have grown rapidly in recent decades and that incoming tourism from China increased from 22.7% in 2011 to 43.7% of foreign visitors in 2014 (H.-S. Kang, 2017). From a linguistic perspective, Korean is influenced by Mandarin, with estimates of 65% of its vocabulary being of Chinese origin (H.-S. Kang, 2017), which could be capitalised upon in teaching and learning. Language teaching could still begin in Grade 3 of primary schools as at present, once children are literate in their first language, but the current overriding emphasis on communicative competence seems misplaced when children have so little chance to use any foreign language outside school. Instead, all languages offered could follow a similar curriculum, with a focus on intercultural understanding and the development of positive attitudes to learning languages rather than achieving specific levels of language competence.

The educational framework in which primary language learning takes place also needs attention. Given teachers' complaints about being overloaded with change from government initiatives, the implementation of any long-term plan for the teaching of English and other languages needs to be carefully phased, with the meaningful involvement of teachers in the process of re-evaluation of languages in the primary education system, as teachers are key change agents in the implementation of any reforms. If developments such as these, carefully considered within their socioeducational contexts, were to be investigated, the outcome might be both more equitable and more positive language learning experiences for young children in primary schools in South Korea. Again, I shall return to further discussion of these issues in the final chapter of this book.

Notes

(1) In this chapter 'South Korea' and 'Korea' are used interchangeably. The chapter does not focus on education in North Korea.
(2) Data from the MoE, available at http://english.moe.go.kr/sub/info.do?m=050102&page=050102&num=2&s=english
(3) Source: https://www.macrotrends.net/countries/KOR/south-korea/gdp-per-capita
(4) Data from Statistics Korea, available at http://kostat.go.kr/portal/eng/press Releases/8/7/index.board
(5) Details of subjects and time allocations in the National Curriculum for all grades are available at http://english.moe.go.kr/sub/infoRenewal.do?m=0302&page=0302&s=english
(6) This policy is sometimes referred to as 'Teaching English in English' or 'TEE'.
(7) 'Native speaker' is a contested term, but as it is in use in the South Korean context (and many others besides), I continue to use it here.
(8) The Teach and Learn in Korea (TaLK) programme recruits college students for extra-curricular English classes, especially in more rural areas, and is not discussed here.
(9) Search 'English Program in Korea' on the internet for details.
(10) See http://www.epik.go.kr/contents.do?contentsNo=84&menuNo=334
(11) Expenditure by subject at the elementary level does not appear to be publicly available.

4 Sri Lanka: Language Education and Peace-Building in Primary Schools

Introduction

Language learning in Sri Lankan primary schools takes place in a country that is renowned for the richness of its cultures, its natural beauty as the 'pearl of the Indian Ocean' and, sadly, a history marred by violence between its two major ethnic communities, the Sinhalese and the Tamils, for much of the past 70 years. The roots of the conflict are complex, but it is important to recognise that 'relations between Tamils and Sinhalas[1] have not always or consistently been antagonistic' (Perera, 2001: 8) across the centuries that both communities have resided on the island. However, particularly since achieving independence from British Colonial rule in 1948, interethnic relationships have often been manipulated by politicians, intent on maintaining their own power, using language allied to economic and sociopolitical difficulties to exacerbate tensions between the communities rather than to diminish them (Perera, 2001). While this may not, at first sight, seem to have direct relevance to language teaching in primary schools, awareness of Sri Lanka's pre- and post-independence history is critical in any attempt to understand the role that language education currently plays in its schools at all levels and which begins in primary schools. Language education policy itself is based on 'a recognition that a fair and amenable language policy in a multilingual nation is a necessary but not of itself sufficient condition for reconciliation and national integration after a period of conflict' (Irshad, 2018: 120). In common with Thailand and South Korea, English is the first foreign (or for some children, more a second) language in the education system but, with two official languages in Sri Lanka, Sinhala and Tamil, children are also required to learn their second national language (2NL) from Grade 1 onwards; that is, Sinhalese children learn Tamil and Tamil children learn Sinhala. Second national language teaching in primary schools is officially intended to promote what is known as 'social cohesion' among a population divided by language, ethnicity and religion. It functions in the context of longstanding national goals for education, initially articulated by the National Education Commission (NEC) in 1992 and reaffirmed in subsequent NEC policy documents, most recently the 2016 *Proposals for a National Policy on General Education in Sri Lanka*. Three of these goals for education (numbers i, ii and vi) are of particular import to the discussion in this chapter, viz.:

(i) The achievement of National Cohesion, National Integration and National Unity.
(ii) The establishment of a pervasive pattern of Social Justice.
(vi) The active partnership in Nation Building Activities should ensure the nurturing of a continuous sense of Deep and Abiding Concern for One Another. (NEC, 2016: 3)

A new education act is currently under consideration which reiterates the substance of these goals in new language:

1.1.1 Developing a Sri Lankan citizen with love and dedication to Motherland through fostering national cohesion, national integrity and national unity
1.1.2 Respecting human dignity recognizing pluralistic nature and cultural diversity in Sri Lanka upholding tolerance and reconciliation
1.1.4 Creating and supporting an environment imbued with the values of social justice and a democratic way of life (NEC, 2017: 1–2)

The second goal is explained as follows:

Sri Lanka is a multiethnic, multi religious and multi linguistic society. Hence, the unity, harmony and peace which have been threatened in the recent past have to be restored and consolidated not by conniving at the ideologies of supremacism and dominance but by realizing the beauty of unity within diversity and mutual respect. For this, bigotry should be avoided, welcoming consultation, compromise and consensus. Every individual ought to be ensured of his/her due and dignified position, by virtue of being a Sri Lankan. (NEC, 2017: 2)

In light of these goals with their focus on social cohesion, harmony and justice, language education in Sri Lankan primary schools is, then, not simply about learning languages. It aims to positively influence the attitudes of young children towards other ethnic communities so as to unite rather than divide them, to promote social justice and to inculcate mutual respect between and concern for others among the communities. In this context it is important to reflect on the social climate in which children grow up, beginning with a brief survey of pre- and post-independence ethnic relationships which continue to shape modern-day Sri Lanka, as well as to consider how schooling in general and language education in particular can make a positive difference to children's lives. Education does not take place in a social vacuum and, without an understanding of the context in which children go to school, we cannot fully comprehend what occurs inside schools.

The Sociopolitical Framework for Primary School Language Education in Sri Lanka

Sri Lanka is a multi-ethnic and multilingual country of 20.36 million people according to the 2012 census, the most recent available. The census records the ethnicity of the population as Sinhalese, Sri Lanka Tamils, Indian Tamils, Sri Lanka Moor, Burgher, Malay, Sri Lanka Chetty, Bharatha and Other,[2] reflecting a diversity resulting from migration, trading and intermingling with colonial populations over the centuries. Of the total population, 74.9% are Sinhalese, 11.1% are Sri Lanka Tamils, 4.1% are Indian Tamils and 9.3% are Sri Lanka Moors. The 'Sri Lanka Moors' tend to identify on the basis of religion, Islam, rather than on language, although most speak Tamil as a first language (Davis, 2018).[3] The division of Tamils into two groups reflects the legacy of the colonial policy of bringing indentured labourers from southern India to work on plantations in the 19th and early 20th centuries. For many years after independence these Indian Tamils were stateless as a result of onerous conditions in the 1949 *Ceylon Citizenship Act* which made it almost impossible for them to obtain citizenship. Many were repatriated to India in the 1960s and it was not until 2003 that the issue was finally resolved with the *Grant of Citizenship to Persons of Indian Origin Act* (although some Indian Tamils had secured citizenship with earlier measures). Paradoxically, this act obscures the origin of both major ethnic groups as neither are indigenous to the island, migrating there long ago from different parts of India. The Sinhalese came to Sri Lanka from northern India and the Tamils from southern India some 2000 years ago and there are competing claims about which group arrived first. This issue, as we shall see, has more than academic importance, but neither Sinhalese nor Tamils are the earliest inhabitants of the island. That distinction belongs to the Wanniyalaeto, a minority group of hunter-gatherers, who arrived between 35,000 and 40,000 years ago and are generally referred to as Sri Lanka's Indigenous inhabitants. Unfortunately, the existence of the Wanniyalaeto is under threat from displacement and a process of either Sinhalisation or Tamilisation, depending on the dominant language of the area in which they live. Continuing discrimination allied to social and economic exclusion does not bode well for their future (Childs, 2017), and their language is classified as 'dormant' by the Endangered Languages Project.[4] It is likely that there are no longer any native speakers of the language, which does not feature in any government documents on language education. Even in the census the Wanniyalaeto are classified in the 'other' category.

In contrast to Wanniyalaeto, Sinhala and Tamil are vibrant languages. Irshad (2018: 109) notes that during the pre-colonial period, 'According to Liyanage and Canagarajah (2014), historical evidence has shown that Sinhala and Tamil had spread across the country and the people of Sinhala, Tamil, and Muslim communities learnt the language of the other community for pragmatic reasons as well as for aesthetic reasons of appreciation of the classical literature of the two languages'. From 1605, successive waves of colonial domination by the Portuguese, Dutch and, most significantly, the British altered the linguistic as well as the sociopolitical landscape of Sri Lanka. The British made English the official language of administration with local languages used only at the lower levels. The colonial education system reflected this linguistic segregation. For the vast majority of Sri Lankans who were able to attend school at all (and even as late as 1927 only 50% of children of school-going age were enrolled), education was in the vernacular and was designed with a socioeconomic purpose, the production of a compliant, mainly agricultural labour force (Brutt-Griffler, 2002). English-medium education was restricted to the children of British expatriates and of local people who served in the colonial administration. The *Free Education Act* of 1945 did little to change the stratified system in the near-term, although inequality was lessened to a small degree by a scholarship system which offered a few rural children the prospect of studying in the English-medium schools and, hence, access to high-status jobs. Sinhala and Tamil retained their importance, however, in a curious outcome of colonial policy in spite of English becoming the language of opportunity and advancement for a small number of Tamils and Sinhalese at this time, as British administrators had to learn and pass examinations in these languages if they wished to be promoted in the colonial civil service (Irshad, 2018).

Post-independence in 1948, the government changed the medium of instruction in Year 1 of all primary schools to Sinhala or Tamil, and from 1953 also progressively in secondary schools. By 1959 all schooling was conducted in children's first language and English was relegated to the position of a subject. Over the same period of time, however, political developments based on ethnicity and religion led to the passing in 1956 of the *Official Language Act* – commonly known as the 'Sinhala Only Act' – which replaced English with Sinhala as the sole official language of the country. Not surprisingly, this was followed by protests by Tamils against the marginalisation of their language, in turn followed by anti-Tamil riots. In response, the government enacted the *Tamil Language (Special Provisions) Act* of 1958 which permitted some use of Tamil in government administration. This lasted until 1972 when the government of the time passed a new constitution which included a provision for Sinhala as the only official language. After demands began to be made for a separate Tamil state in the north and east of the island, Tamil was made a national language, but this did not alleviate dissatisfaction among the Tamil community regarding their social, economic and political position within the country. It was not until 1987 that Tamil was given the status of an official language along with Sinhala, and English was made a link language, in the 13th Amendment to the 1978 Constitution. The constitution proclaims in Clauses (2) and (3) of Chapter IV on language:

Official Language. 18. (1) The Official Language of Sri Lanka shall be Sinhala. (2) Tamil shall also be an official language. (3) English shall be the link language.[5]

As I have noted elsewhere:

The wording seems to be intentionally ambiguous and indicative of a clear language – and thus ethnic – hierarchy. The constitution does not state that 'The Official Languages of Sri Lanka shall be Sinhala and Tamil', which would have given the two languages unequivocal equal status, but retains the original 1978 article with Sinhala first and Tamil inserted in a subsequent clause without the capitalisation for 'official language.' In practice, although Tamil has the status of an 'official language', its place in national life remains subservient to that of Sinhala. (Hayes, 2010: 61)

Through these developments, official language policy appeared to favour the dominance of the Sinhalese majority and act as a means of 'legitimization of power relations among [the] ethno-linguistic groups' (Bekerman, 2005: 2). They did nothing to stop the conflict and by the time the constitutional amendments were passed, the country had already been mired in civil war for four years. While the war was not caused solely by language policy, it was instrumental in marginalising the Tamil community and contributing to a sense that their grievances could not be solved by peaceful means.

The war brought devastation to the country between 1983 and 2009, only ending with the military annihilation of the rebel group known as the LTTE (the 'Liberation Tigers of Tamil Eelam'). The defeat of the LTTE was initially followed by a period of triumphalism by the government of president Mahinda Rajapakse, which had 'won' the war and which was strongly Sinhalese nationalist (Jayawickrema *et al.*, 2010). Rajapakse's attempts to remain in office beyond his two-term limits, through amending the constitution to allow him to run for a third term, were thwarted by the surprise election as president in January 2015 of Maithripala Sirisena, whose success was in part attributed to the lack of progress towards reconciliation with the Tamil minority. Regrettably, meaningful reconciliation was still slow during Sirisena's tenure, with post-war claims of 'Sinhalisation' of the northern and eastern provinces still continuing (Mittal, 2015). Since then, the political situation has not been improved by the election of Gotabaya Rajapakse (younger brother of Mahinda) as president in November 2019. As defence minister in the final stages of the civil war, he oversaw the crushing of the LTTE and has been accused of – and denies – overseeing serious abuses of human rights. 'There is a general skepticism as to whether Gotabaya will create a safe space for inclusion, harmony and social cohesion' (Kapur, 2019: np), a scepticism fuelled by the appointment of his elder brother Mahinda as prime minister and reinforced by his decision to give a presidential pardon to a soldier convicted of murdering eight Tamil civilians during the war[6] (Amnesty International, 2020).

Since the end of the war, apart from the recent establishment of an *Office of Missing Persons* and *Office for Reparations*, meaningful action to address the longstanding grievances of the Tamil minority has not been taken (Amnesty International, 2019; ICG, 2011) and there remains the danger that a failure of post-war reconciliation will lead to history repeating itself and armed conflict breaking out again at some time in the future (Silva, 2018). If this is not to occur, younger generations need to overcome the entrenched interethnic hostility of many of their elders. To reiterate, education in general and language education in particular, beginning in primary schools, thus has an important role to play in long-term reconciliation and the process of peace-building between the communities of Sri Lanka, a necessary precondition if not a sufficient vehicle for the establishment of social harmony (Colenso, 2005). In what follows, I will first discuss the role of language education in promoting 'positive peace', then outline the Sri Lankan education system, next examine research on the impact of 2NL learning on inter-ethnic attitudes among primary school children, and thereafter discuss the place of English in Sri Lanka, its status as an official 'link' language and its teaching and learning in primary schools.

Language Education and 'Positive Peace'

Irrespective of the political situation, educational policies, encapsulated in the *National Policy and a Comprehensive Framework of Actions on Education for Social Cohesion and Peace* (MOESL, 2008), have for many years aimed at establishing the preconditions for 'positive peace' in Sri Lanka. Education for social cohesion aims to replace a culture of violence by 'a culture of peace seen as a culture of human enhancement' (Reardon, 2000: 420). It is not enough for military action to have ceased in Sri Lanka – a condition of 'negative peace' (Harris, 2004) – as this does not in itself remove the causes of conflict. Instead 'positive peace' must be promoted: '*Positive* peace is a condition where non-violence, ecological sustainability and social justice remove the causes of violence' (Harris, 2004: 12). Clearly, the establishment of positive peace in Sri Lanka is not dependent on education alone but is multidimensional, encompassing the resolution of political, social and economic grievances. Even before the end of the war, it was anticipated that 'education's role lies as much in the preparation for, as in the creation of, social harmony' (DFID & World Bank, 2000: 6). Influencing children's attitudes to other communities through 2NL learning is crucial to this preparation. Bush and Saltarelli (2000: 17) note that, as language and linguistic rights are central to harmony in multi-ethnic societies, 'A sensitive handling of linguistic issues can also contribute to the building and maintenance of peaceful relations within and between different ethnic groups'. How are such peaceful relations to be achieved?

Bar-Tal and Rosen (2009) discuss two models of peace education, the direct and indirect models. In the direct model the themes of conflict, the causes and effects of violence, are openly explored in the school classroom. This model has been used in adult education in Sri Lanka in areas previously under the control of the LTTE (Harris & Lewer, 2008). However, it is unlikely at any time in the future to be introduced into Sri Lankan primary schools for two reasons. The first is concerned with the societal, political and educational preconditions for overt confrontation of the ethnic conflict. Direct peace education is a major endeavour which requires 'legitimization, equalization, differentiation and personalization of the rival' (Bar-Tal & Rosen, 2009: 568), but events in Sri Lanka since the military defeat of the LTTE in May 2009 indicate that these attitudes towards the rival do not yet exist. Second, the approach is not appropriate for young children in primary schools who do not possess the emotional or cognitive resources to deal so directly with themes of violence and its consequences. In contrast, indirect peace education has been among the goals of Sri Lankan education for many years, as has been noted (NEC, 1992, 2016). In an indirect model, the conflict is not directly addressed but more general themes of conflict resolution, empathy, mutual respect and tolerance are introduced into the classroom to help build the conditions for peace. Just as with direct peace education, it is claimed that the indirect model can reduce 'collective fear and hatred' and foster 'collective hope, trust, and mutual acceptance' (Bar-Tal & Rosen, 2009: 568). Education generally has been shown to affect implicit and explicit ethnic group attitudes within states (Davis *et al.*, 2007), and 2NL education, if represented as 'an exercise in interculturalism', can constitute indirect peace education, given that 'a central aim in any language learning endeavour is human interaction' (Lo Bianco, 1999: 60). Second national language education should, then, promote mutual respect and understanding among different ethnic groups by providing them with the tools to communicate in each other's languages.

This position was endorsed in the post-war report of the *Commission of Inquiry on Lessons Learnt and Reconciliation* (LLRC, 2011), which recommended:

> 8.237 The learning of each others' languages should be made a compulsory part of the school curriculum. This would be a primary tool to ensure attitudinal changes amongst the two communities. Teaching Tamil to Sinhala children and Sinhala to Tamil children will result in greater understanding of each other's cultures.

> 8.238 The proper implementation of the language policy and ensuring trilingual (Sinhala, Tamil and English) fluency of future generations becomes vitally important. A tri-lingual education will allow children from very young days to get to understand each other. (LLRC, 2011: 310)

The commission welcomed government policy to develop trilingualism among future generations of school children but also noted that it would require resources to be made available to achieve it.

> 8.239 The Commission therefore welcomes the Government initiative for a trilingual nation by the year 2020. To this end the necessary budgetary provisions must be made available on a priority basis for teacher training and staffing. (LLRC, 2011: 310)

The government's *Ten Year National Plan for a Trilingual Sri Lanka: 2012–2022* was endorsed by the Cabinet in February 2012.[7] It contains detailed provisions to achieve the objective of national trilingualism in three phases with a 'participatory monitoring and evaluation system', but outputs from this monitoring system are difficult to find. There are, however, other sources that assess the extent to which the initiative has had an impact at the primary school level and these will be referenced in subsequent sections on 2NL teaching and the teaching of English, following the outline of the education system.

The Education System

Sri Lanka has a free education system which has been instrumental in achieving high primary school enrolment rates and concomitant high literacy rates. In 2018, net primary school enrolment was 99.10%[8] and the literacy rate among the 15–24 year age group was 98.78% with gender parity (98.51% for males, 99.04% for females).[9] Children begin compulsory schooling in Grade 1 at the age of five and must attend until the end of junior secondary school, in Grade 9. The primary phase lasts from Grades 1 to 5, at the end of which children may take the Grade 5 scholarship examination prior to entry to secondary school. Children generally attend schools according to medium of instruction, although there are some bilingual schools and a small number of trilingual schools. Data from the 2020 school census giving basic information on the number of schools, the medium of instruction and numbers of students and teachers are presented in Table 4.1.

Government schools are divided into two categories – 'national' and 'provincial' schools. The designation of 'national' school was introduced in 1985, with schools having to meet certain criteria regarding size, academic standards, facilities and reputation in the community. The first national schools were those that were originally English-medium schools established by missionaries to serve the children of colonial administrators and the local elite. National schools, located in urban areas, are more prestigious than provincial schools, are generally better resourced and are regarded as offering a higher quality of education. Many parents strive to gain access for their children to these schools, if not in Grade 1, then through the Grade 5 scholarship examination which is important in the

Table 4.1 Basic statistics of government schools in Sri Lanka, 2020

Schools

Schools			
All government schools	10,155	**Schools by language medium/s of instruction**	**Schools by student population**
National schools	373		
Provincial schools	9782	Sinhala medium only 6357	1–50 students 1439
		Tamil medium only 3042	51–100 students 1523
Type of school		Sinhala and Tamil	101–200 students 2169
1AB schools	1000	mediums 42	201–500 students 2690
1C schools	1932	Sinhala and bilingual	501–1000 students 1404
Type 2 schools	3224	(S/E) mediums 524	1001–1500 students 398
Type 3 schools	3999	Tamil and bilingual	1501–2000 students 215
		(T/E) mediums 157	2001–3000 students 212
		Trilingual (Sinhala,	3001–4000 students 73
School by gender of the school		Tamil and bilingual (S/E	More than 4000 students 32
Boys schools	145	&/or T/E) mediums 33	
Girls schools	241		
Mixed schools	9769	**School by functional grade span**	
		Grade 1–5 3884	
		Grade 1–8 115	
		Grade 1–11 3204	
		Grade 1–13 1949	
		Grade 6–11 20	
		Grade 6–13 983	

Students — **Teachers**

Students			Teachers	
All students	4,063,685	**Students by language medium/study**	All teachers	249,494
Male students	2,018,151		Male teachers	61,747
Female students	2,045,534	Sinhala medium 2,978,133	Female teachers	187,747
National schools	796,812	Tamil medium 986,156	Graduate teachers	121,569
Provincial schools	3,266,873	Bilingual mediums	Trained teachers	121,796
		(Sinhala-English and	Trainee teachers	4525
Students by type of school		Tamil-English) 99,396	Untrained teachers	1472
1AB schools	1,570,640		Other teachers	132
1C schools	1,076,629	**Students by grade cycle of studying**		
Type 2 schools	750,726		**Teachers by type of school**	
Type 3 schools	665,690	Primary cycle	1AB schools	82,244
		(Grade 1–5) 1,640,647	1C schools	67,837
		Junior secondary	Type 2 schools	61,728
		cycle (Grade 6–9) 1,357,437	Type 3 schools	37,685
		Senior secondary		
		O/L cycle		
		(Grade 10–11) 636,985		
		Senior secondary		
		(A/L) cycle		
		(Grade 12–13) 421,114		
		Special education units 7502		

Grade 1 admissions

Grade 1 admissions				
Grade 1 admissions	319,405	Sinhala medium 239,236	**Grade 1 admissions by type of school**	
Male students	161,853	Tamil medium 80,169		
Female students	157,552		1AB schools	46,539
National schools	25,672		1C schools	72,732
Provincial schools	293,733		Type 2 schools	70,125
			Type 3 schools	130,009

Source: MOESL (2020), www.statistics.gov.lk/Education/StaticalInformation/SchoolCensus/2020

later years of primary schooling. National schools are centrally managed by the Ministry of Education and provincial schools by Provincial Departments of Education. In an attempt to assuage complaints about restricted access to national schools and to redress urban–rural inequity, the government has recently announced plans to increase their number to 1000 (Mudugamuwa, 2019), although this appears to be a decision resulting from a political calculation rather than an educational imperative. The 'type' of school indicates the grades of education provided. All types of school offer primary education, but 3890 of the Type 3 schools offer education only from Grades 1 to 5 with 169 offering education to Grade 8. Type 3 schools have low enrolments and are generally located in rural areas. Almost 30% of schools have enrolments of less than 100 students, and half of these (49.17%) enrol fewer than 50. As is common in many state education systems, small rural schools in Sri Lanka lack the resources and qualified staffing of their larger urban counterparts and the quality of education suffers as a result.

The statistics in Table 4.1 also confirm that the vast majority of students attend schools in either Sinhala or Tamil medium, from entry in Grade 1 to the end of their schooling, largely corresponding to their mother tongue. Although the right of children to be educated in their mother tongue is universally accepted, in the Sri Lankan context the association between mother tongue, religion and ethnicity is harmful to the concept of social harmony, as Davis (2018) notes:

> While schools are officially organized on the basis of language medium and religion, teachers and students widely refer to them by their ethnic affiliations. Schools thus naturalize the conflation of language medium, mother tongue, and ethnicity. (Davis, 2018: 131)

This view is widespread. For example, Wijesekera *et al.* (2019) also comment:

> It is hard to dispute, empirically, the mutually constitutive effect of MTI [Mother Tongue Instruction] (Sinhala/Tamil), ethnic exclusion, ethnocentric identity construction, and the historically divided nation in Sri Lanka. (Wijesekera *et al.*, 2019: 28)

The system of separate schools for each medium of instruction thus denies children from the Sinhalese and Tamil communities the opportunity to interact with each other at school, meaning that 2NL teaching offers the only official prospect for most children to begin to establish a foundation for mutual respect and understanding while they are young.

Whether in Sinhala or Tamil medium, schools follow a common curriculum developed by the National Institute of Education (NIE). The structure of primary education, subjects studied and time allocation per grade are given in Table 4.2. While English does not feature as a separate subject in Grades 1 and 2, it is nonetheless included in the curriculum

Table 4.2 Structure of primary education

Subject/activity	Time per week		
	Key stage 1 (Grades 1 and 2)	Key stage 2 (Grades 3 and 4)	Key stage 3 (Grade 5)
Mother tongue	5.00 h	5.00 h	5.00h
Mathematics	3.30 h	5.00 h	5.00 h
Environment-related activities	5.30 h	6.00 h	7.30 h
English	–	3.00 h	3.30 h
Second national language	30 min	1.00 h	1.00 h
Religion	1.15 h	2.00 h	2.00 h
Morning assembly and religious observances	1.15 h (15 min per day)	1.15 h (15 min per day)	1.15 h (15 min per day)
Interval	1.15 h (15 min per day)	1.40 h (20 min per day)	1.40 h (20 min per day)
Health and physical activities	1.40 h (20 min per day)	2.05 h (20 min per day)	2.05 h (20 min per day)
Co-curricular activities	30 min (in one day of the week)	30 min (in one day of the week)	30 min (in one day of the week)
Optional activities	–	–	30 min
Total	21.15 h	27.30 h	30.00 h

Source: NIE (2018: 26), https://nie.lk/pdffiles/other/eOM%20Curriculum%20Reserach%20 Report.pdf

within Environment Related Activities (ERA) under the nomenclature of 'Activity-Based Oral English' (ABOE), with the emphasis on children and teachers using it 'as a means of communication while children are engaged in activities under the subject ERA' (NIE, 2018: 25–26). Comparing the time allocation for English with that for the 2NL (Sinhala or Tamil), it is apparent that English is favoured throughout the primary phase of education. It is a truism that you cannot learn a language in an hour a day (Lightbown, 2000), still less an hour per week (and only 30 minutes per week in Grades 1 and 2), which brings into question what can be achieved in 2NL teaching and learning with such a limited allocation of time in the primary phase.

Primary school teachers receive training in one of the 18 National Colleges of Education (NCOEs), and follow a two-year academic programme supplemented by a one-year 'internship', which also involves action research, leading to the National Diploma in Teaching. College coursework consists of a professional component (focusing on such things as educational psychology, educational sociology and elements of education) and a general component which focuses on the subjects primary teachers need to teach (this includes 60 hours each for mother tongue and 2NL and 120 hours for English, reflecting the disparity in time allocation for study in the primary school curriculum). There is significant gender disparity in NCOE enrolment with less than 5% of trainees being male, and there are additional concerns that only 50% of trainees are selected on merit with the other 50% coming from 'difficult' districts, presumably whether or not they are academically qualified (Sethunga *et al.*, 2016), which inevitably has an impact on the quality of teaching.

Second National Language Learning and Interethnic Attitudes in the Primary School

The personal accounts of a Sinhalese student and a Tamil student in a bilingual programme recounted in Wijesekera *et al.* (2019) reveal the reality of attitudes held among many young Sri Lankans as they progress through their primary education in schools segregated by medium of instruction.

> When we were young we only associated with Sinhala students and Sinhalese. When I came here and heard Tamil I got scared instantly. I wondered if they would talk to me, I have no place to go. I wondered if something happened I may have to hide somewhere. That's how I felt in the first few days. (A Sinhala student)

> There was a difference. From Grade 1-5 it was like, let's say, we were like from another planet and those people were like from another planet. Though we existed we never got to interact. (A Tamil student) (Wijesekera *et al.*, 2019: 24)

It is these feelings about members of the other community being from another planet that the teaching of the 2NL was designed to redress. Teaching of the 2NL was introduced from Grade 1 as an oral subject in 2007, prior to the end of the civil war. Even though the time allocation is low and as a consequence the degree of proficiency in the language achievable is inevitably limited, introducing the 2NL at an early stage of schooling nonetheless offers the opportunity to influence children's attitudes towards and to promote understanding of and respect for the other community at an age when their interethnic attitudes are still developing. Research in psychology indicates that, in most contexts, around the age of seven children begin to fashion their explicit attitudes to other groups ('out-groups', with their own group known as the 'in-group') in terms of social desirability and there is usually a decline in any existing, explicit negative attitudes to out-groups. Ethnic prejudice is unlikely to occur before the ages of six or seven due to the time required to attain the requisite cognitive development and social experience and the extent to which it forms is argued to depend on three factors (Nesdale *et al.*, 2004): the first factor is the extent to which children identify with their own ethnic group; the second is the extent to which members of their own ethnic group, particularly adults, clearly express their dislike of the out-group; and the third is the extent to which there is a known conflict between ethnic groups in society and a concomitant belief among in-group members that their well-being is threatened by the out-group (Nesdale *et al.*, 2004). Where these three factors coalesce in situations of intractable conflict, children do not moderate their negative explicit intergroup attitudes (see, for example, Teichman & Bar-Tal's 2008 research on children experiencing the Arab-Israeli conflict).

Research to date in Sri Lanka indicates that the objective of 2NL teaching to reduce interethnic hostility among children is not being achieved. Hayes *et al.* (2016) surveyed 402 children at the beginning and end of their Grade 3 and Grade 5 classes in a variety of locations across the country using a trait attribution task, an instrument designed to measure children's implicit attitudes to the other community, and found that, when analysed by medium of instruction, attitudes between the two main ethnic groups, Sinhalese and Tamils, became more rather than less polarised over the course of the year. Further, in a cross-sectional analysis, there was an increase in negative attitudes towards the other ethnic group between Grade 3 and Grade 5. A fundamental reason for the lack of success of 2NL teaching is the acute shortage of teachers proficient in the language they are supposed to be teaching, particularly Tamil. At the end of the war in 2009, data showed that because of these shortages only 45% of schools even offered teaching of the 2NL, and these 2046 schools had just 846 qualified teachers of the 2NL (non-specialists teaching the 2NL were not included in the data) (Aturupane & Wickramanayake, 2011). More recent research indicates that the quality of teaching has not improved in those schools where the 2NL is taught, as we see in Premarathna *et al.*'s (2016) report:

> It is evident that there is considerable dissatisfaction with regard to the competency of teachers in all three languages. In many instances, the research team found the Tamil teacher to be a non-native speaker of Tamil. A majority of teachers also believe that the Sinhala teachers are not proficient enough to teach the language. It is evident therefore that a recommendation should be made to enhance and upgrade the proficiency and competency levels of teachers of all three languages in Sri Lanka. While there were enough English language teachers in the districts in which data were collected, there was a severe lack of Tamil language teachers to teach Tamil in predominantly Sinhalese populated districts. The existing Tamil teachers are hardly capable even of producing an accurate spoken sentence. (Premarathna *et al.*, 2016: 20)

This point was reinforced by the UN Special Rapporteur on minority issues who said at the end of her visit in October 2016 that 'There is a serious shortage of quality and professional language teachers in the schools, and reportedly an additional 6000 language teachers are needed' (OHCHR, 2016). The NCOE specialising in teaching of second languages produces only 270 graduates per cohort for all three languages, while another two colleges offer Sinhala as a 2NL and English alongside a variety of other subjects (Sethunga *et al.*, 2016). Assuming the graduates are equally distributed across languages in the specialist NCOE, it seems obvious that 90 new teachers each year for Tamil as a 2NL and, including graduates from the additional NCOE courses, perhaps 150 for Sinhala will make little impact given the scale of the problem.

If teachers lack proficiency in a language, this has a direct impact on their motivation to teach it as well as the quality of their teaching, and children are, in turn, hardly likely to be motivated to learn it. To compound the problem, children's attitudes are also likely to be influenced by their parents, the second of Nesdale *et al.*'s (2004) three factors. In this regard, Malalasekera (2019) found that while Tamil respondents thought that Sinhala was 'useful' to know as it was necessary for daily life and finding employment, Sinhalese respondents felt that Tamil was 'not useful' as they could function in their daily lives without it, with any Tamils they came into contact with switching to Sinhala, and proficiency in Tamil was not necessary to secure employment. A teacher of Tamil as a 2NL, interviewed by Malalasekera (2019), 'felt there is a lack of interest in learning Tamil among Sinhalese children in general' and the views of her Sinhalese respondents led her to conclude that 'They do not like Tamil and believe their children do not like Tamil. They act on these feelings and beliefs by not using Tamil and not encouraging their children to study Tamil' (Malalasekera, 2019: 59). These negative attitudes towards Tamil as a 2NL exacerbate problems arising from a lack of teachers sufficiently competent in the language and make it very difficult to achieve the government's stated aim of a trilingual nation. In sharp contrast to the Sinhalese attitude to Tamil, both Tamils and Sinhalese expressed the belief that learning English was not only useful, and hence valuable for their children to learn, but also conferred status on those who spoke it. 'Those who cannot speak English are considered inferior to English speakers', as Malalasekera (2019: 64) concluded.

The Status, Teaching and Learning of English, the 'Link' Language

The demand for English in Sri Lankan society stems partly from the same kind of economic imperatives as in other countries worldwide and partly from the effect of its continuing status as a language of the Indigenous elite post-independence. In economic terms, the perceived need for English is epitomised in current World Bank education development projects focusing on 'strategic subjects that are key for economic development such as

English and mathematics' (World Bank, 2018). The number of people in the workforce requiring knowledge of English in their day-to-day employment is, however, harder to determine. The most recent *Labour Demand Survey* published in 2017 does not mention any need for English specifically and only reports that 8.1% of employers felt that 'knowledge of a foreign language' was a skill needing improvement among job seekers (Department of Census and Statistics, 2017). Positions requiring high-level skills in the STEM subjects (science, technology, engineering and mathematics) and those in management, international trade and the tourist industry are most likely to require knowledge of another language, particularly English, but other occupations where there is a skill shortage are much less likely to have this need. The labour demand survey reported that the top three occupations with a skill shortage were sewing machine operators, security guards and 'other manufacturing labourers' (Department of Census and Statistics, 2017), where there appears to be no immediate need for English. A survey by Brunfaut and Green (2019), which yielded just 20 responses from 469 employers with whom contact was made, 19 of them in the most economically developed western province, indicated that varying levels of proficiency in English were required in 17 of the companies. Brunfaut and Green (2019) noted that employers:

> typically indicated that English proficiency was a requirement for top and middle management, staff in supervisory roles or staff in marketing, HR, business development, IT, engineering, and accounts, or for specialised roles such as call centre staff. English was thought to be less crucial for operational roles such as machine operators. (Brunfaut & Green, 2019: 11)

English was also regarded as being important for future economic development, particularly in the service sector and tourism, and for offering prospects of advancement to managerial positions for some individuals. Available evidence indicates, then, that English has a place in particular industries, but mainly in technical and managerial positions, although the perception that English is an important language that all Sri Lankans should acquire remains strong. As noted for other countries, whether this requires that English should be taught in primary schools is another matter.

With regard to its post-independence standing, there is extensive evidence to attest that being a competent speaker of English attracts a higher social status than being monolingual in Sinhala or Tamil. This is true even for teachers, whose status has otherwise diminished over the years (Hettiarachchi, 2013). A teacher interviewed in Hayes' (2010) study discussed the marginalisation he felt as a child growing up in a poor farming family because he could not speak English, saying: 'I think in me there would have been this feeling that I'm denied opportunities, I'm not like others, because I don't have my English or English background. So I thought I should learn it' (Hayes, 2010: 523). Hettiarachchi (2013: 6) also found that in a culturally conservative society, where marriages are still arranged in some families, being an English teacher had value in this respect: 'Even in marriages it matters. People prefer to marry English teachers because of the social status, because of English'. Its higher status is not unproblematic, however. Gunesekera (2005) believes that English is more divisive than even ethnicity:

> In the case of social disparity, the real gulf in Sri Lankan society is not based on religion, ethnicity, money or caste: it is based on language. The gap between those who know English and those who don't know English denotes the gap between the haves and the have nots. (Gunesekera, 2005: 34)

In this way, English has been likened to a 'kaduwa' or sword which divides the country in two and, in this vein, Punchi (2001) disputes its role as a link language except in so far as it unites two privileged groups:

> Since English is a tool of upward social mobility and a passport to the affluent classes, instead of achieving a greater harmony and integration between the majority of Tamils and Sinhalese, it would lead only to a fusion of two thin groups, namely the English educated Tamils and English educated Sinhalese. (Punchi, 2001: 377)

The potential of English to contribute to social harmony among the majority of the population through facilitating interaction in a shared language that is not the mother tongue of either may, then, be more recognised in theory than given substance in practice for the majority. The structure of the education system would seem to sustain this position, as the vast majority of schools are organised on the basis of a single medium of instruction and, hence, children from the different communities never meet at school. The opportunity for Sinhalese and Tamil children to learn in the same English classes, and to participate in the practical realisation of the use of English as a link language, does not exist for most children.

However, all children, whatever their school's medium of instruction, use the same English textbooks which have to be approved by the Educational Publications Department of the Ministry of Education. Like all school materials, these textbooks are required to conform to long-standing directives designed to eliminate bias in several respects. At the turn of the century, even while the war was still raging, the National Curriculum Policy stated with respect to curriculum content that 'there can be no bias in relation to ethnicity, religion, gender or economic deprivation' (NIE & MEHE, 2000: 10). Further, as part of the quality control process, the Curriculum Process Plan required textbooks and other materials to 'be scrutinised for ethnic, religious, gender and economic bias' (NIE & MEHE, 2000: 7) before they could be approved for use in schools. This process recognised that textbooks themselves can carry messages about the social context of the country and relationships between communities when they portray Sri Lankan actors and use Sri Lankan settings. These messages can be both explicit and implicit.

The way in which implicit messages can be carried by textbooks is vividly illustrated by an incident related in Hayes (2002) concerning the textbook series, *Let's Learn English Grades 3–5*. This series was in use for some 20 years and has only recently been phased out, beginning in the 2017 school year with the Grade 3 textbook, with the entire new series now in use for Grades 3–5.[10] *Let's Learn English* was written by a team of Sri Lankan primary school teachers recruited and trained as part of a primary education project funded by the British and Sri Lankan governments. During a recruitment exercise to join another writing team to produce supplementary readers, teachers were asked to look at a page of the textbook (reproduced in Figure 4.1) and to describe what they saw in the form of an artist's brief.

Figure 4.1 Sample page from *Let's Learn English, Pupil's Book, Grade 3*

84 Early Language Learning in Context

One Sinhalese teacher, however, focused her attention on the message she saw represented in the illustration, writing:

> All [the characters] they are in a happy mood. Although they are small children and animals, they show their friendship to the world. Even Kandu [the elephant] is a dangerous animal, it also join with the others like a small child. Ruwan, Pancha, Kandu, Meena, Kusum are sitting in a polite way, but Nizar is not sitting properly. All the boys are wearing shoes and socks. In present world, we don't see most of the children like to share and live friendly. But here we can see their unity. Without peace we can't do anything, like our present situation in Sri Lanka. But this picture is a good example for the people, because they show their unity and peaceful. (Hayes, 2002: 195)

I commented on this:

> It is quite clear from this that the teacher views the scene as promoting peace and unity, one in which children share and live in a friendly way – in specific contrast, the teacher says, to children in the present world. It is also clear that the teacher sees this page as offering a positive example to children in Sri Lanka. According to the teacher, then, the book conveys positive messages about social harmony and about the moral values of sharing and co-operation amongst children. (Hayes, 2002: 195)

There are other implications that we can derive from the teacher's description of the page. When she says 'All the boys are wearing shoes and socks', we can infer that this is not the norm in schools in her experience, and indicates that the children would be from middle-class backgrounds with the means to buy shoes and socks rather than the rural poor who may not have such means.

A second example of implicit messages, also from Hayes (2002), indicates that adults may draw inferences from the materials that the writers themselves did not intend.

> At an early [textbook review] meeting we presented the four characters who would be introduced in the Grade 3 books. The writers had chosen to represent two boys and two girls. These were a Sinhalese boy and girl, a Tamil girl and a Muslim boy [...] It was noted by a monitoring team member that the Tamil girl was the eldest of the four. We were then warned (though the Sinhalese speaker said this was not, of course, a personal opinion) that this could be taken by some to mean that the Tamils came to Sri Lanka before the Sinhalese, thus causing offence to the majority community. (Hayes, 2002: 187)

The view articulated here also illustrates the depth of feeling that is connected to the idea of one particular community having arrived in Sri Lanka before the other, which I alluded to earlier, as this is viewed by some as 'proof' that they have a prior claim to the island. Whether children themselves interpret the materials in either of these ways has, unfortunately, not been investigated, but the fact that the teacher in the first of the examples recognises the presentation of all communities in Sri Lanka as living together in harmony is an indication that the writers' intentions have been met.

Whatever the rationale for learning English and its role in Sri Lanka, what is also important, of course, is whether schools provide the means for children in primary schools to learn the language in their classes. In common with many other countries, there have been longstanding concerns that outcomes for English are poor considering the investments in its teaching. Little has changed since the NEC (2003) commented:

> While English has been a compulsory second language in all schools from grade 3 since the 1940s, the teaching of English as a subject confined to one period a day has not enabled the vast majority of students to communicate in English effectively or to be equipped with language skills to explore the expanding world of learning, resulting in a decline in the quality of higher education. (NEC, 2003: 115)

The continuing difficulties can be gauged by the national assessments of achievement of children in Grade 4. These assessments give early indications of how well students are learning, as measured against expected learning outcomes for the grade using tests based on the framework for each subject.[11] They provide important information given the lockstep nature of the curriculum, as if children fall behind in the early stages they tend to struggle throughout their school careers. The assessment for English for 2015 (MOESL & NEREC, 2016), the most recent publicly available, revealed that there was a wide variety in achievement, with a high percentage of low achievers (7.97% scored below 20 on the test, 15.79% scored 20–29 and 12.71% scored 30–39) as well as high achievers (13.93% scored 70–79, 13.36% were in the 80–89 range and 8% in the 90–100 range). Cumulatively, 36.47% of students were below the pass mark of 40 while 25.29% scored more than 70. Looked at by province and within the provinces, there is continuing heterogeneity. Four of the provinces had marks above the all-island mean with the remaining five below the mean; however, in all provinces the standard deviation in scores was roughly the same (between 25.49 and 23.24) and indicates wide disparities in performance among students. There was also a gender disparity in achievement: the percentage of high achievers was greater among girls and of low achievers among boys, and the male student mean was lower than the female student mean. The report concludes that 'Female students' English language achievement has contributed greatly for the all-island mean to rise' (MOESL & NEREC, 2016: 109). Disparities continue by medium of instruction, with the Sinhala-medium mean of 56.01 being well above the Tamil-medium mean of 47.51, as well as by location. There was:

> variation in achievement among the schools in the different localities. The urban schools have performed better than the rural schools. Their achievement with respect to both mean and median is very much higher than the performance of rural area schools. (MOESL & NEREC, 2016: 116)

Urban area students had a mean score of 61.34 while rural area students had a mean of 49.07. In the urban areas, the highest percentage of students (18.71%) scored between 80 and 89 and in the rural areas the percentage was highest (19.50%) in the 20–29 range.

Another reason for lower than expected achievement by a third of the students at the end of Grade 4 may be, as Little *et al.* (2019) put it, that:

> Educational policy and educational practice inhabit different domains. While guidelines may prescribe the time that should be devoted to the teaching of English (opportunities for teaching and learning), its style, content and practices on the ground (pedagogy) may deviate quite markedly. (Little *et al.*, 2019: 116)

That is, we need to consider not only time allocated to learning but *time lost* from potential learning and the *quality of time spent* on the teaching-learning process. Little *et al.*'s (2019) classroom research found that between 23.2% and 24.8% of teaching-learning time allocated was lost to a variety of non-academic school activities, to teacher absence without cover and to late starts and/or early finishes to lessons. If almost a quarter of allocated time is lost to teaching and learning, it is obviously much harder to meet expected attainment levels, even if all other aspects of the teaching-learning process and its resourcing are satisfactory.

When the assessment for 2015 was compared against that for 2013, it revealed an increase in high achievers across the island and a decrease in low achievers, but the numbers in the lower ranges were still a matter of serious concern. Exacerbating the divide, the percentage of high achievers was greater in urban schools, while the percentage of low achievers was greater in rural schools. The report concludes that 'students' performance at the end of the fourth year of schooling indicates that equal opportunities to achieve the goal of "education for all" had not been successful' (MOESL & NEREC, 2016: 197). The pattern of under-achievement in rural areas is not a phenomenon isolated from the context but reflects underlying socioeconomic inequity. Aturupane *et al.* (2013), using data from an earlier iteration of the Grade 4 test, investigated determinants of academic performance across the country, finding that:

> At the child and household level, educated parents, better nutrition, high daily attendance, enrollment in private tutoring classes, exercise books, electric lighting, and children's books at home all appear to increase learning, while hearing problems have a strong negative effect [this impacts 1–2% of the Grade 4 students]. Among school variables, principals' and teachers' years of experience, collaborating with other schools in a 'school family', and meetings between parents and teachers all appear to have positive impacts on students' scores. (Aturupane *et al.*, 2013: 2)

Perera's (2006) study of the learning of English in a small, disadvantaged primary school suggests that absence of the household and school determinants that increase learning can be seen in a 'culture of poverty' which manifests itself in the children who acquire an adult fatalism from their parents or caregivers that they cannot achieve any other way of life, a 'learned helplessness'. If this is indeed the case across the country for many children in low-achieving schools, then attempting to ensure greater equity in the school variables that influence academic performance would seem to be a logical starting point from which to begin to reduce (and hopefully eliminate) the sense of fatalism brought about by 'learned helplessness'. This is not, obviously, an issue associated with English language teaching alone but nonetheless illustrates that language teaching in the primary classroom is intimately linked with school variables, as well as the context in which the school operates and the socioeconomic position of children, their families and the school in the wider society.

I should emphasise that education retains the power to break through the impact of a 'culture of poverty' and 'learned helplessness' and so offer improved life chances for disadvantaged children. However, this is a task that requires political will and targeted resourcing. Connected to this, Little *et al.*'s (2019) study revealed thought-provoking information about the use of student-centred activities (which are recommended in the curriculum) by particular groups of teachers, in particular types of schools and according to their pre- and in-service training, as follows:

> Student-centred activities were more likely to be observed among teachers who reported using remedial teaching methods more frequently, taught Grade 3 rather than Grade 5 primary and who had been appointed as English teachers. [...] Teachers in rural and estate[12] schools, in schools with more facilities and those who had attended the Primary English Language Programme spent more time on all types of academic task than other teachers. (Little *et al.*, 2019)

The negative influence of the scholarship examination at Grade 5 on student-centred activities is apparent, as is the positive effect of having teachers who are specialist primary English teachers rather than generalists. It also seems that teachers in the smaller, more rural schools are less diverted by non-teaching tasks than those in the larger schools. A specific, long-running, island-wide in-service teacher training programme, a major element of the Primary English Language Programme which prepared the *Let's Learn English* textbooks referred to earlier and which was designed to focus initially on the more rural schools, also appeared to have met some of its objectives in helping teachers to focus on student learning (see also Hayes, 2006).

Another powerful illustration of the potential of education, in this case to overcome the ethnic polarisation that has plagued Sri Lanka, is to be found in Wijesekera *et al.*'s (2019) case study of teachers and students in a bilingual education programme where both Sinhalese and Tamil students study other subjects through the medium of English. Unfortunately, as we have seen in Table 4.1, the numbers of schools with both Sinhalese and Tamil students are very small indeed. Whether it would be possible to expand them island-wide is questionable given the requirement for teachers to be able to teach their subjects effectively in English rather than their first languages. Nevertheless, the case study shows the potential for children from different ethnic communities to come together in a setting that encourages the development of inclusive pedagogical practices 'that enabled the reorienting of exclusionary, ethnocentric identity positioning of students and promoted social inclusivity' (Wijesekera *et al.*, 2019: 30). Success in this endeavour is critically dependent on teachers displaying 'absence of favouritism based on ethnicity' (Wijesekera *et al.*, 2019: 32), i.e. their own ethnicity. Heteroglossic language practices, in which the teachers allowed students 'to shuttle freely between languages to fulfil their academic and communication needs' (Wijesekera *et al.*, 2019: 34) promoted 'membership of a group that is inclusive of all ethnic diverse others' (Wijesekera *et al.*, 2019: 35). Although not specifically stated, the grade of schooling in Wijesekera *et al.*'s (2019) study appears, from the comment of one of the parents, to be Grade 9, but there is no reason *in theory* why the successful practice discussed here could not be replicated in primary grades, beginning once children have become literate in their respective first languages, so that children become more tolerant and respectful of other communities at as early an age as possible. Of course, *in practice*, the programmes would be easier to replicate in well-resourced urban schools and priority would need to be given to improving resources and providing appropriately qualified teachers for rural schools to avoid increasing the divide between the two.

Reflections: Languages in Primary Schools and Social Cohesion

More perhaps than in other countries that we have examined so far, language teaching in primary schools in Sri Lanka is of immense and immediate importance to the future of the country. Education in general and language education in particular may be a part of the solution to ethnic conflict or may be a part of the problem if, either unintentionally or intentionally, it divides and antagonises different groups (Sen, 2007). In Sri Lanka, although the primary educational curriculum is, in theory, supposed to foster an inclusive national identity among children, this was difficult to achieve while the war was being fought (Sørensen, 2008) and has not been achieved since (NEC, 2017). The language-specific divisions in the educational system, in which schools are separated according to medium of instruction with most children being taught in their first language – Sinhala or Tamil – has long, at best, been considered unhelpful in fostering mutual respect and understanding between the communities and, at worst, continues to reinforce ethnic and language differences. While the decision to teach the 2NL to Sinhalese and Tamil children is laudable in principle, as is the objective of a trilingual nation, in practice it seems that language policies have so far had little impact on reducing interethnic hostility. A key reason for this is the lack of adequate resources, most importantly qualified teachers, while the widespread perception among many Sinhalese adults that Tamil is not a useful language for their children to learn does not promote positive attitudes towards its learning even in those schools where teachers are available.

The opportunities offered by using English as a medium of instruction in multi-ethnic classrooms for promoting social cohesion and mutual respect among Sinhalese and Tamil children for each other's language and culture reveal what can be achieved in the right circumstances (Wijesekera *et al.*, 2019). However, a precondition for this approach is an adequate supply of teachers who are able to teach their subjects through the medium of English. Moreover, children in primary schools also need to become literate in their first languages and English as a second language so that they understand the subject content. In the current circumstances, children in the poorer rural and urban schools would be further disadvantaged through such a policy as it is teachers in the larger urban schools, particularly the central schools, who are most likely to be proficient in English as well as their subject content. Although English is seen less as a colonial imposition by younger Sri Lankans and more as a language required for individual economic advancement, the teaching of English at present reflects socioeconomic inequality in the wider society and still acts as a 'kaduwa' or sword dividing the haves and have nots. For the future of the country, enhanced inter-ethnic understanding needs to begin in primary schools through language education, which is only possible if priority is given to better resourcing and more effective teaching of the 2NL. This is likely to require a substantial commitment on the part of the Ministry of Education to increase the number of 2NL teachers, particularly of Tamil. At present much more attention in primary schools is paid to English than to the 2NL, but even here there is unequal access to high-quality teaching, with rural areas and poor urban schools at a significant disadvantage. For both the 2NL and English, the importance of 'a close alignment between curriculum expectations, curriculum materials, classroom realities and teacher education' (Little *et al.*, 2019: 125) also cannot be overemphasised.

Notes

(1) In this chapter I use the more common designation of 'Sinhala' for the language and 'Sinhalese' for the people.
(2) See http://www.statistics.gov.lk/PopHouSat/CPH2012Visualization/htdocs/index.php?usecase=indicator&action=Data&indId=10
(3) The Easter 2019 bombings of churches and hotels in Colombo by Muslim extremists which caused 253 deaths and more than 500 injuries was followed by anti-Muslim attacks, further hampering efforts to foster peaceful relations between the communities of Sri Lanka. As this discrimination is based on religion rather than ethnicity and language, it is not discussed in detail here although the links between religion and

language are recognised. See Davis (2018) for a discussion of Muslims and Sri Lankan language politics.

(4) See http://www.endangeredlanguages.com/lang/3398

(5) See https://www.parliament.lk/files/pdf/constitution.pdf

(6) As this book was going to press in July 2022, mass demonstrations in Sri Lanka against chronic economic mismanagement and accusations of rampant corruption forced the resignation of the government. Gotabaya Rajapakse fled the country and also resigned as President.

(7) The plan is available for download at https://www.yumpu.com/en/document/read/47901672/ten-year-national-plan-for-a-trilingual-sri-lanka-2012-a-2022

(8) See https://data.worldbank.org/indicator/SE.PRM.NENR?locations=LK&view=chart

(9) See http://uis.unesco.org/en/country/lk

(10) The complete new series is available for download at http://www.edupub.gov.lk/BooksDownload.php

(11) These tests assess achievement in students' first language and mathematics as well as English.

(12) 'Estate' schools are those situated on plantations.

5 Equity and Multilingual Diversity in Primary School Language Teaching and Learning in Malaysia

Introduction

In previous chapters on Thailand, South Korea and Sri Lanka, factors such as the washback effect of high-stakes examinations making itself felt even in primary schools, a lack of alignment between the curriculum and what is achievable in the context, rural–urban disparities in access to resources and outcomes, and inadequate resourcing for second languages important in the context have all been identified as having an impact on early language learning in primary schools. The focus of this chapter is the language context of Malaysia, which has its own unique post-colonial language challenges, but where similar factors to those found in other countries may also influence policy and practice in early language learning. English is the principal foreign language taught in Malaysian schools from primary grades onwards, but Malaysia is no different from many former British colonies in that its relationship with the language of the former occupier is both conflicted and contentious. On the one hand, English is now regarded as the language of economic opportunity, essential for a globalised economy, while on the other hand it is a reminder of a past characterised by cultural, political and economic subjugation to a foreign power. The teaching of English also occasions soul searching about its impact on identity and the use of the national language, alongside a contrasting concern about what are perceived to be declining standards in English contributing to a loss of national economic competitiveness. As in Thailand, South Korea and Sri Lanka, the policy response to these and other concerns is usually more teaching of English at the earliest grades in the school system. The chapter begins with discussion of the Malaysian context, outlining its linguistic landscape together with national and educational language policies, which provide the framework within which the teaching of languages in primary schools takes place. Alongside these factors, the chapter addresses the acknowledged rural–urban divide in English language proficiency as well as equity across language groups in the country.

The Linguistic Landscape of Malaysia, National Language Policies and Educational Language Policies

Malaysia is a multilingual, multi-ethnic society where 137 living languages are spoken. There are two distinct land masses, peninsular Malaysia and East Malaysia, separated by some 1500 km of the South China Sea. East Malaysia comprises the states of Sabah and Sarawak on the island of Borneo and the island of Labuan off its western coast. According to 2016 figures from the Department of Information, the population of 31 million is comprised of 61.8% Bumiputera, 21.4% Chinese, 6.4% Indian, 0.9% unspecified 'Other' and 9.6% Non-Malaysian Resident.[1] The designation 'Bumiputera' refers to Malays and other Indigenous groups, while Chinese and Indians were later arrivals, mostly in the European colonial period. The largest group among 'Non-Malaysian Resident' is migrant workers from Indonesia and there is also a significant presence of migrants from the conflict-affected southern provinces of the Philippines in Sabah.

European colonisation followed a pattern familiar in the region with Portuguese settlements being superseded by Dutch, which were then replaced by more widespread British control. The British settlements in Penang, Singapore and Malacca were combined into the Straits Settlements in 1826 and throughout the 19th and early 20th centuries British supremacy was gradually established over the whole of peninsular Malaysia as well as parts of Borneo (the present-day states of Sabah and Sarawak). The advent of British rule brought with it significant changes in the language and cultural make-up of Malaysia. Censuses from 1871 onwards recorded an increase in recruitment of both Chinese labour for the tin industry and Indian labour for rubber and palm oil plantations such that by 1930 Indians made up 20% of the population of the peninsula, Chinese 40% and Malays 40%. These labourers brought their languages with them, of course, and 'British economic and demographic policies were thus important factors in linguistic patterns, regardless of policies specifically related to language use' (Powell, 2002: 219). Chinese settlers also migrated to Sabah and Sarawak during the colonial era and now form the largest non-Austronesian group living in those states. Since independence for peninsular Malaya in 1957 and the formation of a federated Malaysia with Sabah and Sarawak in 1963,[2] the ethnic composition of the country has continued to evolve with Bumiputeras now forming the largest percentage of the population, as we have seen from the 2016 figures.

A total of 41 languages are spoken in peninsula Malaysia, including the migrant Chinese and Indian languages, with around a quarter being dialects of Malay. East Malaysia is home to even greater linguistic diversity with 'around 60 languages spoken in Sabah, including Indigenous Austronesian languages, cross-border Austronesian languages from other parts of Borneo and adjacent islands, and migrant languages' (Pugh-Kitingan *et al.*, 2018: 229). There is a similar range of languages in Sarawak among its 26 ethnic groups. Notwithstanding this linguistic diversity, non-Malay Indigenous languages have little official representation anywhere in the country. The status of Malay[3] as the national language was enshrined in the Federal Constitution at independence, hence it became the language of administration post-independence, and later the language of education. The importance of Malay as a unifying language among the diverse groups in the country assumed greater importance after ethnic clashes in peninsular Malaysia in May 1969, which the government argued 'were caused by the undoubted economic backwardness of the Malay population, a legacy of British neglect during the colonial period' (Brown, 2007: 320). As a result of these clashes, and a fear of them being repeated, government policy has influenced minority language groups to feel

> that the children need to learn Malay well before they are introduced to another language. When the students enter school, the curriculum and language in which they learn to read is Malay, the national language. Then after two or three years, they are able to have a class in their mother tongue. (Smith, 2003: 62)

Prioritisation of the national language has had an unintended, albeit foreseeable, impact on first language vitality among Indigenous minority groups as well as acting as a factor in high levels of school drop-outs, particularly in the states of Sabah and Sarawak which have 80% of Malaysia's minority language students (MOEM, 2013b). In Sabah, only one Indigenous language, Kadazandusun, has been offered in schools, beginning as a pilot programme in 1997 but only from Primary 4 and not as a medium of instruction (MOI). By 2000 it was being taught in 440 schools across the state, irrespective of whether it was the child's home language or not (Smith, 2003). Other Indigenous groups in Sabah such as the Iranun have been working to develop materials so their language may be taught in schools (Smith, 2003), but the Ministry's priority remains for all children first to become proficient in Malay and for English to become a strong second language. The situation for minority language teaching is similar in Sarawak, where the Minority Rights Group (2018) notes:

> The prominent role of Malay as the country's national language has led it to almost completely supplant English and indigenous languages, particularly Iban, in schools and government. Though English is still taught widely, Iban is only taught as a subject in one school in Kuching [the state capital], and in less than half of the state's primary schools which have more than 50 per cent Iban students. This language preference, which

appears discriminatory in the context of Sarawak, has contributed greatly to the increased marginalization of many indigenous peoples in terms of access to employment opportunities predicated on fluency in Malay, and may also be contributing to an extremely high level of school drop-outs. (Minority Rights Group, 2018)

The consequence of the policy for many children in East Malaysia (and this applies to a lesser extent in the peninsula too) is not just that they have to learn two new languages when they enter primary school, Malay and English, but that often they lose attachments to their home language and culture. Appell (2000) commented of the Rungus of Sabah that:

> The schooled generation now makes fun of their elders who carry on the old traditions when they can. They have become a source of ridicule rather than a source of knowledge, wisdom and cultural history. (Appell, 2000: 15)

Subtractive rather than additive bilingualism has thus been a concern for some time for many smaller minority groups throughout the country, which find it difficult to receive any education in their first language. This contrasts with the situation for the larger Chinese and Indian minorities, which long ago established schools teaching in their own languages, Mandarin and Tamil, and which are now run as 'national-type'[4] primary schools with Malay taught as a compulsory second language. While there is strong cross-community support for a national language policy in order to maintain the social cohesion of the country, an unfortunate side-effect of the policy to prioritise Malay has nevertheless been 'an increase in Chinese and Tamil schools catering to the demands of these ethnic groups, who believe that these schools are more culturally and linguistically suited to their communities' which, in turn, 'appears to have contributed to racial polarization, with national schools having mostly Malay children, and Chinese schools mostly Chinese and Tamil schools all Indian children' (Hashim, 2009: 40). Unfortunately, the trend has not eased and, as the Ministry of Education (MOEM, 2013a: E-12) has admitted, 'ethnic stratification in schools has increased'.

As in Sri Lanka, Sri Lanka if children do not mix with their peers from other communities, it is difficult for them to develop a genuine understanding of each other's cultures and a sense of identification as members of a national rather than a primarily ethnic group. The Malaysian government is well aware of this, acknowledging in the most recent Education Blueprint that 'As student environments become more homogeneous, there is a growing need for the Ministry to create avenues for students from different school types to interact' (MOEM, 2013a: E-12) and that 'To foster unity, it is important for students to interact and learn with peers and teachers from various ethnic, religious, cultural, and socioeconomic backgrounds' (MOEM, 2013a: E-12). At the time of the writing of the Blueprint, however, it seemed that funding constraints were hampering efforts to promote inter-ethnic interaction through programmes such as the 'Student Integration Plan for Unity' (Rancangan Integrasi Murid Untuk Perpaduan, RIMUP, in Bahasa Malaysia).

The policy to recognise Malay as the national language after independence and to introduce it progressively as the MOI in national schools was begun in 1970 in the first year of primary school and completed across the school system in peninsular Malaysia by 1980 and in Sabah and Sarawak by 1985. Inevitably this led to a change in the level of proficiency in English among school leavers as the former colonial language was relegated to the status of a school subject, taught from Grade 1 onwards. Nationally, the degree of proficiency in English tends to run along generational lines, with those who received their primary schooling prior to the change of MOI from English to Malay being most proficient and tending to bemoan the language standards of younger generations (Gill, 2012). The perceived necessity for English in a globalised economy, and the impact of lack of competence in English on economic development, is usually at the forefront of these complaints. Gill (2012: 56) concluded that:

> One of the main challenges that resulted from the focus on Bahasa Malaysia in the educational system was a generation that was fluent in Bahasa Malaysia but weak in English. This resulted in one of the main problems facing the nation to this day – that of the unemployment of graduates, particularly from the public universities who had to look for employment in the private sector, where English is the main language of communication. (Gill, 2012: 56)

The official view on English language proficiency and economic needs has not changed in recent years, with members of the Ministry of Education's English Language Standards and Quality Council (ELSQC) writing of 'a fundamental problem faced by our young people today. They have to cope with a rapidly changing and increasingly globalised world and job market which requires them to communicate effectively in English at a much higher level than before' (Don & Abdullah, 2019). However, other research reveals that English is only one of several factors involved in graduate employability. In a survey of 571 HR personnel, the most prominent reason for new graduates being rejected after interviews was 'unrealistic salary demands'; the second was 'bad character, attitude and personality of the jobseeker'; 'poor command of English language' came third, followed by 'lack of good communication skills, and lastly 'too choosy about the job or company they wish to work for'. Overall, the employability factors were summarised as 'the students' problems relate more to attitude than capability' (Research Team, 2013: 46).

Adding to the complexity of attitudes towards English, there exists a sense among the Malay community that speaking English is somehow a betrayal of their ethnic identity. As Ting (2003: 205) put it, 'The Malays are particularly wary of speaking English to another Malay because

English is often perceived as subtracting from their Malay identity by their community'. This is a longstanding attitude and can be seen at least in part as a consequence of 'the religious, cultural, and linguistic identity ascribed to the Malays in the Federal Constitution of Malaysia, which defines them as people who practice Islam and the Malay culture and who speak the Malay language (Article 160)' (Rajadurai, 2010: 94). The constitutionally enshrined priority for Malay indirectly leads to a closing off of opportunities for communicating in English and the prospect of alienation from their home communities for those who wish to do so; not only that, but lack of opportunity to use English lessens the chances of achieving the necessary proficiency to be accepted into elite English-speaking communities in the country (Rajadurai, 2010). In contrast, negative attitudes of this kind are not replicated among Malaysian Chinese and Indian communities which generally see instrumental value in acquiring English, as an economic necessity, in much the same way that they see acquiring Malay as a political necessity (Rajadurai, 2010). Such an attitudinal divide among the communities exacerbates linguistic polarisation in the country and educational language policy has become highly contested. The end result is that, while successive governments have continued to place emphasis on English for economic reasons, they have failed to resolve the tension with Malay and linguistic nationalism, seeming to have

> forgotten that language planning and education policy should not rest on economic considerations but on the recognition of and respect for linguistically expressed cultural identities. For Malaysia, this is important when coming up with a solution to the educational questions without creating racial and ethnic tensions or conflict. (Hashim, 2009: 49)

The dangers of making changes solely in response to perceived economic needs can be seen in reactions to the government's decision to reintroduce English as an MOI for maths and science starting in the first year of primary and secondary schools in 2003. Although the policy aimed to improve English language levels as well as outcomes in science and maths, it appeared to have the opposite effect. Students found it difficult to understand subject content in English; hence teachers reverted to teaching in Malay (Rashid *et al.*, 2017), and results in the Ujian Penilaian Sekolah Rendah (UPSR), the primary school leaving exam, actually decreased in science and maths across all schools (Zaman, 2019). Further, the change of MOI exacerbated the achievement gap between urban and rural schools (Gill & Shaari, 2019). After several years of the policy, large-scale protests by rural Malays occurred,[5] with protesters complaining that it disadvantaged their children and contributed to worsening inequalities between rural and urban schools. Taken together with concerns about the impact of the policy on the national language, the government felt compelled to reverse the policy in 2009, not long after full implementation had been reached. While, in reality, English and Malay largely operate in different domains, the perception remained that the MOI policy posed a threat to the vitality of Malay. This perception, and the failure to take sufficient account of the rural–urban divide in access to English in the environment and children's motivation to learn it, which were vital for successful implementation, led to political consequences that the Malay-dominated government could not ignore and brought about their change of course.

Nevertheless, in spite of the failure of the English as an MOI policy for maths and science, the government continued to maintain its emphasis on English in other ways, with a new policy initiative in the 10th Malaysia Plan (2011–2015), designated as the 'Memartabatkan Bahasa Malaysia Mengukukhan Bahasa Inggeris' (MBMMBI) or the 'Upholding Bahasa Malaysia and Strengthening English Programme'. This programme attempted to reconcile the tensions between upholding the national language and promoting English as a language necessary for economic development. Within MBMMBI, additional contact hours were allocated to Malay and English in primary schools, which satisfied both those groups who wanted to strengthen the national language and those who wanted greater proficiency in English. However, the new policy caused disquiet among some Chinese vernacular school supporters who felt that it endangered Mandarin. The additional hours were thus only implemented in Malay language national schools and Tamil-medium national-type schools (Rashid *et al.*, 2017).

As the 10th Malaysia Plan approached a close, the government initiated a 'National Education Dialogue'. A series of town hall meetings were held across the country, involving over 10,000 people, with responses taken into account in the preparation of plans for reform (Hanewald, 2016). Wholesale education reform was then initiated with the *Malaysia Education Blueprint 2013–2025: Pre-school to Post-secondary Education* (MOEM, 2013b). Within the Blueprint, among the skills and attributes that students are deemed to need is 'Bilingual Proficiency', articulated as follows:

> Every child will be, at minimum, operationally proficient in bahasa Malaysia as the national language and language of unity, and in English as the international language of communication. This means that upon leaving school, the student should be able to work in both a bahasa Malaysia and English language environment. The Ministry will also encourage all students to learn an additional language. (MOEM, 2013b: E-10)

This objective was operationalised in the 'Eleven shifts to transform the system' contained in the Blueprint, where 'Ensure every child is proficient in Bahasa Malaysia and English language' came second only to 'Provide equal access to quality education of an international standard' (MOEM, 2013b: E11–12). The aim is to attain 100% basic literacy in Bahasa Malaysia and English among children after three years of school. The scale of the task with respect to English can be seen in scores reported in the Blueprint on the Sijil Pelajaran Malaysia (SPM) exam at the end of secondary Grade 5, where results among the different school types are all well below 50%, with only 23% of Bumiputera, 42% of Chinese and 35% of Tamil students reaching the required standard in English (MOEM, 2013a: E-23). Nonetheless, the Ministry's expectation in the 2013–2025 Blueprint is to transform the teaching and learning of English through remedial coaching for students who fall behind, expanded opportunities for greater exposure to the language and the 'upskilling' of English teachers. The Ministry's ELSQC subsequently provided a framework for implementation of the *Malaysia Education Blueprint* in a 'Roadmap' for reform (ELSQC, 2015). The Roadmap will be discussed in the following sections where attention will be turned to the implementation of government reform initiatives in primary schools over the years, how they have been received by teachers, and their outcomes.

The Primary Curriculum and the Teaching of English

As of 2020, there were 7779 primary schools in Malaysia, of which 3674 were classified as rural and 4105 as urban, providing education to 2,740,180 children (MOEM, 2020). In common with many other countries, most (70.5%) of the 236,070 primary teachers were female (MOEM, 2020). Children begin compulsory primary schooling at the age of seven for a period of six years (many may also attend pre-schools but this is not universal). As previously noted, the schools are divided into two categories, 'national' primary schools and vernacular 'national-type' primary schools, with national-type schools (SJK – *Sekolah Jenis Kebangsaan*) using either Chinese/Mandarin (hence SJKC) or Tamil (SJKT) as the MOI, while national primary schools (SK – *Sekolah Kebangsaan*) use Bahasa Malaysia. Before proceeding to secondary schools, students in Year 6 are required to sit the Primary School Achievement Test (UPSR – *Ujian Pencapaian Sekolah Rendah*), although they do not have to pass the English component in order to progress.

The current primary school curriculum, the *Kurikulum Standard Sekolah Rendah* (KSSR), was introduced in 2011 and emphasises higher order thinking and problem-solving skills, for English as well as other subjects. It also instituted school-based assessment to reduce the emphasis on national exams. KSSR has since been revised and implementation of the revised curriculum began with primary Year 1 in 2017. KSSR increased the time allocated for English in SK from 240 minutes a week in Years 1–3 and 210 minutes a week in Years 4–6 to 300 minutes for both stages of primary school. In SJK the increase was from 60 to 150 minutes for Years 1–3 and from 90 to 180 minutes for Years 4–6 (ELSQC, 2015: 168). In spite of the increase in class hours in KSSR, the ELSQC maintained in its *English Education Reform in Malaysia: The Roadmap 2015–2025* that 'Learners currently do not have sufficient engagement time with English in order to gain familiarity with the language and confidence in using it' (ELSQC, 2015: 171). It is not clear whether this refers to out-of-class engagement or allotted lesson time, but it may also be a reflection of how the time is actually spent in the classroom as much as it is of the time available. The ELSQC (2015) noted that lessons in primary schools continued to be teacher dominated and that there was limited use of English in the classroom. Not surprisingly, attainment falls below expectations. While the objective is for children to reach A1 on the CEFR by the end of Year 3 and A2 by the end of Year 6, a study of proficiency in English in 2013 found that only 22% of the children surveyed in Year 6 had reached A2, 34% were at A1 and 32% below A1; at the higher levels of the CEFR scale, 12% of children attained B1 and 1% B2 (ELSQC, 2015: 22). The proficiency outcomes at Year 6 also highlight that children in rural schools perform less well than those in urban schools (a pattern that is, not surprisingly, consistent across later years too).

Assessment of teachers' proficiency in the same study found that 29% were below B2 (independent user) on the CEFR, but the ELSQC commented that the teachers sampled were not representative of the total population and 'the results are likely to present a somewhat optimistic impression of the overall situation' since, for example, 'about 31.7% of teachers currently teaching English in schools are not English optionists' (ELSQC, 2015: 169). The study thus indicates significant concerns over teachers' English language proficiency and their capacity to implement the curriculum as intended, as well as children's under-attainment and an urban–rural divide in achievement. This divide does not appear to be related to quality factors such as the allocation of educational resources, although the school climate in rural primary schools has been found to be less positive than in urban primary schools, which may be related to the socioeconomic background of the students and teachers' perceptions of them (Othman & Muijs, 2013).

While there is concern over teachers' proficiency and students' achievement in English, specifically, it is important to note before going any further that in many other – and arguably more important – respects the Malaysian education system has been transformed since independence in 1957, when more than half of the population had no formal schooling, only 6% had secondary education and a mere 1% post-secondary education. By 2011 near universal primary enrolment had been achieved, and 87% of children were in lower secondary and 78% in upper secondary schooling (MOEM, 2013a: E-4). These achievements correlate with the progressive change in MOI from English to Bahasa Malaysia. There are also many instances of excellent performance across the system, with Malaysians recently winning medals at the World Robot Olympiads, the International Exhibition for Young Inventors and, for English specifically, the English-Speaking Union International Public Speaking Competition (MOEM, 2013b: 1–3). Nonetheless, it is equally important to note that the indicators of excellence are not representative of all regions and sectors in the country. Inequity in achievement remains – and not just in English proficiency; hence, one of the primary objectives of the *Malaysia Education Blueprint* is 'to halve the socio-economic, urban–rural, and gender achievement [girls outperform boys by the end of primary school and the gap continues to widen thereafter] gaps in student outcomes by 2020' (MOEM, 2013b: 2–3).

Curriculum Change, Teachers and Context

The objectives for KSSR English are not entirely new, as we can see by comparing the overall aims for KSSR with its predecessor, KBSR (*Kurikulum Baru Sekolah Rendah* or New Primary School Curriculum), which was first introduced in 1983. KBSR 'aims to equip learners with basic skills and knowledge of the English language so as to enable them to communicate, both orally and in writing, in and out of school' (KPM, 2001: 2), while KSSR 'aims to equip pupils with basic language skills to enable them to communicate effectively in a variety of contexts that are appropriate to the pupils' level of development' (MOEM, 2015: 5). KBSR was designed to be learner centred with the teacher as a facilitator, similar to KSSR's focus on 'Learner-centred teaching and learning' which was allied to 'Fun, meaningful and purposeful learning' (MOEM, 2015: 6). The emphasis on English for communication first introduced in KBSR was designed to bring about a paradigm shift in teaching methods, promoting communicative activities in the classroom to replace the teaching of grammar in a structural approach. However, macro-level planning of goals for the KBSR curriculum was not matched by micro-level realisation in its implementation, as the research showing limited use of English in many classrooms illustrated (ELSQC, 2015). Furthermore, KBSR did nothing to prevent – even worsened – a socioeconomic divide in the achievement of proficiency in English, with Azman (2016) commenting:

> Conceptually, the CLT [communicative language teaching] approach as conceived should have produced competent users of the English language. Instead its implementation had created a distinct chasm in the society, between the urban and the rural as well as between categories of socio-economic status. It is indeed unfortunate that in the twenty years (1983–2003) that the CLT approach [in KBSR] was implemented, proficiency in the English language was increasingly influenced by socio-economic factors rather than teaching efficacy. (Azman, 2016: 69)

KSSR is also supposed to play its part in minimising the link between proficiency in English and socioeconomic status which the government itself acknowledges is a problem (ELSQC, 2015; MOEM, 2013b). Azman's (2016) depiction of a 'chasm' between rural and urban and rich and poor, which was at the root of the demonstrations against the teaching of maths and science in English in 2009, is explicitly recognised in the Roadmap for reform where the focus on dimensions of equity is unequivocal.

> We have to ensure that the new programme enables children from poor rural backgrounds to succeed in English, that the style of teaching and learning is appropriate for boys as well as girls, and that the programme makes equitable provision for children from different ethnic backgrounds. (ELSQC, 2015: 53)

The problem of the proficiency in English of students in rural schools being significantly below the expected grade level is, of course, just one element of their under-achievement but, because of the policy-level attention paid to the importance of English, its place in the over-arching educational goal of reducing rural–urban inequity attracts disproportionate attention.

Moreover, while there is a significant achievement issue in English in rural schools generally, the achievement level of children in non-Malay Indigenous (or 'Orang Asli'[6]) primary classrooms is even more problematic. In 2012, less than 15% of Indigenous children passed the UPSR English exam according to statistics from the Department of Orang Asli Development (Mihat, 2015). In his study of the implementation of KSSR in Indigenous primary classrooms in one Malaysian state, Mihat (2015) lays bare the difficulties experienced in these schools with the curriculum for English. For example, 60% of the teachers surveyed felt that the learning objectives by the end of primary schooling were 'too ambitious for indigenous pupils to achieve' (Mihat, 2015: 6). Further, 60% of teachers felt that the KSSR syllabus for English failed to cater for the home language background of Indigenous children, while 84% believed that the textbooks used failed to provide guidance on how to 'accommodate the activities to pupils of lower proficiency' (Mihat, 2015: 7). One of the major issues teachers identified was that the syllabus assumed an initial level of literacy in Year 1 which Indigenous children simply did not have, partly because of their limited participation in pre-school programmes and partly because of the lack of a written form of their home languages. In a context where the children's home language is not the language of schooling, where children are said to be typically less interested in schooling and even attendance is an issue (these factors are, of course, interrelated), the question of the relevance of a third, foreign language taught in schools from the earliest stages to Indigenous children's lives and educational experience assumes even greater importance in considerations of rural–urban inequity.

Curriculum objectives are, of course, mandated by the Ministry of Education, but it is apparent from classroom-based research such as Mihat's (2015) that they do not take sufficient account of the everyday realities experienced by many teachers, particularly those in rural and other underprivileged areas. Similar classroom difficulties with the implementation of KSSR to those found by Mihat (2015) are to be found in other studies. Hardman and A-Rahman (2014), for example, report that primary school English teachers had challenges with:

> the problems of having to manage large classes of pupils with mixed learning abilities, low levels of proficiency in the English language, the need to get through specified content in the curriculum and the pressures to prepare the children for end-of-year assessments [as well as] not enough support provided to aid the implementation of the communicative approach and that there was a mismatch between the curriculum and how it was assessed [...] discussions with the teachers revealed that the teachers were unsure of what the term interactive learner-centred teaching meant in practice. (Hardman & A-Rahman, 2014: 270)

When teachers such as those in Hardman and A-Rahman's (2014) study feel that their students are not capable of understanding the English they are supposed to be teaching, they fall back on using their shared first language in the interests of children in school achieving at least some level of comprehension of the input. This is what most responsible teachers would do and is not a new phenomenon, identified in many studies over the years (see, for example, Ali, 2003; Othman & Kiely, 2016).

Despite being at the heart of the implementation process for any curriculum reform, teachers in Malaysia – and they are far from unique in this respect – seem not to have been involved in the development of the curriculum they are expected to teach, still less to have been consulted on the magnitude of the changes that they are required to make in their classroom teaching (Rashid *et al.*, 2017). Hardman and A-Rahman (2014) conclude in their study of teacher implementation of KSSR that:

> the new primary English curriculum in Malaysia has been introduced with insufficient consideration being paid by policy-makers to the key role of teachers in enacting curriculum reforms and to the major shifts in beliefs and classroom practices that have to be brought about for their successful implementation in the classroom. (Hardman & A-Rahman, 2014: 273)

This conclusion is reminiscent of Havelock and Huberman's lament – and also reminds us that little seems to have changed in educational planning since it was made more than 40 years ago – that:

> Those designing, administering and advising on [curriculum and other educational] projects do not generally have to make very many changes *themselves. Their* task remains the same. It is *others* who will have to modify their behaviours and very often to modify them rapidly in fairly significant ways, and with little previous or even gradual preparation. These are typically the kind of rapid and massive changes which planners or administrators or advisers would never plan, administer or advise for *themselves.* (Havelock & Huberman, 1977: 159)

If teachers are not adequately consulted, the opportunity is lost to take account of the classroom realities that Mihat (2015) and Hardman and A-Rahman (2014) report which, in turn, makes it more difficult to realise the objectives that the Ministry has for the primary curriculum. Inevitably this then feeds into a public discourse of 'declining standards' rather than a critical evaluation of the curriculum itself and the means by which it is developed and implemented.

The discourse of declining standards may perhaps be what led the ELSQC to support teaching other subjects in English, despite the difficulties experienced with earlier iterations of English-medium instruction for maths and science, which exacerbated rural–urban inequity, and seemingly contrary to the focus of the Roadmap for reform on equitable provision across rural and urban areas, as well as across ethnic backgrounds (ELSQC, 2015). The Roadmap (ELSQC, 2015) explains that:

> For selected schools science and mathematics can also be taught in English. Having subjects like these taught in English will gradually bring about dual language instruction which will improve students' learning of both English and Malay. However, this recommendation for the increase in the engagement hours for English must be compatible with maintaining the position of Malay as the national language. (ELSQC, 2015: 329)

As a corollary of this recommendation, it doesn't take much foresight to see that those 'selected schools' that will be allowed to offer subjects in English are likely to be the best resourced and most prestigious schools in urban areas. Indeed, the criteria that schools have to fulfil to be allowed to run 'Dual Language Programmes' (DLPs) since 2016 under the MBMMBI are that they should have sufficient resources, the principal and teachers should be in favour of running DLP, parents should also be in favour of the programme, and the school's performance in Bahasa Malaysia should be on a par with or better than the national average (School Advisor, 2021), virtually guaranteeing that few rural schools will be running them. (As of 2018, there were 654 of the more than 7700 primary schools running DLPs but no information was given as to their locations in the Ministry's annual report on the implementation of the Education Blueprint [MOEM, 2019].) In addition, with the requirement for 'sufficient resources' to be available, it is likely that these selected schools will have had fewer, if any, teachers who featured among the two-thirds of 70,000 English teachers who failed to meet the Ministry's required CEFR C1 proficiency level in nationwide testing conducted in 2012 (ELSQC, 2015; Hiew, 2016).

Teacher's English Language Proficiency, Pedagogical Skills and Continuing Professional Development (CPD)

The issue of English teachers' language proficiency levels is one that figures large in government documents. The Ministry of Education's 'upskilling' programmes have been designed to meet the target of a minimum level of C1 for all English teachers in the 2016–2020 phase of the Education Blueprint where the focus is on 'introducing structural change' (ELSQC, 2015). Teachers' language proficiency is not just a concern for the Ministry, though, but also garners a great deal of attention in the public discourse. For example, a newspaper headline interpreted teachers' failure to meet the required proficiency levels as '70% of English teachers not fit to teach' (The Star, 2013), equating competence to teach simply with English language proficiency. In response to these teachers' failure to meet the mandated standards when they sat for tests, the Ministry developed training programmes with a principal focus on language proficiency and an ancillary focus on classroom methodology. In one of these, a major programme called 'ProELT', teachers in urban and suburban areas had to attend four hours of courses for 44 weeks outside school hours, while teachers in rural areas had to attend a course with eight weeks of face-to-face training, with 30 contact hours per week, supplemented by eight weeks of independent learning via a computer-mediated programme, also with 30 hours of learning time per week.

From 2012 to 2015 the ProELT programme was outsourced by the Ministry to the British Council Malaysia, which recruited native-speaker trainers to run the courses using a standardised course book, *English for Teaching*. The use of native English speakers in ProELT and other training programmes such as the 'English Language Teacher Development Project' (ELTDP),[7] which ran from 2011 to 2015 and in which local teachers were mentored by the native speakers in school clusters, is a source of controversy among Malaysian English language teaching specialists. For example, a report on the Malaysian English Language Teaching Association (MELTA) forum on native speakers at their annual international conference in 2010 concluded that:

> The measure to bring in native speakers as trainers undermines the legitimacy and expertise of home-grown talent. Malaysia already has local English language academics and teachers who are expert users of the language, possessing the same levels of linguistic and pedagogical knowledge as native speaker teachers [...] By not including these Malaysians in this programme, the country is sending out a message that Malaysians are not good enough or will never be good enough to become self-reliant. (MELTA, 2010: 2–3)

MELTA's submission to the Ministry to work in partnership with any native speakers deployed was not taken up, however, and both ELTDP and Pro-ELT relied on British Council recruited native speakers.

The Pro-ELT courses were attended by 5000 teachers nationwide in 2012–2013 and 9000 teachers in 2014–2015.[8] Primary and secondary teachers of English attended courses together rather than being separated into groups according to the educational level at which they taught. The overall success of ProELT courses in enhancing teachers' language proficiency is difficult to determine. For example, the Ministry's Annual Report for 2014 highlighted '10,502 English Language Teachers trained under ProELT programme' (MOEM, 2014: 14), and then went on to discuss the programme in more detail as follows:

> In 2014, a total of 10,502 teachers were selected to attend the programme, with the aim of moving up teachers by one proficiency band level on the Common European Framework of References for Languages (CEFR).

> The result of the Aptis[9] test conducted at the end of the ProELT programme showed a total of 519 out of 591 (87.8%) teachers have successfully improved from Band B1 to B2, and 1,716 out of 3,979 (43.1%) teachers have improved from B2 to C1. Overall, out of 4,579 teachers that completed the programme and sat for the post-Aptis test, a total of 2,244 teachers have improved one proficiency level, and another 166 teachers have improved two proficiency levels. (MOEM, 2014: 22)

With only 4579 teachers completing the programme and sitting the test out of 10,502 selected to attend, it is not clear whether the remaining 5923 teachers – more than half of those selected – did not complete the programme or simply did not take the test. Further, although there were good results for the smaller number of teachers who came in with a B1 level improving to B2 (87.8%), the figures for the far larger group of teachers who had B2 on entry attaining the desired C1 level were much less impressive (43.1%). There is no discussion of why these results should be so different. The lower numbers attaining C1 are also worrying from another perspective if the Ministry proceeds with its policy for teachers who fail to meet this target proficiency standard, viz.:

> Teachers who do not meet the minimum proficiency standard after attending the training course will be given up to two years to make the necessary improvements. [...] Those who still do not meet the proficiency standard will be tasked to teach other subjects or redeployed. (MOEM, 2013b: 4–13)

Information on whether failing teachers later met the standard, or whether there has been any redeployment of teachers from English to other subjects, is not readily available but, if teachers are being redeployed, the logical corollary is that an equivalent number of qualified English teachers who do have the mandated language proficiency level would need to be recruited to make up the shortfall. This would have a potentially significant knock-on effect on the supply of new primary school English teachers required from initial teacher-training courses.

The strong emphasis on language proficiency in the Education Blueprint, while perhaps understandable from a policymaker's perspective, is still essentially reductionist, equating effective English teachers purely with being proficient English speakers. While a good command of the subject matter is undeniably important for teachers of any subject, effective teachers are more than just experts in their subject matter. However, it is notable that when teachers were selected to attend ProELT, this was done solely on the basis of their language proficiency scores and did not include any assessment of their teaching skills. Hiew's (2016) study of the impact of ProELT in the eastern state of Sabah showed that this single criterion for selection for the 'upskilling' courses had a profound impact on teachers' self-esteem, especially for more experienced teachers who complained that they were forced to attend irrespective of their classroom performance in schools. As one of Hiew's (2016) interviewees put it:

> I don't understand why we have to attend this course after sitting for the Aptis test when, furthermore, some of us have been teaching for quite long and we have performed well in school without sitting for that evaluation. So, does that mean we are evaluated by just that test? We have performed, you know. I have performed. I told [the trainer]. 'I have performed. I dare to say that because I really have performed. I have increased my school's UPSR result. I have students who were not B or A, but they got B or A. I have very weak students. I got 5 students who we didn't expect to pass. They passed. So that means I know I have performed. I have used my own method. I have used a lot of activities. That means I spent so much time, but still that is not enough?' (Hiew, 2016: 193)

Hiew (2016: 351) notes that there was a general perception among teachers that ProELT was only 'for linguistically and instructionally incompetent teachers', hence it is hardly surprising that she summarised the emotional impact on many teachers of being selected for the courses in Sabah as 'feeling *degraded, embarrassed, demotivated, inferior* and less confident' (Hiew, 2016: 351, italics in original).

In addition, while the ancillary objective of ProELT was to develop teachers' classroom methodology, the grouping of primary with secondary teachers resulted in many teachers feeling that the courses did not meet their needs, with primary teachers in particular thinking, 'this course seems to be more suitable for secondary level' (Hiew, 2016: 172). In her analysis of the ProELT course book, Hiew (2016: 351) also criticised 'the irrelevant program content which were mostly non-transferable into the teachers' lessons due to misalignment between the modules and the national curriculum specifications'. Moreover, some teachers' perception of the course was that it was little more than preparation for retaking the Aptis test rather than helping them to improve their teaching. One teacher remarked:

> I find that they're preparing us for the Aptis test, which I find the test doesn't have any connection with our teaching and learning. What has it got to do, you know? That's what makes us very angry because if there's a connection to it, okay I understand. But there's nothing. No connection at all. (Hiew, 2016: 161)

While many participants commented that they sought to make the course content relevant to their classroom contexts, it appeared to be largely incumbent on them to do this for themselves rather than relevance being a feature intrinsic to the course material as teachers would have expected. Hence, as a whole, the experience of the ProELT programme, at least as far as the teachers in Hiew's (2016) study in Sabah were concerned, was often demotivating and of little relevance to their classroom needs – the very antithesis of what an effective CPD programme should be. The Sabah experience is unfortunately not an isolated one, and available evidence suggests a long-term failure to address teachers' needs in other CPD programmes, notably those intended to implement the new curricula of KBSR from 1983 onwards, KSSR from 2011 and its revised version from 2017 onwards.

CPD and the Implementation of KBSR and KSSR

Regular professional development programmes are designed by the Teacher Education Division of the Ministry in accordance with its Continuous Professional Development Master Plan (CPDMP) (Rashid *et al.*, 2017). The typical training mode is prescriptive, with teachers 'spoon-fed and instructed in what they should do in the classroom, which gives them little opportunity to tailor the instructional approach to meet the needs of their students' (Rashid *et al.*, 2017: 108). Kabilan and Veratharaju (2013: 332) similarly characterise professional development programmes in Malaysia as being 'very centralized, dominated by cascade-type programmes (top-down) that neglect teachers' interests and needs'. The outcomes of Kabilan and Veratharaju's (2013) research with teachers in 1561 randomly selected urban and rural primary schools across the country underscored the importance of basing professional development on the needs of teachers and their students and they warned that 'Ignoring the teachers' voices would cause more serious repercussions as teachers may feel neglected and resist any reforms introduced' (Kabilan & Veratharaju, 2013: 333).

Resistance to the reforms may indeed have contributed to the low level of impact of the large-scale training programmes to implement both KBSR and KSSR, resulting from the design of the training programmes themselves which, in spite of taking place some 30 years apart, was remarkably similar. From a planning perspective, when a new curriculum has to be introduced nationwide there is always likely to be tension between the policymaker's desire to deliver all the required information about the new curriculum as efficiently as possible, a short-term objective, with teachers' expectations that they will not only understand the curriculum content but also come to terms with how to teach it, a long-term process. Neither KBSR nor KSSR resolved this tension successfully.

Hardman and A-Rahman (2014) describe the process for KSSR as follows:

> The training programme was designed to be cascaded down to schools to ensure national coverage, starting with workshops at the national level for state-level trainers lasting five days. The state-level trainers were in turn expected to train a teacher representative from each primary school in their state over a three-day period. The trained teachers were then expected to cascade the training back to all teachers of English in their school over a three-hour period using a pack of resource materials provided at the state-level workshop. (Hardman & A-Rahman, 2014: 261)

The system was comparable for KBSR, where each state sent subject specialists to Kuala Lumpur for a course during which they were provided with information about the new curriculum. Once back in their states, they organised courses for 'key personnel' from each educational division in the state who, in their turn, organised courses for teachers. Courses for teachers lasted a week and were devoted to the whole curriculum for that year. In that week, English as a subject was allotted just seven training hours (Hayes, 1995). Unsurprisingly, Ibrahim's (1991: 125) research into the impact of these courses concluded that 'The evidence suggests that the courses had a surface effect but not the impact that could bring deep assimilation of all the KBSR features'. It is paradoxical that any education system, and Malaysia is far from alone in this, that has introduced a school curriculum focused on learner-centred teaching, should continue to rely on transmissive CPD programmes which do not take account of the way teachers-as-adults learn, specifically in relation to making learning experiences personally meaningful (even though this is usually mandated as a curriculum objective for their students). It is little wonder that the type of cascade model employed by KBSR and KSSR has been routinely criticised for diluting the training as it progresses down the cascade (Hayes, 2000). In the separate cases of curriculum implementation, there has been a failure to consult teachers about their needs during the development of the CPD programmes. Both programmes have relied on a transmissive approach rather than one that is transformational, failing to recognise that 'CPD is more likely to be successful if it promotes teachers' critical capacity to reflect on their own work, their self-esteem, their autonomy to innovate and their creativity – outcomes which transmissive CPD is neither designed for nor able to achieve' (Hayes, 2019: 157). Instead of teachers being seen as partners in improving the educational experience for children in schools, they seem to be viewed simply as implementers of policies and classroom methods decided upon by others. While the curriculum itself may have the potential to provide a fulfilling educational experience for children in schools, it cannot fulfil that potential unless teachers are convinced of its value, lending weight to Ali *et al.*'s (2011: 149) view that 'national-level planning needs to be complemented by micro-level work to create desirable language policy outcomes'.

Reflections: Socioeconomic Disparities in English Language Learning, Vernacular Language Endangerment and Multilingualism

Educational language policy has been instrumental in democratising schooling in Malaysia since independence. Not only has it enabled children to be educated in one of the country's three principal languages from the beginning of primary school, but language policy has also fostered universal proficiency in the national language, Bahasa Malaysia, which has helped to promote unity and suppress the ethnic tensions that gave rise to communal riots in 1969. At the same time, there has been a decline in general levels of proficiency in English which was entirely foreseeable given its change of status from an MOI to a subject but which remains the cause of much public debate. The necessity for English to be taught in schools from primary Grade 1 onwards continues to be predicated on a link between success in a globalised economy and nationwide proficiency in the English language. This link has not been adequately scrutinised, nor have claims that proficiency in English is also necessary because it is the principal language of business within Malaysia. One could argue that this latter factor may be a historical legacy and that once the generation of business leaders educated through the medium of English departs the system, Bahasa Malaysia – spoken by everyone – may replace English as the language of business within the country even if English remains useful as a means of international communication.

Since its replacement as an MOI in national schools by Bahasa Malaysia and in national-type schools by Chinese and Tamil, the current goals for proficiency in English do not appear to be realistic in the existing sociocultural, sociopolitical and socioeconomic conditions. Azman (2016) sums up the challenges that the education system faces as it implements the latest reforms designed to raise educational standards generally and to produce students proficient in both Bahasa Malaysia and English in particular:

> the success of any reform and its initiatives for ELE [English language education] can be hampered by extenuating socio-cultural factors that pose as obvious challenges such as socio-economic disparities that causes limited access to opportunities in a multicthnic society, and fears of vernacular language endangerment among multilinguals. Other related factors such as teachers' English proficiency as well as quality of pedagogy and materials can also hinder progress of the implementation. (Azman, 2016: 75)

There thus appears to be a lack of congruence between curriculum and contextual factors and the end result of macro-level planning in which teachers are not involved can be seen in their everyday, micro-level experiences as they mediate between educational language policies and children in schools. As Azman (2016) has noted, the changes in classroom practice envisaged by the introduction of KBSR in 1983 towards more learner-centred, communicative teaching failed to take root, and Hardman and A-Rahman (2014) show that the early stages of implementation of KSSR did little to change the situation some 30 years later, as they comment on

> the need for teachers of English in Malaysian primary schools to broaden their pedagogic repertoire beyond the use of rote, recitation, instruction and exposition, to include high-quality dialogue and discussion in whole-class, group-based and individual activities, where pupils are expected to play an active role by asking questions, contributing ideas and explaining and demonstrating their thinking to the teacher and peers. (Azman, 2016: 273)

That classroom practices seem to have changed little since the implementation of KBSR in the 1980s is not teachers' 'fault': it is not just the result of a deficiency in language proficiency or teaching skills or even a lack of application on their part as is often suggested in the public discourse. In their study of educational language planning in Malaysia, Ali *et al.* (2011: 163) conclude that the outcome of students' 'limited proficiency achievement was attributable to, among other factors, the sociolinguistic make-up of the society, the communicative resources and constraints, and the relevance of communicative competence as a goal'. They went on to say that 'It is hard to be optimistic about the outcomes of the new policy which simply does not take account of these realities on the ground' (Ali *et al.*, 201: 163). Although Ali *et al.* (2011) were referring to the then new policy of the 'Upholding Bahasa Malaysia and Strengthening English Programme', their conclusion seems equally applicable to the implementation of KSSR and the ELSQC's (2015) *Roadmap 2015–2025* for reform. The constant cycle of reforms which attempt to achieve the same objective is unproductive, especially when teachers are not sufficiently consulted on changes they are required to implement. As Rashid *et al.* (2017: 103) note, 'The government's constant "tinkering" with the education system is confounding to many stakeholders, including teachers, as the changes are implemented without input from relevant parties'. The latest round of reforms yet again attempts to initiate wholesale changes in teachers' classroom practice. As well as changes to the curriculum itself, the reforms have increased the time allocated for English in primary schools, although this is unlikely to contribute to enhanced outcomes unless there are changes in the enabling conditions promoting the use of English in the wider society beyond the school. Ali *et al.*'s (2011) conclusion seems still to hold true:

> Although Malaysia is a multiethnic and multilingual society, where English may be considered essential for wider communication, the reality is that English is not essential for everyday communication, since all citizens are required to learn and use BM, the national language. This sociolinguistic reality makes the goal of English-in-education policy that

> requires students to be able to communicate in English somewhat para-
> doxical: students need to practise and communicate in English to develop
> communicative competence, but this communication in English in real
> life is unnecessary, unnatural and, to some extent, undesirable. (Ali *et al.*,
> 2011: 155)

In these circumstances, the curriculum may remain too ambitious for the context, as Azman (2016) and Mihat (2015) have also suggested. Given that curriculum reforms for teaching and learning English have consistently failed to meet their objectives in the last 40 years, perhaps a broader conceptualisation of language learning in the primary school would be beneficial instead of an all-consuming focus on English as a second language. English could become one of several languages children could opt for, instead of a compulsory subject. There could be an increased emphasis on the teaching of the languages of instruction in national-type (SJK) primary schools – Chinese and Tamil – to children in national (SK) primary schools. At present, Malay is taught as a second language in all SJK schools but Chinese and Tamil are only elective subjects in SK schools, with information on the numbers of national primary schools actually offering them not readily available. Were these languages to be offered more widely and taught sensitively, it might act as a first step in reducing the ethnic homogenisation in schools that the Ministry of Education has acknowledged as a concern in the Education Blueprint (MOEM, 2013b) and could be used as a stimulus to promote greater interaction with 'students and teachers of every ethnicity, religion, culture, and socioeconomic background' (MOEM, 2013a: E-12), which as we have previously noted the Ministry sees as 'imperative' in achieving national unity. The Ministry already intended to 'improve student access to learning an additional language, subject to availability of resources' (MOEM, 2013b: 7–20) by 2020, with the major additional languages identified as Chinese, Tamil and Arabic; however, this was alongside the goal of proficiency in Bahasa Malaysia and English rather than, as suggested here, with English as co-equal to the other additional languages. A broader conceptualisation of language learning would have the additional advantage of creating more opportunity for Indigenous languages other than Malay to be taught from the early grades, rather than English, in areas where those languages are prevalent – which could, in turn, enhance achievement levels as children would have access to more learning opportunities in their first language. At present only three Indigenous languages – Kadazandusun, Iban and Semai – are offered as elective subjects in primary schools (MOEM, 2013b), even though there are numerous other Indigenous languages spoken across the country by minority communities which, as noted at the beginning of this chapter, do not feature at all in the school curriculum.

Of course, all of these suggestions offer only hypothetical opportunities for a more positive language learning experience for children in primary schools but it is nonetheless apparent that the current prioritisation of English is not achieving the outcomes expected across the country and that, increasingly, proficiency in English is correlated with socioeconomic status (Azman, 2016; ELSQC, 2015; MOEM, 2013b). Continuing with more of the same type of policies to improve English teaching and levels of achievement at the primary school level (and beyond) which have failed to have an impact since the 1980s and expecting different outcomes is not realistic and is itself an argument for a different approach to be given serious consideration.

Notes

(1) See https://www.malaysia.gov.my/portal/content/30114
(2) Singapore, which had been self-governing since 1959, also became part of the Federation but left it in 1965.
(3) Both 'Malay' and 'Bahasa Malaysia', itself sometimes shortened to 'BM', are used in the literature and I use them here interchangeably. 'Bahasa' means 'language' in English.
(4) In Bahasa Malaysia these are 'Sekolah Jenis Kebangsaan', abbreviated as 'SJK' plus 'T' for Tamil and 'C' for Chinese medium. Malay-medium government schools are known simply as 'Sekolah Kebangsaan' or 'SK'.
(5) See https://www.thestar.com.my/news/nation/2009/02/01/more-protests-against-policy-to-teach-in-english
(6) The Orang Asli are Indigenous inhabitants of peninsula Malaysia, as are Malays, but Malays are a politically, economically and socially dominant group while the Orang Asli struggle to maintain a forest-dwelling, hunter-gatherer lifestyle and experience high rates of poverty.
(7) For further information on ELTDP from the training provider's perspective, see https://www.britishcouncil.my/eltdp-native-speaker-project---east-malaysia
(8) See https://www.britishcouncil.my/programmes/education/teachers/pro-english-language-training
(9) This is a standardised English language test designed and administered by the British Council which is mapped to the CEFR.

6 Early Language Teaching and Learning in Ontario, Canada and Finland: Experiences of Bilingualism and Multilingualism

Introduction

In the country case studies considered so far in this book, arguments have been made that the prioritisation of English as the first foreign language taught in primary schools is based on a questionable premise of nationwide economic necessity, pursues unrealistic objectives of communicative proficiency given the circumstances of teaching, learning and English language use in the context, diminishes language diversity, contributes to maintaining – if not increasing – structural inequity in education and society at large and, generally, is singularly unsuccessful in achieving its stated aims. This chapter turns the geographical focus away from Asia to Western countries, providing a comparison both with the teaching of French in a Canadian province and the teaching of foreign languages in Finland in basic education. The chapter endeavours to ascertain whether any of the factors identified as affecting the teaching of English as a second or foreign language in previous chapters are also pertinent to the teaching of English and other languages in Finland or to the teaching of French as a second language (FSL) in Canada, as well as whether there are other factors that have an impact on language learning outcomes for young learners in these countries. Both Canada and Finland have high-performing and generally equitable educational systems and both are also committed to bilingualism at the national level.

In Canada, the context in which English and French became co-equal official languages is first outlined, as is the wider linguistic landscape of the country. Education in Canada is a provincial responsibility and so, after delineating the national context of language policy and practice, the chapter concentrates on early second language learning in Ontario, the most populous province in the country, and the author's academic home for the last 15 years. In Ontario, FSL is a mandatory subject taught in all schools in the province from Grade 4 to Grade 9. Unlike with English in other countries discussed in this book, French is not regarded as an economic necessity in Ontario; rather, its official status results from a federal political commitment to the language and its provincial educational standing flows from that. The discussion in the chapter will examine attitudes towards French and whether the objectives in the Ontario school curriculum for the teaching of what is known as Core French – distinguished from French immersion schooling – are realised at the classroom level.

Following the discussion of the teaching of French in elementary schools in Ontario, attention will turn to the teaching of foreign languages in basic education in Finland, another country that is officially bilingual, in Finnish and Swedish. Children are able to study two optional as well as two compulsory languages (including the mandatory second official language) in basic education but, although they have the opportunity to study a variety of languages as their first compulsory foreign language (starting in Grade 1 since 2020), the vast majority opt for English and the numbers studying other languages have stalled. This situation continues later in life and, at present, more Finns between 18 and 64 have proficiency in English (90%) than in the second official language, Swedish (71%), and only 37% have proficiency in German, the third most popular language (Ministry of Education and Culture, 2017). The Finnish Ministry of Education and Culture has, in response, developed policies to promote greater diversity in the languages students choose to study and has focused on a 'national language reserve' as 'a way to prepare for any rapid changes in language needs' (Ministry of Education and Culture, 2017: 6) and is also opting to recognise a broader conception of language proficiency given that 'even a small amount of proficiency is still proficiency, which individuals can be motivated to build upon later' (Ministry of Education and Culture, 2017: 6–7).

Canada: Languages, Language Policies and Language Practices

Modern-day Canada, a country of some 38 million people, began life as a federation of four self-governing British colonies in 1867. Over the ensuing decades the federation expanded to include a further six provinces and three territories, covering land from the Pacific Ocean in the west to the Atlantic Ocean in the east and northward up to the Arctic Ocean. The distinction between provinces and territories is constitutional, with the former exercising constitutional powers in their own right and the latter exercising powers delegated by the federal parliament. Territories receive much of their operational funding directly from the federal government due to the 'economic, social and demographic realities linked to their challenging geographical situation' (Government of Canada, 2021). Canada's independence was achieved incrementally. In 1931 it gained control over its own foreign policy, but it was not until 1982 that the UK's Canada Act provided for the 'repatriation' of the constitution and the country was deemed to have full political independence.[1] Colonial links remain, however, and the country is a constitutional monarchy with the UK's Queen Elizabeth II also being Queen of Canada, although a head of state whose powers are devolved to a Canadian Governor-General.

Since 1867 English and French have been in use in the federal parliament and the courts, but it was not until 1969 with the *Official Languages Act*, a response to rising separatist sentiment in the province of Québec, that English and French were recognised as equal throughout the federal administration, giving citizens the right to receive federal services in the official language of their choice. Language rights are enshrined in the *Canadian Charter of Rights and Freedoms*, part of the *Constitution Act* of 1982, which also provides for educational rights for English-speaking children in the French-speaking province of Québec and French-speaking children in other parts of the country. As a federal act, the *Official Languages Act* does not apply to provincial administration or private business, and only New Brunswick among the provinces and territories has passed its own *Official Languages Act*, which actually preceded the federal act by a few months in 1969. Across Canada, there is considerable support for bilingualism, with eight out of 10 people surveyed in 2016 agreeing that more needed to be done so that young people could become bilingual, with similar strong support for English and French being taught in all elementary schools nationwide (OCOL, 2016). This is not matched by actual levels of bilingualism among those with English as a mother tongue according to the 2016 census which recorded a bilingualism rate of 9.2%, an increase of just 0.3% from the previous census in 2011. In contrast, levels of bilingualism among those with French as a mother tongue were 46.2%, up from 44.4% in 2011 (Statistics Canada, 2017b: 4). While levels of French-English bilingualism could be regarded in one respect as a success, they are also taken in Québec to indicate that the status accorded to French as the primary language of the province is under threat from English. Indeed, the provincial government tabled a bill in May 2021 that would enshrine Québec's status as a nation within Canada in the constitution and declare its official language to be French (McKenna, 2021). At the time of writing, January 2022, the bill continues to undergo clause by clause consideration in committee stage but its passage in some form seems certain given the provincial government's majority in the Assemblée Nationale du Québec. Critics of the bill complain that it focuses on restricting English language rights rather than 'improving the quality of French in schools and supporting people to strengthen their French language skills' and ignores the reality of immigration of multilingual newcomers to the province for whom neither French nor English are mother tongues as well as the opportunity to strengthen Indigenous languages (Eliadis, 2021). The bill and the response to it reflect deep historical tensions over Québec's status as a French-speaking province within majority English-speaking Canada, tensions which have in the past turned into violence. It is notable that in the last referendum on Québec sovereignty in 1995 there was only a very narrow majority of 50.58% of voters (on a record 93.52% turnout) who were in favour of remaining part of Canada (Gall, 2015).

Neither English nor French are, of course, indigenous to Canada but both are colonial settler languages. There are far more Indigenous languages, but these have much smaller numbers of speakers. The 2016 census recorded 70 Indigenous languages from 12 language groups spoken across the country, with the largest, Cree (from the Algonquian family), having 96,575 speakers and the smallest, Kutenai, just 170 speakers (Statistics Canada, 2017a). There are different numbers given for Indigenous languages by different bodies, with UNESCO identifying 90 living languages. What is not in dispute is that three-quarters of these languages are endangered, with many being critically endangered (Government of Canada, 2019). In two of the three territories (but none of the 10 provinces), a number of Indigenous languages are recognised as official languages. In Nunavut, alongside English and French, there is statutory protection for an Indigenous language, Inuktitut, a term which covers all dialects used by Inuit in the territory (Department of Culture and Heritage, n.d.). In the Northwest Territories, uniquely in Canada, 11 official languages are recognised, nine of which 'belong to three different Indigenous language families: Dene-Athapaskan (Chipewyan, Gwich'in, North Slavey, South Slavey, and Tłı̨chǫ), Inuit (Inuinnaqtun, Inuktitut, and Inuvialuktun), and Algonquian (Cree)' (Indigenous Languages and Education Secretariat, n.d.) with the other two being English and French. Official recognition of Indigenous languages is particularly important given that, although the name 'Canada' is said to come from the Huron-Iroquois word 'kanata' (meaning a village or settlement), the Indigenous peoples of Canada have been marginalised ever since French and then British hegemony was established over their traditional lands and they were subject to policies which attempted to assimilate them into the dominant Euro-focused society and deprive them of their languages and cultures. The legacy of discrimination persists, as Amnesty International (2021) notes:

> Despite living in one of the world's wealthiest countries, Indigenous families and communities in Canada continue to face widespread impoverishment, inadequate housing, food insecurity, ill-health and unsafe drinking water. Indigenous peoples have demonstrated extraordinary resilience in the face of historic programs and policies such as the residential school program that were meant to destroy their cultures, but they must still live with the largely unresolved legacy of the harm that was done. (Amnesty International, 2021)

Giving official status to Indigenous languages is a necessary though not sufficient step in redressing historical injustices. A further step towards maintaining Indigenous linguistic diversity in Canada was taken in 2019 with the passing of the *Indigenous Languages Act* which commits the government to supporting and funding Indigenous-led language revitalisation and maintenance initiatives. Time will tell whether this act will achieve its objectives, but action is urgently needed to arrest the decline in Indigenous language vitality. Friedrich (2021) notes:

> In 2016, 15.6 percent of Indigenous people in Canada affirmed that they could converse in an Indigenous language – a rapid decline from 21 percent in 2006. Furthermore, large disparities exist between distinct Indigenous peoples living within the country: 64 percent of Inuit, 21 percent of First Nations peoples and, far behind, only 2 percent of Métis people respectively confirmed their language proficiency. (Friedrich, 2021: np)

The situation is complicated by the generational divides in proficiency. Data from the 2016 census revealed that '35.6% of First Nations seniors could speak an Aboriginal language, compared with 24.5% in the 25-to-64 age group, 16.5% in the 15-to-24 age group, and 15.8% in the 0-to-14 age group' (Statistics Canada, 2017a: 7). Despite the preponderance of young people in First Nations communities, resulting in 'twice as many First Nations children (45,135) as seniors (22,125) who could speak an Aboriginal language' (Statistics Canada, 2017a: 7), there is still only one in 10 children who speak an Indigenous language and the total numbers of speakers spread across the 70 Indigenous languages is alarmingly small. Indigenous languages will remain endangered unless younger Indigenous peoples are enabled easily to learn their ancestral languages, which is where education in the first language, bilingual education and/or second language education in elementary schools has a role to play.

This brief account of the status and current state of Indigenous languages serves to lend some context to Canada's linguistic diversity at the national level. It provides only a partial picture, however, as the country is also home to numerous other immigrant languages apart from the two dominant, official languages of English and French. Many of these languages have numbers of speakers that far surpass those of Indigenous languages. Data from the 2016 census (Statistics Canada, 2018) revealed that, although English was still the primary mother tongue of the majority of Canadians with 19.46 million speakers, there were more Canadians with a non-official language as a mother tongue (7.32 million) than there were with the other official language, French, as a mother tongue (7.16 million). Data also show that the 7.32 million people speaking an immigrant language at home represent 21.1% of the population which is an increase of 14.7% from 2011 to 2016.[2] In Canada's largest city, Toronto, the top five immigrant languages (with numbers of speakers) were Cantonese (267,155), Mandarin (246,210), Punjabi (196,605), Tagalog

(164,030) and Urdu (161,685). In Montréal, the largest city in the province of Québec, the largest immigrant language was Arabic (191,960 speakers) while the second largest was Spanish (145,650 speakers).

Consideration of Indigenous and immigrant languages thus reveals that the picture of Canada as an English-speaking country with one French-speaking province, Québec, where 'English and French are a fundamental characteristic of the Canadian identity' (OCOL, 2021), is a gross oversimplification of the language complexity and diversity in the country. Language diversity is a particular feature of major cities, with Toronto, the country's largest city, recently being named the world's most diverse.[3] The major implications of growth in immigrant language diversity, which is likely to continue to increase, are that many children will enter formal schooling with a non-official language as their home language and may begin the learning of a second official language in elementary school without being fluent in a first official language. With, as noted earlier, education in Canada being a provincial rather than a federal responsibility, the discussion in ensuing sections will be largely restricted to second language education policy and practice in Ontario, the country's most populous province with a population of 14.755 million people, 38.78% of the national total (Statistics Canada, 2021).

Elementary Schooling, Languages and Language Education Policy in Ontario

The Canadian school system is commended internationally for consistently high scores on international assessments such as the Programme for International Student Assessment (PISA) for 15-year-old students. For example, in the 2018 PISA assessment, Canada ranked 6th in reading, 12th in mathematics and 8th in science with scores well above the OECD average. It was also among the countries categorised as having 'world-class school systems [which] deliver high-quality education across the entire system', which means 'for example, average reading performance was higher than the OECD average while the relationship between socio-economic status and reading performance was weaker than the OECD average' (Schleicher, 2019: 20). This included performance among the growing school population with an immigrant background (35% in 2018, up from 24% in 2009) where first-generation immigrant students performed only slightly less well than non-immigrants in reading but second-generation immigrant students scored higher than non-immigrant students (Parkin, 2019). The scores for Ontario, the province under discussion in this section, for the three subject areas assessed by PISA, were all slightly higher than the national scores.

Children in Ontario are required to begin school at the age of six but may also attend government-provided kindergarten at no cost from the age of four. Education is provided by four systems: the French public system, the French Catholic system, the English public system and the English Catholic system. Ontario has an optional – and growing – French immersion programme, about which much has been written and which has an international reputation as a success (Cummins, 2014; Genesee, 2007), but the proportion of students in French immersion programmes was still only 11.7% of the student population in 2018–2019 across all grades (CPF, 2020). That the immersion programmes are also not without their challenges can be seen in the student retention rate to Grade 12, which in 2018–2019 was just 38% of the original cohort in Grade 1 (CPF, 2020). Discussion here, however, focuses on the English public system, the largest in the province, and 'Core French' (CF), where French is taught as a compulsory second language according to a common curriculum from Grade 4 to Grade 8. By the end of Grade 8, students are expected to have received a minimum of 600 hours of instruction, usually in daily classes of 30–40 minutes. Students are also required to earn at least one credit in FSL in high school, without which they cannot obtain their high school diplomas, and most students take this in Grade 9. In contrast to the considerable research into French immersion programmes, 'research on the CF student experience remains relatively scarce. Since 2000, only 23% of Canadian FSL research investigating students in the Kindergarten to Grade 12 context has focused on CF learners' (Arnott, 2019: 520).

What research there is into CF indicates, unfortunately, a wide gap between the rhetoric of bilingualism and the reality of achievement in French in schools. Most students in the province who study in the CF programme discontinue it as soon as they are able to, at the end of Grade 9. The retention rate to Grade 12 is a mere 6% (CPF, 2020). There is widespread dissatisfaction with the CF programme. Knouzi and Mady (2014: 62) note that it is 'associated with poor results for the students [...] and marginalisation of the teachers', while Cummins (2014: 1) comments that 'policy-makers have largely ignored the fact that most core French programs produce meager results for the vast majority of students'. Similar to outcomes in English as a foreign language programmes in previous country case studies in this book, students report that they are unable to express themselves in the language and feel that they have insufficient opportunity to interact with speakers of French (Lapkin *et al.*, 2009). Most worryingly, Cummins (2014) observes that there is little difference in achievement whatever the starting grade:

> Few differences were observed regardless of whether students started learning French in Kindergarten, Grade 1, 3, 4, 6, or 8. In other words, one year of Core FSL produced equivalent outcomes to 7+ years, suggesting that core FSL during those years was not particularly effective. (Cummins, 2014: 2)

If this is the case, children's time is being wasted in CF beyond one year of instruction, and the implication is that a radical reconceptualisation of how French – and/or other languages – should be offered in elementary schools is urgently needed. There is an obvious paradox to an education system which is both generally equitable and able to deliver high levels of success in reading, mathematics and science in the PISA assessments yet is unable to deliver more than the most basic achievement in FSL with the same students. This experience echoes that of many countries where English is taught as a foreign language.

The curriculum and the status of FSL teachers and teaching

The Ontario school curriculum is founded on general principles which recognise that the student population is diverse and that all students should see themselves reflected within the curriculum. In the preface to the FSL curriculum, the Ministry envisions 'elementary schools for the twenty-first century' as places in which 'It is important that students be connected to the curriculum; that they see themselves in *what* is taught, *how* it is taught, and how it *applies* to the world at large' (MOEO, 2013: 3, emphasis in original). Within this, French is regarded as important because 'The ability to speak and understand French allows students to communicate with French-speaking people in Canada and around the world, to understand and appreciate the history and evolution of their cultures, and to develop and benefit from a competitive advantage in the workforce' (MOEO, 2013: 6). Unlike with the teaching of English as a foreign language in many countries, although the economic value of proficiency in French is recognised, it is not prioritised as a national economic necessity but seen as a competitive advantage for individuals. Also, again unlike with the teaching of English in many countries such as South Korea, there is no high-stakes examination at the end of high school where performance in the language helps to determine university admission. Instead, in Ontario, university admission is based on grades awarded by subject teachers in the last two years of school and, as previously noted, only a Grade 9 credit in French is required for high school graduation.

Pressure to do well in French is, hence, much less and its importance devalued in comparison with other subjects, a fact mirrored in how the language is perceived and treated in schools. Studies on CF over the years have consistently reported that FSL teachers feel marginalised since they teach across the age range in elementary schools, are often without their own classrooms, unlike grade-level teachers, receive little support, and their lessons can even be cancelled if the school has other priorities (Arnott, 2019; Knouzi & Mady, 2014; Lapkin *et al.*, 2009). Such feelings of 'marginalization leads the CF teacher to question her professional identity and creates a hierarchy that is ultimately internalized by the CF teacher and accepted in the wider community' (Knouzi & Mady, 2014: 77). The consequence is a negative impact on classroom learning and children's attitudes to the language. Arnott (2019: 533) concluded that 'Negative student attitudes toward the CF learning situation have continually emerged as a significant factor affecting student retention, suggesting that student motivation is inextricably linked to the way that CF programs are delivered'. The curriculum for CF, last revised in 2013, advocates an instructional approach with the goal of students being 'able to enjoy communicating in French throughout their lives' (MOEO, 2013: 31) and is overtly communicative and task based:

> Action-oriented and communicative approaches to teaching FSL focus on meaning over form; emphasize meaningful interactive activities; centre on communicative language needs; and, when possible, highlight authentic tasks within the context of a classroom environment. While the communicative approach centres on communicating in the target language, the action-oriented approach requires students to perform a task in a wider social context. (MOEO, 2013: 31)

These recommendations for 'action-oriented and communicative' classroom methodology are similar to those for English as a foreign language in the previous case studies in this book. Also similar are the outcomes in that, in spite of these instructional expectations for a communicative approach, many students report that they are unable to converse in French after their mandatory six years of study, that CF is too focused on formal grammatical aspects of the language, that French is not spoken enough in their classes, and that because teachers provide translations into English to promote understanding, they have no incentive to attend to the French to which they are exposed (Arnott, 2019). The reasons given for her decision to discontinue French after Grade 9 by a focus group participant in Arnott's (2019) research, who had direct experience of both CF and French immersion, are instructive:

> One is just that it's bringing my overall average down. Two, I have flip-flopped back and forth [between core and immersion], so I have a good idea of what it's like in both areas. Something I found is that immersion teachers on average are more motivated, they're better teachers ... the teacher I have right now is probably the best teacher I have ever had because she speaks French but all the Core teachers I've had would say something in English and they'd say it in French and then you listen to the English and you tune out the French. (Arnott, 2019: 531)

While judicious, principled use of the first language as a resource in the FL classroom may have a positive effect on the learning of an FL (Cook, 2001), if, as seems to be the case here, teachers are over-dependent on a recourse to translation, the first language then replaces any learning of the second language and the impact is counter-productive. CF teachers who translate French into English may do so in order to promote understanding of the French among their students, but rather than motivating them, they appear to demotivate them.

To counter demotivation and to enhance outcomes, innovations in CF teaching methods in elementary schools have been advocated, of which the Accelerated Integrative Method (AIM), combining the use of techniques such as gestures and drama with a strong initial focus on oral second language production, has been widely used since it was first proposed by Maxwell (2001). However, the results of research into the use of AIM have been disappointing, generally showing no difference in proficiency in French or attitudes towards the language in AIM and non-AIM classes, although in one study of Grade 8 classes in Ontario only 25% of AIM students said they used English in their classes compared to 50% of non-AIM students (Mady *et al.*, 2009). Research into the effectiveness of particular methods elsewhere has tended to be, at best, inconclusive, so it is not surprising that Arnott (2017: 259) concluded that 'Research on AIM to date reflects the inconsistent findings of other studies that looked for links between method implementation and language proficiency'. Flexibility in the use of methods according to students' needs in the context of teaching is likely to be most productive, i.e. there is no one best method for all students in all circumstances in FSL in Ontario, just as with ESL/EFL in other contexts.

The comments of the student in Arnott's (2019) research cited earlier that 'immersion teachers on average are more motivated, they're better teachers' alert us to another factor in the experience of CF in Ontario which is becoming more of an issue of concern in the system: the 'best' teachers of French are more likely to teach in immersion programmes or high school than in CF classes. Until recently, the language proficiency of teachers of FSL has not been the urgent concern exercising government policy that it is in countries such as Thailand and Malaysia for teachers of English, but teacher shortages have placed a strain on school boards in the recruitment of qualified French teachers and the situation is likely to worsen if nothing is done to increase the supply of graduates from teacher education programmes. In its survey of FSL teacher supply and demand across Canada, the Office of the Commissioner of Official Languages noted that 'The school board personnel interviewed unanimously reported experiencing a shortage of teachers with adequate linguistic and cultural competencies, knowledge of second-language teaching and knowledge of the Common European Framework of Reference (a framework which provides standardized competency levels for language learners)' (OCOL, 2019: 8). Further, 'teachers with less experience in French are being "relegated" to teaching Core French or elementary level classes, while more proficient teachers go on to teach French immersion or high school level classes' (OCOL, 2019: 16). If the practice of placing the teachers with less experience in French in CF classes continues, it will inevitably exacerbate the marginalisation of CF in elementary schools in Ontario which will, in turn, increase student demotivation and associated achievement.

Multilingualism, Language Diversity and FSL

As we have seen, there is a continuing increase in diversity of languages spoken in Ontario, with 28.8% of the population reporting a mother tongue other than an official or Indigenous language in the 2016 census as opposed to 26.6% in 2011. However, this language diversity is not always seen as an asset nor capitalised on in the school system. Cummins (2014) notes that few provinces 'have developed coherent policies regarding the multilingual realities of schools and communities' and Ontario has even 'articulated restrictive policies in relation to multilingualism by prohibiting use of languages other than English and French as mediums of instruction except on a short-term transitional basis' (Cummins, 2014: 1). Oddly, this prohibition is at odds with longstanding recommendations about the role of the first language in learning a new language of instruction found in other government documents in the province. For example, official resources for newcomers to Ontario providing information about the school system deal with 'Learning a new language' and have recommendations that align closely with what research tells us about bilingual learners (COPA, 2018):

> You can provide opportunities for your children to continue learning their first language while learning a new one. Continuing to talk with your children in their first language, or in the usual language of communication within your family. Children who express themselves well in their first language find it easier to learn a new one.
>
> Encouraging your children to continue to read and write in their first language. Teachers find that students who read and write well in their first language learn to read and write in their new language more quickly. They also find that students are more able to keep up in science and math. (COPA, 2018: 17)

Similarly, the Ministry's own policy documents on *Supporting English Language Learners* state that English language learners 'present a rich resource in classrooms throughout the province' (MOEO, 2008: 3, 8):

> Students who see their previously developed language skills acknowledged by their teachers and parents are more likely to feel confident and take the risks involved in learning a new language. They are able to view English as an *addition* to their first language, rather than as a *substitution* for it. [...] There are numerous positive outcomes that result from continuing to promote the ongoing use and development of ELLs' first languages. Respect and use of the first language contribute both to the building of a confident learner and to the efficient learning of additional languages and academic achievement.

However, the extent to which these policy statements are realised in the classroom is not clear. Baltus and Belhiah's (2013) study of ESL elementary school teachers in Ontario reported on the tension between classroom teachers wanting to ensure curriculum coverage while ESL teachers were focused on students' language needs, and that ESL teacher-student contact time was insufficient. Brubacher (2013) similarly noted the problems caused by curriculum demands and concluded that the structure of schooling itself made it difficult to take account of children's prior experiences and respond to their needs.

Certainly, the promotion of second language dominance among potential young bilingual immigrants starts very early, even in pre-school, where Chumak-Horbatsch (2008: 24) found that language practices led to 'preschoolers' weakened L1 and hasty embrace of L2'. More recently, a CBC report indicated that young children are still encouraged to use the dominant second language rather than their first language in pre-school settings so they do not 'fall behind' when they start formal schooling where the second language is used (Chan, 2021). These language practices actively discourage multilingualism, promote assimilation to a restricted conception of Canadian linguistic identity, and are strikingly at odds with the principle advanced in the school curriculum that students should 'see themselves in *what* is taught' (MOEO, 2013: 3), as well as being contrary to the guidance found in official policy documents. The devaluing of students' home languages leads to their loss over time and flies in the face of research which indicates that children are quite able to learn more than one language when they are raised in bilingual or multilingual environments in which the languages make sense to them in their contexts of use (Werker & Byers-Heinlein, 2008). It appears that children's first language being accepted as a 'rich resource in classrooms throughout the province' remains a work in progress. However, in spite of a lack of appreciation of their first language resources, students in Ontario who speak a non-official language at home (generally referred to as 'Allophones') are more receptive to notions that learning French is an aspect of Canadian identity and hence more willing to invest time and effort in CF than their Canadian-born counterparts (Mady, 2010). Grade 9 Allophone students in Mady's (2010) study also said that their parents encouraged them to do well in French as much as in other subjects, which was in contrast to 'the Canadian-born participants [who] have understood from their parents that French is of less importance than other subjects' (Mady, 2010: 576).

While achievement in CF is very poor and immigrant languages underutilised as a resource, Indigenous languages are even more marginalised in the Ontario elementary school curriculum. The curriculum for 'Native languages' in Grades 1–8 has not been revised since 2001. A positive factor, at least in theory, is that the programmes, where they exist, are not restricted to Indigenous students (MOEO, 2001):

> The program is open to all Native and non-Native students who want to learn a Native language and develop a better understanding of the culture of which that language forms part. Non-Native students enrolled in

Native language programs will enjoy the benefits of cross-cultural education. By learning about a culture that is different from their own, they will both expand and enrich their view of the world and gain a better understanding of their own culture. At the same time, they will develop a deeper appreciation of and respect for the identity, rights, and values of others. (MOEO, 2001: 4)

The languages the curriculum specifies as being approved are Cayuga, Cree, Delaware, Mohawk, Ojibwe, Oji-Cree and Oneida (MOEO, 2001), and individual school boards decide which, if any, are to be offered. Ultimately, the Indigenous languages offered depend on a school's location. For example, the Kawartha Pine Ridge District School Board, which covers the traditional territory of the Michi Saagiig Nishnaabeg people and includes three Indigenous communities acknowledged to be vibrant,[4] offers Ojibwa[5] classes in three elementary schools as well as an evening school. The Halton District School Board's website section on its 'International and Indigenous Language (Elementary) Program' includes a link to an external provider where 11 international languages (from Arabic to Urdu) are offered beyond the regular school day but no Indigenous languages. Elsewhere, the Niagara District School Board's *Indigenous Education Report 2019–20* only stated that during its first 'Elementary Student Voice' event, 'Many students expressed an interest in learning Indigenous languages' (DSBN, 2020: 3) but none was offered. Partly, of course, this will be as a result of a province-wide shortage of teachers fluent in Indigenous languages which is a serious constraint on maintaining, let alone expanding, the programmes that do exist. Other constraints on the programme concern the amount of classroom time allotted to teaching the languages, specified as a minimum of 20 minutes a day for Grades 1–3 and 40 minutes a day for Grades 4–8, which is unlikely to lead to significant learning if only the minimum is given, as well as the stipulation that 'When a school board decides to offer a Native language program at the elementary level, it should take into account that the program must be offered through to the end of secondary school' (MOEO, 2001: 5). This last constraint is likely connected to the regulation that allows students who enrol in an Indigenous language to be exempted from taking CF classes, which also must be offered through to the end of secondary school, but, of course, it is a severe impediment to Indigenous languages being offered at any level if teacher shortages are already an issue.

Before reflecting on bilingualism in Ontario, I now contrast the experience of one province in Canada with that of Finland, which is also a bilingual country with two official languages at the national level.

Finland: Languages, Language Policies and Languages in Education

Finland is a comparatively small country of 5.53 million people. Until 1809 it was a part of Sweden. It then became an autonomous Grand Duchy of Russia, declared independence in 1917 and became a republic in 1919. It has two national languages, Finnish and Swedish, the status of which is enshrined in Section 17 of the 2000 Constitution. Finnish is the largest language with 4.81 million people speaking it as a first language, while 288,000 speak Swedish (Statistics Finland, 2021). Of the other Indigenous languages of Finland, the three varieties of Sámi have had official status since 1992 in the Sámi native region of Enontekiö, Inari and Utsjoki, and the northern part of Sodankylä, with 2008 people using it as a first language according to 2020 figures (Statistics Finland, 2021). Section 17 of the Constitution also states that 'the Sámi, as an Indigenous people, as well as the Roma and other groups, have the right to maintain and develop their own language and culture'.[6] The government at the federal level is bilingual and government services must be offered in both Finnish and Swedish.

At the basic municipal level, however, the country is not necessarily bilingual and the choice of language to be used depends on the languages of the inhabitants. According to Section 5 of the *2003 Language Act*, a municipality is bilingual if either at least 8% or 3000 of the inhabitants speak a minority language; if the minority drops below 3000 and comprises less than 6% of the inhabitants, the language status of the municipality changes to unilingual.[7] Of a total of 310 municipalities, 33 are bilingual, 18 with Finnish as the majority and 15 with Swedish as the majority language (Statistics Finland, 2020). There are also 16 Swedish unilingual municipalities in the Åland archipelago (Statistics Finland, 2020), where Finnish is largely absent from daily life. In mainland Finland, in spite of the increasing use of Finnish among Swedish speakers, the fear that Swedish would be wholly replaced does not appear to be happening and few Swedish-speaking Finns have shifted to a Finnish identity (Sjöholm, 2004). On the other hand, among the Finnish-speaking community, there has been a growing decline in the use of Swedish as a second language, with Ringbom (2012) reporting that:

> L2 use of Swedish, Finland's other national language, which is spoken by a little over 5% of the population, has been increasingly replaced by English. At school, the choice of a second language for nine-year-olds is open, but more than 90% of the pupils in Finnish-language schools choose English. (Ringbom, 2012: 491)

When they begin school, children are educated in their first language, Finnish, Swedish or Sámi in the Sámi region. With a focus on equity and equality, education is free from pre-primary through to higher education and the vast majority of students attend government schools, with only 2% attending private schools (FNAE, 2020). Education begins at the age of six with one year of pre-primary education before children enter basic education which lasts from Grade 1 to Grade 9. Since 2020, learning a second language has been mandatory from the second semester of Grade

Table 6.1 Second/foreign languages in basic education in Finland

		Mandatory or optional language	Starts	Languages usually studied
Basic education	A1 language	Mandatory	Grade 1	English (Finnish for Swedish-speaking Finns)
	A2 language	Optional	Grades 4–5	German, French (English for Swedish-speaking Finns)
	B1 language	Mandatory	Grade 6	Second national language (unless studied in an A1 or A2 syllabus)
	B2 language	Optional	Grades 7–9	German, French

Source: Adapted from Mustaparta (2008) and the Finnish National Agency for Education website, https://www.oph.fi/en

1 (previously it was mandatory from Grade 3), but all children in basic education are still required to learn both national languages at some stage in their schooling. Language teaching provision in basic education is summarised in Table 6.1.

There is also provision for immigrant languages to be taught in schools to children who are in what is known as 'preparatory instruction', a stage of integration into Finnish schools lasting from six months to two years. While the principal focus is on Finnish (or Swedish) as a second language to allow children to continue with their education in mainstream classes as soon as possible, there is also scope for teaching the students' mother tongues. Municipalities who offer immigrant languages in school receive a government subsidy provided that there are a minimum of four students in these classes, which can be offered either during or after preparatory instruction. Mustaparta (2008) reported that, even more than a decade ago, some 50 immigrant languages were being taught, with Russian, Somali, Albanian, Arabic and Vietnamese as the most common, and that around two-thirds of immigrant children attended mother-tongue classes. Immigration to Finland has increased in recent years but more recent information on the languages taught in schools is not readily available. However, the Institute for the Languages of Finland reports that there are now more than 150 languages spoken in the country.[8] Figure 6.1 shows the immigrant languages with the largest number of speakers in 2020.

Finnish Education and International Comparisons

Like Canada, Finland is a country that has traditionally performed well in international assessments. Indeed, in the early iterations of PISA when it headed the rankings, Finland was the object of a huge wave of international attention with, for example, more than 100 delegations from other countries visiting in 2009 to try to find how it managed to reach such

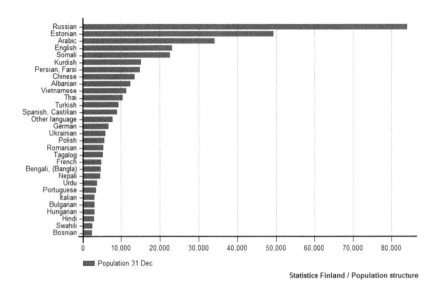

Figure 6.1 Immigrant languages with largest number of speakers, 2020
Source: Statistics Finland, https://www.stat.fi/tup/maahanmuutto/maahanmuuttajat-vaestossa/vieraskieliset_en.html

high achievement levels (Burridge, 2010) and thus to replicate them in their own educational systems. Finland's time at the very top of the rankings did not last, however, and in response to a fall in 2012 the then Minister of Education declared, 'The general downturn in learning outcomes shows we must take strong action to develop Finnish education' (Taylor, 2013). The minister's comments seem somewhat alarmist given that Finnish performance in PISA has remained strong across the years. In the 2018 assessments, Finland had the same score as Canada in reading (520), scored slightly less in mathematics (507 compared to 512 for Canada) and slightly higher in science (522 compared to 518). All these scores were well above the OECD average of 487 for reading, 489 for mathematics and 489 for science.[9] Moreover, while there was a correlation between socioeconomic status and performance in Finland, as elsewhere, this was less strong than in many other countries:

> Socio-economic status was a strong predictor of performance in mathematics and science in all PISA participating countries. It explained 12% of the variation in mathematics performance in PISA 2018 in Finland (compared to 14% on average across OECD countries), and 10% of the variation in science performance (compared to the OECD average of 13% of the variation). (OECD, 2019: 5)

As we noted earlier, 'The most impressive outcome of world-class school systems is that they deliver high-quality education across the entire system' (Schleicher, 2019: 20), and Finland joins Canada in the list of countries where 'average reading performance was higher than the OECD average while the relationship between socio-economic status and reading performance was weaker than the OECD average' (Schleicher, 2019: 20).

Finland also does well in other important indicators. Finnish students seem comparatively happy, with 78% of them saying that they were satisfied with their lives, 11% greater than the OECD average, while 91% of students reported sometimes or always feeling happy and only 4% always feeling sad. The OECD (2019) noted that:

> In most countries and economies, students were more likely to report positive feelings when they reported a stronger sense of belonging at school and greater student co-operation. Students were more likely to express sadness when they were bullied more frequently. (OECD, 2019: 7)

The school climate is clearly important in promoting student learning as students need to feel safe and valued at school if they are to learn well. Also important is the quality of learning time, rather than simply the quantity. In this respect, Finland was a leader in PISA 2018, with students having the fewest learning hours per week yet having high achievement. In contrast, to illustrate that longer hours do not necessarily lead to higher achievement, the United Arab Emirates had the longest study hours but learning outcomes were poor. As Schleicher (2019: 20) says, 'The lack of a correlation between the amount of learning time and learning outcomes illustrates that learning outcomes are always the product of the quantity of learning time, and the quality of learning and the instructional environment'. Thus, adding additional classroom hours, as some education systems do when faced with lack of progress in reaching achievement goals, will not necessarily lead to improved learning unless what happens in that time and in the surrounding school environment is also conducive to promoting language learning. Neither is continual standardised testing to check that children are reaching predetermined achievement levels a guarantee of higher standards. Finland is rare among countries in not having national-level examinations until the end of general upper secondary education. Until that point, all assessments are conducted by teachers on a continuing basis. Even the grades for the final basic education certificate at the end of Year 9 are awarded by teachers (FNAE, 2018). With shorter learning hours than other countries and no standardised testing but consistently high achievement levels, Finnish education seems something of a 'miracle' in the eyes of other countries (Niemi *et al.*, 2012) but, as Simola (2005: 456) pointed out after Finland received international praise for its early PISA success, far from being a miracle, 'it is unequivocally attributable to the excellent Finnish teachers and high-quality Finnish teacher education'.

Finnish teachers are members of a highly respected profession, one that is both attractive to students leaving school and highly competitive to enter at university, particularly teacher education for the early years. Paronen and Lappi (2018) note that:

> Of all teacher education programmes, the one for class teachers [in Grades 1-6] is the most difficult to gain admission to. Since 2011, only 10 to 11 per cent of the applicants have been admitted. In 2016, the proportion of applicants admitted to class teacher education was smaller than the proportion admitted to medical or law faculties. (Paronen & Lappi, 2018)

Teachers are required to have Masters' degrees, a factor that is directly linked to their higher status and, as Hargreaves *et al.* (2007) explained, something of an anomaly in international experience:

> Although internationally evidence for status gains associated with higher levels of qualifications is mixed, one clear example is Finland, where the status of teachers and education in general has risen dramatically in recent years alongside the requirement that all teachers are qualified at masters' level. (Hargreaves *et al.*, 2007: 83)

Even though teaching has high status and it is often more difficult for school leavers to enter teacher education programmes than medicine and law, once they qualify, teachers are paid less than doctors and lawyers (although slightly more than police officers), indicating that factors other than remuneration make teaching an attractive profession (Paronen & Lappi, 2018). In this respect, trust in teachers' professionalism is very important. Teachers have autonomy to teach according to their students' needs within a core curriculum which sets foundational goals and allows teachers to decide on their own methods and materials, which is clearly valued by them (Muhonen, 2017), as is the lack of constant inspection and other oversight found in some other countries. Paronen and Lappi (2018) report that:

> Teachers are accountable to themselves and the learners, not to external bodies. Teachers are not formally evaluated, and there are no inspections of schools or learning materials. The absence of national tests until the end of general upper secondary education also gives teachers the privilege to concentrate on learners and their learning instead of preparing them for external evaluation. (Paronen & Lappi, 2018: 9)

The fact that teachers have a great deal of freedom to interpret the curriculum to suit the needs of the group of children they are teaching, and that they are not regularly administering standardised tests to ensure that children are meeting expected standards, contributes to them feeling more appreciated within society at large as well as giving them more space to fulfil their students' learning needs. Moreover, trust between teachers, children and their carers that what is happening in the classroom is not only enjoyable but leads to positive learning outcomes enables teachers to feel free to get on with teaching with support rather than interference from outside the school.

What teachers do in the classroom is based on the national core curriculum, which specifies general learning objectives, adapted to suit local municipal and school requirements. The core curriculum was revised in 2014 and implemented in 2016 for Grades 1–6, giving schools ample time to prepare their local curriculum in accordance with the general specifications of the core curriculum. There are, for example, five broad components to the English as a foreign language A syllabus for Grades 1–6 (FNBE, 2016) is as follows:

- Growing into cultural diversity and language awareness.
- Language learning skills.
- Evolving language proficiency, interaction skills.
- Evolving language proficiency, text interpretation skills.
- Evolving language proficiency, text production skills.

Each of these has objectives and key content areas related to the objectives, with the three components of 'evolving language proficiency' taken as one area, and additional 'objectives related to the learning environments and working methods' provided. Also given are broad 'assessment criteria' for all of the component objectives, with A2.1 on the Finnish version of the CEFR included as the target level for 'evolving language proficiency'. However, assessment is not so much outcomes oriented as 'encouraging in nature and provides the pupils with opportunities for becoming aware of their skills, developing them, and focusing on modes of expression that are natural for them' (FNBE, 2016: 299). Hence, the curriculum is genuinely learner centred in forms of assessment as well as in its openness to interpretation by individual teachers who are relied on to know what is best for the groups of children they teach.

With no external or standardised testing of children until the end of high school, national-level evidence of children's learning outcomes is generally rare. An exception is the large-scale evaluation conducted in 2013 by the Finnish Education Evaluation Centre, *Outcomes of Language Learning at the End of Basic Education in 2013* (Hildén *et al.*, 2015). This evaluation sampled students in 600 Finnish-speaking and 61 Swedish-speaking schools to assess the extent to which they had achieved the objectives of the 2004 national curriculum for languages by the completion of their basic education at the end of Grade 8. Based on a Finnish-designed, modified version of the CEFR, the evaluation found that 78% of children studying Syllabus A English reached 'good' proficiency, specified as a minimum of A2.2, in speaking and 72% in writing, while 67% reached 'good' proficiency of a minimum B1.1 in listening and 62% in reading. Of the students who reached 'good' proficiency in speaking, 64% reached B1.1 or higher on the scale. Students from urban areas performed better than students from rural areas, and students from Swedish-speaking schools performed higher than the sample average (Hildén *et al.*, 2015). Performance in other languages was also assessed – Swedish, French,

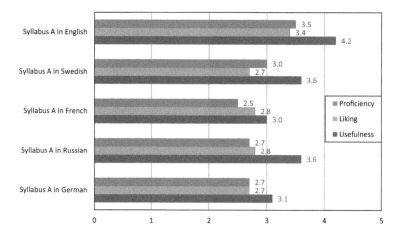

Figure 6.2 Students' opinions of studying Syllabus A languages
Source: Hildén et al. (2015: 22).

Russian and German. Students taking Syllabus A French performed less well than those taking English, even though the target for 'good' proficiency levels in French were lower than those for English. In speaking in French, 56% of students achieved 'good' proficiency of A2.1, 46% achieved A2.1 in writing, 48% achieved 'good' proficiency of A2.2 in listening and 66% in reading (Hildén et al., 2015).

Students were also surveyed on a 5-point scale about their feelings about how useful the languages they learnt were, whether they liked them and their perceptions of their own proficiency. The results (see Figure 6.2) show that students learning English perceived it to be more useful than other languages, they liked studying it more than students who took other languages and they were more satisfied with their own proficiency in the language. This preference for English and less favourable attitudes towards other languages is an issue that the Finnish authorities are concerned to address.

English and Foreign Language Diversity in Basic Education

Finland prides itself on the number of languages children can potentially study in school – up to four in basic education – but the increasing dominance of English as the first foreign language in schools is a growing cause of concern for educators who have been arguing for some time for much greater diversity in the languages actually taught (Ringbom, 2012). The Finnish National Agency for Education (FNAE, 2019) has also highlighted the issue of diversity:

> The narrowing language repertoire of Finns has become a matter of concern and has for a long time been a challenge also for language teaching professionals. How can we help pupils and their guardians understand

the value of diverse language skills? How can we motivate pupils to learn more languages? How can we inspire them to start their language studies with a language other than English? (FNAE, 2019: 1)

Lack of language diversity is reflected in the fact that more than 90% of Finnish-speaking children study English as their mandatory A1 foreign language, while Swedish-speaking children study Finnish. The proportion of children studying French or German as an A1 language has been stuck at 1% for some years and the proportion of children studying an optional A2 language was only 27% of Grade 5 pupils in 2017; even fewer Grade 8 or 9 pupils study an optional B2 language, just 17% in 2017 (FNAE, 2019). Within these groups, there is also significant gender inequity, with girls more likely to study a variety of A1 languages (Swedish, French, German, Russian or Spanish) than boys, who mostly choose English, and girls also study A2 languages more than boys (FNAE, 2019). There is also a gender imbalance in teachers, with more than 90% of teachers of English, French, German, Russian, Spanish and Swedish in basic education in 2016 being women (FNAE, 2019). As a whole, the FNAE notes that 'many pupils seem to find it unnecessary to learn any other languages' than English and that 'studying optional languages has been on the decline for the past twenty years' (FNAE, 2019: 1). Ringbom's (2012) conclusion still appears to be valid:

> Among decision-makers as well as the general public in Finland there is still a fairly common mistaken belief that having to learn several languages confuses learners. Too many people still hold the view that in Finland people should speak Finnish, and in communication with any foreigner, English should be enough. For researchers, much work remains to be done to convince these people of the advantages of a more diverse language education policy. (Ringbom, 2012: 492)

The need for change in the persistent attitude in the wider community that 'English should be enough' informed the Ministry of Education and Culture's (2017) report, *Multilingualism as a Strength: Procedural Recommendations for Developing Finland's National Language Reserve*, where 'The reasons for the one-sidedness of language choices can be attributed to both a lack of municipal resources and attitudes in schools and households. Language studies are not seen as being an investment in individuals and society' (Ministry of Education and Culture, 2017: 8–9).

Since the publication of this report, there is some evidence that attitudes are beginning to change. The 'Government Key Project for Languages' (FNAE, 2017) aims to promote greater diversity in language learning. Among the project initiatives, 'language showers' in pre-primary education correlate with more varied choice of the first compulsory foreign language in basic education. Using play and activity-based techniques, children who participate in language showers are introduced to a wide variety of languages for an hour each week. Every eight weeks the language changes. Chukhlantseva (2020) reported that in the city of Tampere children were able to study English, Swedish, German, French, Spanish, Russian, Japanese and 'several other' languages and that one in three children went on to choose a language other than English as their A1 language in primary school. However, long-term change requires sufficient teachers of diverse languages to implement policy recommendations, and it is naturally easier to offer greater diversity of languages in schools in more densely populated areas, and in those with more languages in the community, than in sparsely populated, more rural areas. The end result is that there has been an increase in regional differences in the study of optional languages, which FNAE (2019: 1) regards 'as an issue of equality and [should] be taken into account at both the local and national level'.

Even if equitable access to different languages were to be achieved, children themselves still need to be encouraged to value languages other than English, which has a more prominent place in their environment through television and the internet than any other foreign language. In practice, this means that it is their parents who need to support participation in initiatives like language showers in pre-primary education and then follow this up by encouraging their children to learn languages other than English later on, given that the preference for English is ultimately a response to the position of the language in society beyond the school. Perceptions of the connection between English and globalisation and internationalisation are as powerful in Finland as in other countries and influence parents to prioritise English. The belief that 'English is enough' thus filters down to children in school through their parents and is reinforced by their own experiences. Mustaparta (2008) maintains that:

> Children have high motivation to learn English, because they hear it on children's programs on TV. And when they grow up, they get surrounded by youth culture not only on TV, but also in the Internet. Parents understand that whatever the child chooses to do after basic education it is necessary to be able to speak and understand English. They also realize that anyone who is interested in [a] good position in society must have good skills in English. (Mustaparta, 2008: 3)

To progress beyond the prioritisation of English, Finland is intent on recognising and developing proficiency in multiple languages – including immigrant languages – as part of its 'national language reserve', all of which can be drawn upon as circumstances require. The Ministry of Education and Culture (2017) is also seeking to expand notions of proficiency, moving away from the idea that there is a set target in terms of proficiency and recognising the importance of other, associated language skills, commenting that:

> We have perhaps become accustomed to thinking of language proficiency in excessively broad terms, comprehending all areas. In reality, different

situations require different verbal communication skills and different aspects of language proficiency: oral or written, producing or understanding. Even though gaining a solid foundation in the development of language proficiency is indeed important, it must be recognised that even a small amount of proficiency is still proficiency, which individuals can be motivated to build upon later. Language proficiency also typically fosters intercultural skills and mutual understanding, which is why it is important in terms of social cohesiveness and international relations. (Ministry of Education and Culture, 2017: 6–7)

The notion of developing a diverse 'national language reserve' is an important one, which has the potential to move the narrative away from the all-consuming focus on English. The Ministry's target is that 'By the year 2025, a majority of pupils will choose a language other than English as their compulsory A2 language' (Ministry of Education and Culture, 2017: 2), and early indications are that, if resources are available, the policy can indeed help to bring about this shift (Chukhlantseva, 2020).

The Ecology of Schooling in Finland

The teaching and learning of foreign languages in schools is part of an educational ecosystem. Success cannot be achieved unless all parts of the system are working efficiently and in harmony towards the same end. Further, like all ecosystems, education is adapted to the particular circumstances of the context. In this respect, Finnish academics caution that international observers who seek to learn from – and even say they wish to replicate – Finnish success cannot just copy its policies and systems but need to study it from a historical perspective and understand how it developed in response to its changing sociocultural and political context over time (Simola, 2005). Even in Finland itself, as Halinen (2018) explains, the 'eco-systemic' concept of education is not always understood by the wider public.

The public debate in traditional and social media reveals how difficult it is to perceive the eco-systemic character of education or the curriculum. Very often, the discussion focuses only on one element of education and does not promote the ability to see the connections between different elements: for instance, discussing student assessment without understanding its connection to the new learning conception, or discussing goals and competences without connecting these to the agreed value basis or the school culture. One of the central strengths of the Finnish curriculum development is its explicit eco-systemic approach to education. (Halinen, 2018: 87)

The 'agreed value basis' and 'school culture' are, in turn, a part of the surrounding sociocultural ecosystem as Simola (2005) has emphasised, which itself is inevitably affected by socioeconomic factors. Hence, to understand the teaching of foreign languages in schools, the preference for

English although other languages are available, and the apparent success in achieving widespread fluency in English in Finland necessitates going beyond the parameters of the curriculum, instructional hours, starting ages and teacher qualifications, important though they are, to encompass the place of the language and attitudes towards it in society at large. In this respect, also important is a recognition that where English is used, it is not perceived to be threatening the vitality of Finnish and Swedish, 'but rather a process in which English is taken up and used by Finns in a variety of ways, in order to serve their own discursive, social, and cultural purposes' (Leppänen *et al.*, 2011: 24–25). Finns have multilingual conceptions of themselves and English is part of the repertoire of languages they use for different purposes in different domains.

The process of developing a multilingual identity and repertoire of languages begins in school but is continually in the process of formation beyond school, both in the surrounding environment and over time into adulthood. Mustaparta (2008) explains how English permeates Finnish students' experience in a way that other languages do not.

> The media – TV and Internet – plays a decisive role in the popularity of English in two ways. Through media we get the idea – and illusion – that all the rest of the world speaks English, and therefore we must also be able to communicate in English, if we want to communicate with people from other cultures. And through the media we learn English by hearing and reading it on a daily basis. On the other hand, other languages are studied less and less despite promotion campaigns and programs for the diversification of language studies. Other languages do not play the same role in our mind and daily life. They are perceived as something extra, probably something for the future. The reward they promise in our mental picture is smaller. There are less opportunities to hear other languages, and probably therefore learning them is a bigger effort. We may feel that we are working hard but do not get the same reward we get with English. We might occasionally hear the language spoken on TV, but get frustrated, because we do not understand. If we could hear the language as often as we hear English, we would have a different experience. (Mustaparta, 2008: 3)

An ancillary factor in the popularity of English may be the role that online video-gaming plays in experience with English for some young learners. In other Scandinavian countries such as Sweden, research has shown that frequent gamers (playing for five hours or more a week) had greater English vocabulary levels than non-gamers, with the learners in this case being between 11–12 (Sylvén & Sundqvist, 2012) and 15–16 years of age (Sundqvist & Wikström, 2015). Similarly, research in Denmark with younger learners, aged 8–10 years, found that gaming with English input, whether spoken or written, correlated with greater vocabulary levels than for non-gamers (Hannibal Jensen, 2017). In Finland, however, much of the research into the impact of gaming on English skills is with older age groups (secondary school and university students) with a paucity of research with young learners, particularly in refereed publications. Such research as there is with young learners seems to support the findings from Sweden and Denmark. For example, in a BA thesis, Rajala (2019) investigated the gaming experiences of students in Grades 4–6 and found from their self-reports that there was a positive impact on English skills, most notably vocabulary acquisition, but that this 'was overall seen more in extramural use rather than in the school environment' (Rajala, 2019: 16). In a comparative study of 11–13-year-old students in Finland and Vietnam for a Master's thesis, Tran (2017) found that Finnish learners generally believed that English was not just acquired in school but that informal learning outside school was important. This informal learning was not restricted to gaming but included accessing the internet, listening to music and watching TV. The vast majority of Tran's (2017) Finnish respondents thought their informal learning had a significant impact on their English skills. Tran's (2017) research seems to align with that of Peters *et al.* (2019: 752), who found in reviewing the evidence into out-of-school learning that 'The positive effect of gaming has seemed to be less pronounced in studies in which gaming was but one variable in addition to reading, TV viewing, or listening to songs'. This indicates that it is perhaps a variety of forms of out-of-school exposure to English that is important rather than just one form such as online gaming. The wide access to English in Finland, as Mustaparta (2008) said, is the critical factor.

It is against this backdrop that the Finnish Ministry of Education and Culture has developed policies which are designed to lessen the dominance of English as the first foreign language in schools. However, if progress is to be made towards this goal, policies alone are not sufficient. The experience of English suggests that success in promoting diversity in language learning is likely to be dependent on access to the languages beyond the school as much as within it. Nevertheless, if there is indeed a clear need for languages such as Russian, German, Spanish and Swedish in Finland, as Hildén and Kantelinen (2012) maintain (and other languages that are entering the environment too), the Ministry's focus on a 'national language reserve' is a significant step towards developing a wider conception of multilingualism to counter the overemphasis on English to the detriment of other languages which is prevalent in Finland as in so many other countries.

Reflections: Contrasting Experiences of Bilingualism and Multilingualism

Enhancing language diversity in elementary schools in Ontario

Unlike in the contexts previously examined in this book, there is not the overwhelming emphasis given to a need for proficiency in French for the national economy in Canada that is given to English elsewhere. Although bilingualism is generally regarded as an asset in principle, there are only a minority of job postings that state that French-English bilingualism is actually required in employment – only 8.8% in 2014 (Workopolis, 2015) – and these tend to be restricted to public service appointments and customer service jobs. With little actual requirement for employment, it is hardly surprising that Arnott (2019) found that the economic benefits promoted for bilingualism did not resonate with students of FSL which 'also calls into question its power to motivate students to continue learning French in school – or perhaps more importantly – to override the demotivating factors that students identified related to the delivery of CF programs' (Arnott, 2019: 535). However, although there is no priority given to economic associations in the teaching of French as a compulsory subject in Ontario elementary schools, it remains as much a political imperative as is the teaching of English in Thailand, Korea, Sri Lanka and Malaysia, with Cummins (2014: 2) remarking that 'The ideological commitment to teach both official languages, regardless of the success of this endeavor, trumps the evidence of ineffectiveness'. Given the poor outcomes in CF over the years, a different approach to learning French – and other languages – in elementary school seems to be warranted, one that takes advantage of 'the multilingual realities of schools and communities' in the province and one that also enhances the value of learning Indigenous languages beyond the few communities in which they are currently found. Programmes to develop more teachers of Indigenous languages inevitably take time, but using community speakers of Indigenous languages as expert resources in collaboration with grade-level teachers could provide a short-term solution. In addition, more time needs to be made available in the curriculum to teach the languages, and a flexible policy which allows children to learn an Indigenous language in elementary school even if it is not possible to continue with it in high school would allow younger children at least to begin to develop basic language knowledge, as well as growing in appreciation of Indigenous peoples and cultures.

For CF itself, if it is to remain in the curriculum, as the ideological commitment to a bilingual Canada dictates, its status in schools and in the wider community is in need of considerable improvement. Overcoming the marginalisation of CF teachers in elementary schools is not just an issue for the teachers themselves but one for the entire school staff as well as an English-dominant society beyond the school gates. Attitudinal changes take time but might be promoted by adopting a more flexible approach to the teaching of additional languages in the system. In elementary schools, rather than unattainable proficiency goals in French alone, an approach that takes advantage of linguistic resources in the community and that promotes a love of language learning and appreciation of other cultures and ways of thinking and living among children, whatever the language, might also lead to a greater appreciation of French in the long run. At present the *Ontario Education Act* only allows instruction in English or French during the school day. If a school wishes to offer other languages, they have to be taught in a 30-minute extension to the school day or outside school hours, additional time for which teachers are not paid. Hence, other languages are likely to be thought of as an 'add-on' to the curriculum until this practice changes. In other provinces which historically have had fewer Francophones, such as Alberta, partial immersion programmes in which 50% of school programming can be offered in another language exist for Arabic, Chinese, German, Italian, Japanese, Punjabi, Spanish and Ukrainian, with entry points at Grade 1 or Grade 4.[10] This does not mean that French is neglected: its importance as an official language is acknowledged and there are also French-medium schools and French immersion programmes offered. In other schools in Alberta, French may be offered but it is optional, not mandatory. At present, as we have seen, the retention rate for CF in Ontario schools beyond the mandatory Grade 9 is just 6% and many students fail to see the value of the language. The system is failing children, who are developing negative attitudes towards French rather than acquiring the benefits that come from learning French that the curriculum specifies, i.e.:

> The ability to speak and understand French [which] allows students to communicate with French-speaking people in Canada and around the world, to understand and appreciate the history and evolution of their cultures, and to develop and benefit from a competitive advantage in the workforce. (MOEO, 2013: 6)

Continuing with an approach that has been failing for many years is self-defeating.

Second language learning in Finland in and beyond the primary school

From the perspective of some of the other governments referred to in this book, Finland is in the enviable position of being placed third out of 100 countries in the 2020 rankings of the *EF English Proficiency Index*. Since the assessments began in 2011, Finland has consistently been among the top 10 countries, with a 'very high proficiency' score. Even though the basis for these rankings, a self-selected sample of adults wishing to learn English who took EF's free online 'Standard English Test' or one of their placement tests, has been the subject of criticism, it remains true that many governments, particularly in South-East and East Asia, place great store in them as indicators of their country's relative success and failure in achieving national proficiency in English. Furthermore, governments allow these outcomes to influence the policies they develop for school language teaching even at the primary level, assuming that the earlier children start learning English, the sooner their populations will attain widespread English proficiency. However, although the education system in Finland provides high-quality education in foreign languages as well as in other subjects, Finnish success in learning English is not, as we have seen, solely dependent on what happens in schools. For many years it has been apparent that 'English is a language which many learners acquire outside the classroom' (Ringbom, 2012: 496), and that it is not for young children that this is most marked, but that 'For young adults in particular, the use of English becomes well motivated and socially significant: English has an important role in constructing new forms of expertise and social relations' (Ringbom, 2012: 506). The amount of language exposure and the opportunities for language practice beyond the school are important features of the social context in Finland, which build on the high-quality basic education provided by well-qualified teachers who have autonomy to interpret a core national curriculum to best suit the needs of their particular groups of students in a classroom environment focused on learning and not testing. This combination of educational and social factors ultimately provides fertile conditions for Finnish children to develop high levels of proficiency in English and, hopefully, will also exist for other languages to enable them to develop similar levels of proficiency in them in the years to come.

Notes

(1) See https://www.canada.ca/en/intergovernmental-affairs/services/provinces-territories.html
(2) Detailed information on the enormous variety of languages spoken across the country can be easily accessed through Statistics Canada's website and the interactive bubble charts and tables for each province and metropolitan areas within the provinces. See https://www12.statcan.gc.ca/census-recensement/2016/dp-pd/dv-vd/lang/index-eng.cfm
(3) There are over 230 nationalities residing in Toronto, and 51% of its population was born outside the country. See https://www.bbc.co.uk/sounds/play/p03v1r1p
(4) See www.kprschools.ca
(5) The alternate spellings Ojibwe and Ojibwa are as written in the original sources.
(6) There is no English language version of the Finnish Constitution. Information here is taken from the newsletter of the Office of the Commissioner of Official Languages, Canada. See https://www.clo-ocol.gc.ca/newsletter_cyberbulletin/finl_e.htm
(7) Information here comes from an unofficial translation of the 2003 *Language Act*, available at https://finlex.fi/en/laki/kaannokset/2003/en20030423.pdf
(8) See https://www.kotus.fi/en/on_language/languages_of_finland
(9) See https://www.oecd.org/pisa/PISA-results_ENGLISH.png
(10) See https://education.alberta.ca/international-languages-k-6/programs-of-study/

7 Rethinking Early Language Learning in State Sector Education Systems

Early Language Learning, Education and United Nations Goals

The discussion in this book paints a generally disheartening picture of early language learning in primary schools in many state sector education systems, particularly the learning of English, but one that the evidence indicates is nonetheless realistic. Within this overall gloomy picture, however, there are more than sufficient instances of good practice which provide directions for a productive way forward, one in which more young learners can have successful language learning experiences. My contention, based on the evidence presented in previous chapters, is that because of the widespread failure of early language learning to meet its stated objectives there is an urgent need to rethink policy and practice, particularly in contexts where the foreign language currently chosen is an international language – usually English – which has no or little place in the society outside the classroom for most learners. In this final chapter, I review the main arguments derived from the case study chapters and suggest ways in which early language learning may be made more meaningful for both teachers and children as well as producing more positive outcomes. I maintain that educational language policies that focus on enhancing intercultural understanding through an appreciation of diverse languages, especially those that are easier to access in the local environment, are to be preferred to policies aiming to develop widespread proficiency in English as an international language which is, ultimately, likely to benefit only children from higher socioeconomic groups, leaving the children of the poor even more marginalised. The analysis in previous chapters indicates that this is an issue in Malaysia, Thailand and Sri Lanka, manifested in particular in an urban–rural divide.

Recognising the marginalisation of the children of the poor in some countries, it is worth reminding ourselves at the beginning of this final chapter that all of the countries discussed in this book have ratified the UN Convention on the Rights of the Child,[1] according to which (Article

28.1), 'States Parties recognise the right of the child to education, and with a view to achieving this right progressively and on the basis of equal opportunity, they shall, in particular: (a) Make primary education compulsory and available free to all' (UN, 1989: 12–13). This objective has, by and large, been achieved in the countries discussed in previous chapters,[2] but other articles in the convention present more of a challenge in implementation. For example, Article 29.1 declares:

States Parties agree that the education of the child shall be directed to:

(a) The development of the child's personality, talents and mental and physical abilities to their fullest potential;
(b) The development of respect for human rights and fundamental freedoms, and for the principles enshrined in the Charter of the United Nations;
(c) The development of respect for the child's parents, his or her own cultural identity, language and values, for the national values of the country in which the child is living, the country from which he or she may originate, and for civilizations different from his or her own;
(d) The preparation of the child for responsible life in a free society, in the spirit of understanding, peace, tolerance, equality of sexes, and friendship among all peoples, ethnic, national and religious groups and persons of indigenous origin;
(e) The development of respect for the natural environment. (UN, 1989: 13)

Similarly, and more recently, in 2015 all 193 member states of the United Nations adopted the 2030 Development Agenda which included 17 Sustainable Development Goals (SGDs), among which SDG 4 concentrates on 'quality education', with Target 4.1 on 'free primary and secondary education' stating:

By 2030, ensure that all girls and boys complete free, equitable and quality primary and secondary education leading to relevant and effective learning outcomes.[3]

Both Target 4.1 of the SDGs and Article 29.1 of the Convention on the Rights of the Child indicate that providing equitable, quality education which maximises each child's potential should be a major objective of a state school system. Without quality education, it is extremely difficult to ensure that schooling is developing 'the child's personality, talents and mental and physical abilities to their fullest potential', as the Convention on the Rights of the Child avows, or that education is promoting respect for children's 'cultural identity, language and values' and preparing them for 'life in a free society, in the spirit of understanding, peace, tolerance, equality of sexes, and friendship among all peoples'.

Even though these general goals for education systems promote universal ideals of equity, the valuing of Indigenous languages and intercultural understanding, ideals to which governments have subscribed by endorsing the Convention and the SDGs, they do not inhibit the development of educational policies which are also appropriate to their local contexts. Equally, within this overall, internationally agreed framework, context-appropriate policies for early language learning may also be based on generalisable characteristics about more effective language policy and practice while respecting the culture of teaching and learning in the society in which they are embedded. Nonetheless, while respecting cultures of teaching and learning, it is important not to represent any culture as static and immutable. As Williams (2010: 17) says, 'Culture has a dynamic quality, even though different aspects of culture may change at different rates'. Hence, while education is often an instrument of socialisation of children into a country's existing culture(s), it is also an agent of change at the same time. Exposure to other cultures through languages will inevitably have an impact on the worldviews of children learning those languages in ways that may be large or small.

With this concept of education as an element of a society's dynamic culture in mind, any suggestions made here for improved, perhaps idealised, policy and practice in early language learning will need to be reinterpreted for implementation in particular socioeducational and cultural contexts, although with the interests of *all* learners rather than just the children of higher socioeconomic groups at its heart. This book is not a 'how to' teacher's guide and so the suggestions are of necessity more general than specific, needing to be given substance and elaborated for particular contexts by educators who work within those contexts.

Revisiting the Economic Rationale: Languages, National Economies and Education

Languages, trading partners and schooling

In Chapter 1 of this book, I introduced the argument that in many countries worldwide the case for developing widespread proficiency in English for national economic purposes is dubious. In the four Asian countries discussed in Chapters 2–5 – Thailand, South Korea, Sri Lanka and Malaysia – governments routinely claim that the country needs widespread proficiency in English in order to be competitive in global markets, despite there being little empirical information on the extent to which any foreign language is needed in their economies, in which sectors, by whom or for what purposes. If we take South Korea as an example, Chang *et al.* (2006), when reporting on research into lowering the starting age for teaching English in primary schools there, wrote that:

> there appears to be little readily-available, empirical data on actual language use in any sector of the economy. A study of English language use in various sectors of the economy would benefit policy making by providing a sounder data base for the development of school language policy as well as for language planning in society as a whole. (Chang *et al.*, 2006: 116)

No such study of actual language use in the Korean economy appears to have been conducted since this was written. Even in a country where there is some related data, as we noted in Chapter 4 for Sri Lanka, the *Labour Demand Survey* published in 2017 reported that 8.1% of employers felt that 'knowledge of a foreign language' was a skill needing improvement among job seekers but English was not mentioned specifically and this was offset by the top three occupations with a skill shortage being sewing machine operators, security guards and 'other manufacturing labourers', occupations with no apparent need for English (Department of Census and Statistics, 2017).

With national language audits for the economy scarce, to say the least, one could perhaps approach the issue of educational language policy through linking it to the language(s) of a country's largest trading partners. If we did this for South Korea, we would find that the country might benefit by focusing more attention on learning Mandarin, as 27% of its exports went to China in 2020, than on English, given that the United States received only 15% of its exports and other English-speaking countries such as Australia (1.2%), Canada (1.1%) and the UK (0.91%) much less. There would be a case for learning Vietnamese too as 9.8% of South Korean exports went to Vietnam in 2020.[4] Reducing the emphasis on English and making the teaching of these other languages more readily available in schools might have the added benefit of reducing the stress associated with achieving proficiency in English which, as we saw in Chapter 3, dominates children's schooling from primary school through to when they sit the College Scholastic Ability Test (CSAT) to determine which university they attend. We also noted that, in South Korea, English examination scores function more as a gatekeeper to employment than anything else and that, in reality, 'most companies rarely use English while they work' (Cho, 2014: 8), which makes the case for greater diversity in languages taught in schools (and examined in the CSAT) even more compelling.

Using this same reasoning regarding trading partners, Thailand would also seem to benefit from having a more diverse foreign language focus in its schools. While 15% of its exports went to the United States in 2020, almost as much (13%) went to China and 10% went to Japan.[5] While an additional 4.3% of exports went to Australia and 1.4% to the UK, a trilingual focus on English, Mandarin and Japanese to meet the needs of the economy would still seem to be a more practical language education policy for Thailand than a monolingual focus on English. In neighbouring Malaysia, the largest trading partner in 2020 was China with 17% of exports.[6] Singapore, which has English as one of its four official languages and as the medium of instruction in schools, was its second largest with 15% of exports, but here Malaysia could make use of its similar multilingual background as an advantage to communicate with Singaporeans in their other three official languages of Malay, Mandarin and Tamil rather than English with which, as we commented in Chapter 5, Malaysia has a 'conflicted and contentious' relationship as a former British colony.

Current economic realities notwithstanding, it is also important to remind ourselves that it commonly takes children eight years to go through basic education (and a further four if they complete high school), and so basing primary school language education policy solely on the utility and surrender value of proficiency in any particular language(s) at a distant time when children eventually move into the workforce is always likely to be a speculative enterprise. Hence, what is important in all contexts is that young children should not be thought of as future units of production for government economic planners for whom proficiency in a foreign language – most often English – is simply a required tool for global economic competitiveness. Focusing on purely utilitarian reasons for learning in this way is hardly likely to foster love of language learning in children for its own sake, let alone promote any of the other goals enshrined in the UN Convention on the Rights of the Child.

The quality of education and economic development

In contrast to the lack of a proven link between foreign languages taught in school and national economic competitiveness, there is, as I said in the opening chapter of this book, a well-established connection between the quality of basic education as a whole and national economic development (Grant, 2017). This has been known for many years. Some 40 years ago, Colclough (1982) reviewed recent research at that time and summarised the benefits of investing in primary education, which went beyond the economy to other aspects of social development:

> The main case for investment in primary schooling is that it makes people more productive at work and in the home. It goes well beyond the attainment of short-run consumption or equity goals, and, far from being an obstacle to higher rates of economic growth, it helps to achieve them. In addition, primary schooling facilitates the attainment of other objectives of social policy, particularly in the fields of fertility control, improvements in health, nutrition, literacy and communications, and the strengthening of national culture. (Colclough, 1982: 181)

Experience since then has not altered this conclusion, only reinforced it. Thus, it is more important for children to receive a high-quality general education and to develop transferable analytical and problem-solving skills which they can use flexibly in the future than to acquire proficiency in a single language such as English. In previous chapters, we have seen that unequal access to high-quality general education has repercussions both for individual life chances and for national economic development. This is a major concern in Thailand (Fry, 2018; World Bank, 2015) and Sri Lanka (Dundar *et al.*, 2017) in particular. Furthermore, notwithstanding the rhetoric about its economic need in Thailand, the lack of widespread proficiency in English has not impacted its ranking in the 2021 Institute for Management Development (IMD) World Competitiveness Index where it was 28th, a ranking that compares well with its ASEAN neighbours Malaysia (25th) and Indonesia (37th), and is consistent with its performance in earlier years – 29th in 2020, 25th in 2019, 30th in 2018, 27th in 2017 (Leesa-Nguansuk, 2021). If a lack of widespread proficiency in English was as harmful to national economic competitiveness in the era of globalisation as is so often claimed, one would have expected Thailand's ranking to have been on a downward trend over this time period. Yet, while lack of English itself is not mentioned as a risk factor in its report, the IMD noted that there was considerable scope for improvement in Thailand's education and healthcare systems if it wished to enhance its competitive edge economically (Leesa-Nguansuk, 2021). As we noted in Chapter 2, the need to improve the Thai education system has also been identified by other external agencies such as the World Bank.

English alone, then, is not enough to enhance global economic competitiveness. There is ample evidence to indicate that proficiency in English only enhances learners' life chances if it is accompanied by employment-related skills in particular sectors which have value in the economy rather than being of value by itself (Azam *et al.*, 2010; Erling, 2015). To reiterate the point made by Ricento (2018: 221) in Chapter 1 of this book, 'the role and utility of English worldwide is a vehicle for some people, in some economic sectors, mainly the knowledge economy, but is generally not connected to socioeconomic mobility for the vast majority of the global workforce'.

English and socioeconomic status

The link between the quality of education generally, the levels of achievement in English and socioeconomic status has been a recurrent theme throughout this book. Evidence indicates that teaching English in primary schools in many countries is associated with 'inequality in the distribution of learning opportunities amongst various socioeconomic groups' (Hayes & Chang, 2014: 22), with the poorest groups receiving the fewest opportunities. Even in countries with high achievement levels in basic education, such as South Korea, English still functions as a way for 'the privileged classes [to] conserve the established class structure to the disadvantage, if not detriment, of the other classes' (Song, 2012: 17). In other countries such as Thailand and Sri Lanka where, as we have seen, there is a struggle to provide high-quality education across the whole system, an inevitable consequence is inequitable access to high-quality English language teaching. Moreover, in those countries that have a colonial association with English, not just countries that have less well-resourced education systems such as Sri Lanka but those with better resourced systems such as Malaysia, high levels of proficiency in the language primarily remain the preserve of the urban elite who use it as a marker of their social status and a means to maintain their privilege (Azman, 2016; Gunesekera, 2005).

Regrettably, the English proficiency levels that indigenous elites attained when English was a medium of instruction in the colonial era in Malaysia and Sri Lanka are habitually assumed to be the norm that their education systems as a whole should attain in post-colonial times, reflected in complaints – typically from older English-educated generations, as Gill (2012) observed for Malaysia – about a decline in standards in the language which ignore the basic fact that if English is just one subject among many in the curriculum, the conditions for development of language proficiency are not the same as when it was being used to teach all the subjects. Furthermore, such complaints ignore the fact that throughout the colonial era proficiency in English was not widespread among colonised populations. In Malaysia, Stephen (2013: 5) noted that the effect of these colonial-era educational divisions persisted post-independence.

> Graduating from an English-medium school accorded one an elite standing in urban society and those who could afford such schooling for their children were mostly the Malay aristocrats, along with rich Chinese traders and Eurasians. By the late 1940s, English had become the lingua franca of the English-educated Malayans and the society in postcolonial Malaya was divided into the English-speaking versus the non-English speaking, which meant, in effect, the elite versus the non-elite. (Stephen, 2013: 5)

In contrast, Malay-medium education 'came to be looked on as the poor man's education' (Stephen, 2013: 5), a stigma that Malaysian governments have removed since independence with the change in medium of education from English.

There was a similar situation in Sri Lanka, where the final census under colonial rule in 1946 recorded that only 7.4% of the population had the ability to speak English, with 0.2% speaking English only, 2.9% speaking English and Sinhala, 1.9% speaking English and Tamil, and 2.4% speaking English, Sinhala and Tamil (Department of Census and Statistics, 1952, cited in Coperahewa, 2009: 93). In post-colonial Sri Lanka, the politicisation of national language policies contributed to a 26-year civil war, as we discussed in Chapter 4. In part, the proclamation in the Sri Lankan constitution in 1987 of English as a 'link' language was designed to promote greater inter-ethnic harmony between Sinhalese and Tamil communities. As we also saw in Chapter 4, in practice there is potential benefit for interethnic harmony from Sinhalese and Tamil children studying together through English which can promote 'membership of a group that is inclusive of all ethnic diverse others' (Wijesekera *et al.*, 2019: 35). However, widespread realisation of this potential cannot be accomplished when most communities are separated along ethnic lines and is a possibility only in large urban communities with a significant minority population. Hence, until the unlikely prospect of greater inter-ethnic integration is achieved at the community level, proficiency in English in Sri Lanka will continue to function as a marker of socioeconomic status, symbolising 'the gap between the haves and the have nots' (Gunesekera, 2005: 34), just as it did in the colonial era. This social reality calls into question the emphasis placed on the teaching of English in primary schools. If the goal is interethnic harmony, it would seem to be more urgent to seek ways to enhance the provision of second national language education in primary schools, particularly the teaching of Tamil to Sinhalese children, and to work to counter prejudice among adults, than to focus on English as a link language.

The evidence from the chapters on Thailand, South Korea, Sri Lanka and Malaysia indicates that the teaching of English in their education systems has failed to develop the intended widespread high levels of proficiency in the language which, as Erling (2015: 64) maintains, 'is why it is so important to situate a discussion about the role of English language skills in employability within a description of the wider social and educational context'. Erling (2015: 64) goes on to argue that 'If issues of access, quality and the labour market are not given significant attention, English language skills will only increase the growing disparity between the advantaged and the disadvantaged – and will not enable those most in need of development opportunities to enhance their capabilities'. Or, as Bruthiaux (2002: 292) put it more bluntly: 'For deeply poor populations in many countries, education of the most basic type remains a pipe dream, and English language education an outlandish irrelevance'. Arguments that teaching English at the primary level will improve achievement levels across education systems and enhance the life chances of children from lower socioeconomic groups are not reflected in the reality of their lives.

English and aspiration

Nonetheless, in spite of the contrasting experiences of achieving proficiency in the language among different socioeconomic groups and the resulting contribution to social inequality for the disadvantaged, English still functions as an aspirational language for most parents in all the non-English speaking countries examined in this book. Parental influence – or 'parentocracy', as Enever (2018) has tellingly labelled it – is a crucial determiner of attitudes towards the teaching of specific languages in schools, either largely positive in the case of English in the majority of non-English speaking countries or largely negative in the case of Tamil as a second language in Sri Lanka and French in Ontario, Canada. From an educational standpoint, it may well be more in children's interests to develop a positive attitude to learning other languages as an outcome of primary school rather than proficiency in a specific global language, but parental views that regard attaining proficiency in this global language as vital for their children's future, a key element of their social capital, cannot simply be discounted. As the National Curriculum Framework in India put it: 'The level of introduction of English is now a matter of political response to people's aspirations rather than an academic or feasibility issue' (NCERT, 2005: 38). This 'political response' is applicable to most contexts in which English is the first foreign language in primary schools. Given such parental attitudes, any attempt to diversify the languages taught in primary schools also necessitates associated public information initiatives to promote an appreciation of the value of learning languages other than (or even in addition to) English among adults in the wider society. Parents' aspirations for their children might then expand to include varied bi/multilingualism and language choice would become less political. Initiatives to influence parents' attitudes could take as their starting point conclusions from Erling's (2015) review of research on English and employability, which

> reminds us that there are economic returns from all languages, and evidence suggests that it is multilingualism – and not English language skills on their own – that allows societies to prosper. It is therefore important that governments and societies value all of the languages used among their societies, and recognise their potential value for use in education and economic ventures. (Erling, 2015: 64)

Unless the possibility of economic returns from multilingualism is effectively communicated to the parents of children entering school, they are unlikely to support their children's participation in language classes other than English even when they are made available and no matter how little English their children actually learn at school. This argument is equally true for changing negative attitudes towards the learning of French among the English-speaking community in Ontario, discussed in Chapter 6, and critical if the negative attitudes to Tamil among Sinhalese children in Sri Lanka that we discussed in Chapter 4 are to be improved.

Early language learning and communicative needs

At present, then, the aspirational value of English taught as the first foreign language is not matched by high levels of achievement in the educational systems discussed in this book, with the exception of Finland where children's school learning is supported and additional learning opportunities arise outside the classroom. Elsewhere, however, children living in contexts where English is the first, and often the only, foreign language in schools and who receive minimal exposure to the language outside the school will always find it difficult to see the value of learning it if that value is couched in terms of a need to communicate in the language when they leave school, and that need does not match with their own lived experience. Byram (1989) concluded more than 30 years ago that:

> If we justify language teaching – and motivate pupils – solely, or even just mainly, by putative communication needs and those needs turn out to be non-existent, then the justification disappears – and most of the motivation with it. When we attempt to persuade pupils by this appeal to relevance and appropriateness, and they argue that they do not and will not have such communicative needs – or, what has the same effect, cannot imagine themselves as having such needs – then we are pre-programming our work for failure. (Byram, 1989: 11)

This standpoint is articulated in the words of a Thai teacher I interviewed who reported to me that her students could not see beyond working on the family farm and often said to her, 'Oh Ajarn,[7] why do I have to learn English? Because I just go to the farm and there is no-one, no farang [foreigner] to talk with'. These students' circumstances are replicated in many other contexts, although the type of local post-school employment available may change, and so it is hardly surprising that, despite the massive investment by governments in its teaching, there is continued failure to achieve stated objectives in terms of communicative English language proficiency in so many state education systems.

As we have seen repeatedly in this book, poor outcomes in English subsequently occasion much discussion of 'declining standards' and a great deal of national soul searching about how the standards can be improved. This occurs every year in South Korea and Thailand, for example, when the *EF English Proficiency Index* rankings are released. However, rather than questioning the underlying principles of the approach to teaching and learning languages in their education systems, the response to continued failure to achieve proficiency targets by the end of primary school for students (as well as other stages of schooling) is usually to offer more of the same failed approach, i.e. lowering the starting age to earlier primary grades, even to pre-primary where it is available, and/or increasing the number of hours per week of instruction. In India, the National Curriculum Framework cautioned against 'extend[ing] downwards the very system that has failed to deliver' (NCERT, 2005: 38), but this appears to be precisely what is happening in many countries which are, as a consequence, 'pre-programming our work for failure'.

The arguments in this book lead to a conclusion that, rather than focusing on hypothetical communicative needs and unattainable proficiency targets in a particular international language, a more productive starting point for early language learning might be to prioritise the general educational value of including other languages in the school curriculum, such as expanding children's worldview and developing tolerance of different peoples through promoting an appreciation of other cultures. Enhancing proficiency in a specific foreign language could be left to later stages of schooling and might be more successful if it were building on a positive attitudinal base to language learning generally which had been developed in earlier years. There is even some evidence that older children may be faster at learning languages because of their greater use of cognitive strategies and more advanced literacy skills (Myles, 2017), which supports an emphasis on focusing on proficiency targets later in the educational cycle.

Unfortunately, there is increasing resistance to viewing education in anything other than strictly utilitarian terms. In Thailand, even at the turn of the century, Witte (2000) was writing of competing visions of the purpose of education.

> One could ... characterize the goal conflict in the Thai education system as just another facet of the 'overall dominating contradiction between, on the one hand, education as an instrument which is utilitarian and pragmatic ... and the humanistic ... approach, with its broader and holistic ambitions' (Gustavsson, 1997: 240), a contradiction which is as old as education, but has been revived with a new urgency in the face of globalization. (Witte, 2000: 242)

With regard to English as a foreign language, adopting the increasingly dominant utilitarian and pragmatic approach in response to globalisation has been profoundly unsuccessful in many countries. After a decade or more of instruction from the earliest years of school, far too many students end up reacting like the Thai student who said, 'whenever I see English words or meet English speakers I can only look and smile' (Hayes, 2016: 83), or worse, as in South Korea, after 'years of arduous toil [...] English falls among students' most loathed subjects' (Moon, 2014: 207). Outcomes such as these are the very antithesis of what foreign language education should produce.

A way forward: National language reserves

This book contends that the main concern of policy for early language learning should always be the educational and developmental welfare of the children in schools rather than assumed communicative needs for future economic reasons. When they begin school, most children – at least once they have overcome their initial shock at the strangeness of the new environment – are excited to be there and have immense curiosity about learning new things. Where foreign languages are offered in the early years, the education system should make the most of children's natural curiosity so that they maintain an eagerness to learn about the world through the lens of new languages and cultures which persists beyond primary school. Early language learning should instil in children a desire to learn *more* languages as they grow, not stifle their interest through over-focus on a single language taught in a way that has little meaning for them: to a certain extent, the choice of language(s) to learn in primary schools is secondary to the actual possibility of being able to learn other languages. Of course, there are some young learners for whom the emphasis on English is positive, especially if they have access to a range of opportunities to engage with the language beyond the classroom. This appears to be the case in Finland and doubtless will apply elsewhere too. Unfortunately, in many other countries the access is often restricted to higher socioeconomic groups, as we have seen in Malaysia, South Korea and Sri Lanka.

Nonetheless, as we saw in Chapter 6, Finland is concerned by the trend to select English and neglect other languages in schools. In response, it has initiated a policy of developing a 'national language reserve' which provides children with the opportunity to experience multiple languages for short periods while they are in kindergarten. This offers a possible way forward to begin to break an over-dependence on English as the first foreign language in school systems. Allied to a broader conception of language proficiency whereby any amount of a language learned is seen as a basis for later learning, the concept of a national language reserve has the additional advantage that it can appeal to those worried about the economic implications of language learning in schools as it provides a way to prepare for future, unforeseeable changes in language needs in society at large. In the Finnish example, the multilingual approach to teaching foreign languages begins in kindergarten, but in systems where pre-primary education is not universal it could equally well begin at the primary level. The practice of 'language showers' can capitalise on any languages available in the community, such as Indigenous non-official languages, immigrant languages or languages of neighbouring states. If there is no expectation that any particular proficiency level is to be attained but, instead, there is a focus on enthusing children with a desire to learn languages and to learn about the world through languages, there is the prospect that the approach will provide a positive attitudinal foundation for success in further language learning later in the school cycle. Early indications in Finland are that the experience of language showers increases the number of children going on to study a language other than English as their first compulsory foreign language in primary school (Chukhlantseva, 2020).

Revisiting Issues of Curriculum, Policy and Practice

Basic principles for the early language learning curriculum

However a foreign language curriculum for primary schools is conceptualised, whether through 'language showers' or longer term study of one or more languages, it needs to take account of children's cognitive, physical, social and emotional development as well as the desired subject matter. For example, Vosniadou (2001: 8–27) discusses 12 interconnected principles which are foundational for learning in schools, viz.:

(1) Learning requires the active, constructive involvement of the learner.
(2) Learning is primarily a social activity and participation in the social life of the school is central for learning to occur.
(3) Children learn best when they participate in activities that are perceived to be useful in real life and are culturally relevant.
(4) New knowledge is constructed on the basis of what is already understood and believed.
(5) Children learn by employing effective and flexible strategies that help them to understand, reason, memorize and solve problems.
(6) Learners must know how to plan and monitor their learning, how to set their own learning goals and how to correct errors.
(7) Sometimes prior knowledge can stand in the way of learning something new. Students must learn how to solve internal inconsistencies and restructure existing conceptions when necessary.
(8) Learning is better when material is organized around general principles and explanations, rather than when it is based on the memorization of isolated facts and procedures.
(9) Learning becomes more meaningful when the lessons are applied to real-life situations.
(10) Learning is a complex cognitive activity that cannot be rushed. It requires considerable time and periods of practice to start building expertise in an area.
(11) Children learn best when their individual differences are taken into consideration.
(12) Learning is critically influenced by learner motivation. Teachers can help students become more motivated learners by their behaviour and the statements they make.

Hence, for early language learning, it is far from a question of simply deciding which elements of a language to teach in which grade, and which structures or vocabulary items are required for which functions. If education systems mandate a language curriculum for children in the early years, it has to take account of learners' internal cognitive factors which interact with environmental factors within collaborative, meaningful learning environments to promote successful learning. Yet, most foreign language curricula focus only on language items with the goal of achieving a particular proficiency level by the end of primary school. This level is increasingly tied in a growing number of countries to the Common European Framework of Reference (CEFR), as we have seen in previous chapters.

The influence of the CEFR

In Malaysia the expected level by the end of primary school is A2 on the CEFR, in Thailand by the end of Grade 6 the target is A1 and A2 by the end of Grade 9, and in Finland the target is A2.1 (first stage of basic proficiency) for receptive skills and A1.3 (functional elementary proficiency) for productive skills by Grade 6 on a Finnish version of the CEFR. In Sri Lanka, the Teacher's Guide for Grade 3 English (NIE, 2017) has 19 'can do' statements and associated 'performance standards' for the students to achieve. Although a number of 'basic competencies' not related to the English language itself, such as 'competencies relating to personality development', e.g. 'Values such as integrity, tolerance and respect for human dignity' (NIE, 2017: iii), are also included in the guide, there is no assistance for the teacher in planning how these important competencies might be realised by the 'can do' statements and associated language.

Some educational systems, such as Finland's, have modified the CEFR, but it is important to note that the CEFR standards themselves were not originally developed with young learners in mind but 'were formulated drawing from a corpus of adult language use, failing to capture the essential features of children's early foreign language (FL) experiences' (Enever, 2011: 9). Perhaps in response to how the CEFR is being used around the world, a recent update and extension to the framework makes clear that 'provision of common reference points is subsidiary to the CEFR's main aim of facilitating quality in language education and promoting a Europe of open-minded plurilingual citizens' (Council of Europe, 2020: 28). The update also emphasises that 'it is important to underline once again that the CEFR is a tool to facilitate educational reform projects, not a standardisation tool' (Council of Europe, 2020: 29), as well as providing a number of broad objectives, viz.:

> The CEFR sets out to be comprehensive, in the sense that it is possible to find the main approaches to language education in it, and neutral, in the sense that it raises questions rather than answering them and does not prescribe any particular pedagogic approach. There is, for example, no suggestion that one should stop teaching grammar or literature. There is no 'right answer' given to the question of how best to assess a learner's progress. Nevertheless, the CEFR takes an innovative stance in seeing learners as language users and social agents, and thus seeing language as a vehicle for communication rather than as a subject to study. (Council of Europe, 2020: 29)

Yet, in prescribing the attainment of certain CEFR levels by the end of specific school grades, educational systems are, in actual fact, using the framework as a tool for standardisation.

Communicative language teaching and 'native speakers'

In addition, the focus in language curricula on what learners 'can do' with a language as a vehicle for communication is strongly associated with communicative language teaching (CLT) and its task-based learning and teaching (TBLT) offshoot which constitute the dominant pedagogic paradigm in English language teaching worldwide. CLT is, in turn, linked to an English-only policy in classrooms and privileging of the 'native speaker' in many school systems. We have seen in Chapter 3, for example, that in South Korea the policy of 'Teaching English through English' was developed on the basis that if teachers would only speak English for most of the lesson time, children would then become more competent speakers of the language. This view is common, even though research and classroom experience indicate that approaches that stigmatise the use of the first language in English lessons when teachers and students share a common first language are counter-productive, preventing young learners from using 'already established cognitive and social structures when learning the TL' (Rabbidge & Chappell, 2014: 12).

The native speaker continues to be privileged in teacher training too. In Chapter 5, in Malaysia, we saw that the 'Pro-ELT' and 'ELTDP' continuing professional development (CPD) programmes for teachers were contracted out to an organisation that emphasised its ability to provide native-speaker trainers. In Thailand, in Chapter 2, the Regional English Training Centres were staffed by native speakers who ran the CPD courses. While the native speakers in the Thai training centres were assisted by local teachers who were being trained as 'master trainers', there was no formal plan for them to continue to run the centres once the native speakers left and the training project was wound up.

In contrast to these examples, a welcome counterpoint to the CLT and native-speaker trend is offered in Sri Lanka where the new primary school textbooks for English state that 'no particular ELT approach was specially considered' and that teachers 'are requested to be creative and independent to select the best possible methodology to achieve success in teaching and learning' (NIE, 2017: i), while 'using accepted SL Pronunciation' (NIE, 2017: viii) is included in the 'can do' syllabus statements.

The negative impact of privileging native speakers, with the neo-imperialist associations of English rendering it a particular problem, cannot be underestimated. Again, we have seen that native speakers as teacher trainers on CPD programmes for English, no matter how well-qualified otherwise, usually do not speak the language of the community well (if at all) and do not have the context-specific expertise that local trainers have, both of which are crucial to an understanding of what happens in the classroom and thus to any attempts to modify teachers' classroom practice. Privileging native speakers as trainers also 'undermines the legitimacy and expertise of home-grown talent' (MELTA, 2010: 2), as the Malaysian English Language Teaching Association put it. If Malaysia has trainers and teachers who possess

> the same levels of linguistic and pedagogical knowledge as native speaker teachers [...] By not including these Malaysians in this programme, the country is sending out a message that Malaysians are not good enough or will never be good enough to become self-reliant. (MELTA, 2010: 2–3)

Similarly, policies to recruit native speakers of English as teachers in primary schools in a number of Asian countries negatively affect the standing of local teachers. As I wrote in an interim evaluation of the Regional English Teacher Training Project in Thailand:

> If spoken English is seen as the preserve of the 'native speaker' and Thai teachers of English are not provided with opportunities to present themselves as models of successful second language learners, English is unlikely to be seen as a language which Thai students can master. (Hayes, 2017a: 25)

Nonetheless, in Thailand in 2020 the then Minister of Education announced that the Ministry intended to recruit a further 10,000 native-speaking English teachers, in addition to the 7000 already in the country and, focusing on the folk-belief that young children are able to learn foreign languages easily, 'The Education Minister said he would like to focus his initial reform efforts on young Thai children as he felt that it was here that Thailand could reap the greatest benefit' (O'Connor, 2020: np). Whether the policy will be continued by the latest Minister of Education, because of the difficulties caused by the Covid-19 pandemic which began in early 2020 and which made international recruitment extremely challenging, remains to be seen. However, given that 'the teaching-learning relationship is *the* crucial variable for improving learning outcomes and increasing the relevance of education' (UNESCO, 2009: 101), it is difficult to see how foreign teachers will be able to develop the same kind of relationships with young learners as Thai teachers, who share a first language and culture, are able to do, and thus it must be doubtful that they will have any significant impact on the learning of English in Thai primary schools in the instructional time that the curriculum allows. The use of native speakers is also likely to increase inequity in primary schools as it is the smallest, more rural schools or those in the poorest urban areas that will be unable to attract or retain native speakers.

Standardised curricula, local needs, local responses and local languages

Inequity is already present in many education systems, as previous chapters have shown. In some ways, inequity is built into the system through the very process of standardisation which is, paradoxically, predicated on the assumption that it will ensure that all children, whichever school they go to, will have the opportunity to achieve the same outcomes. Standardisation is the norm across most school systems but, rather than ensuring equal outcomes for students as intended, its lack of recognition of the uniqueness of individual schools inadvertently fosters the opposite. UNESCO (2009) notes:

> A curriculum based on the standardization of learning processes and contents – a 'one size fits all' approach – is not desirable, since it does not serve learners' needs in the context of their lives. Indeed, national models

of school education, and the very notion of standardized learning processes, have sometimes created immense gaps between what pupils learn and what they live. Although inspired to some extent by the principle of universality, which prescribes equal educational opportunities for all, in practice such an approach results in unacceptably high levels of educational failure, particularly among pupils from deprived or disadvantaged backgrounds, for whom school education is seen as being disconnected from their own experiences and concerns. (UNESCO, 2009: 97–98)

Thus, quality education for all children is more likely to be achieved if the school curriculum allows for flexibility in response to local needs so that local teachers can interpret curriculum competencies in ways that relate more closely to their students' lives, making knowledge meaningful to them through connecting it to their environment. Indeed, the UNESCO report maintains that learning has to be local and applicable to children's lives if it is to be successful, explaining that:

> Quality education is thus essentially about learning rooted in local environments and focused on broader knowledge and competencies applicable to learners' lives. It also opens up new horizons and enables learners to bring local knowledge into creative contact with knowledge from other cultures. In terms of curriculum development, 'bringing the real world into schools' applies to both content and form, which entails the development of multicultural and multilingual curricula, based on multiple perspectives and voices and on the histories and cultures of all groups in a given society, including minorities. (UNESCO, 2009: 100–101)

A local approach to learning other languages can take the focus away from unattainable proficiency goals and promote a creative relationship between local knowledge and knowledge acquired through these other languages. The approach argues against an exclusive focus on an international language such as English and supports the proposal that enhancing intercultural understanding through an appreciation of diverse languages, especially those that are easier to access in the local environment, is a sounder objective for primary school education than attempting to reach a certain level in an international language based on an inappropriate framework. We have seen in previous chapters how linguistic minorities such as the Rungus of Sabah and the Iban of Sarawak in East Malaysia and the Lahu and Patani Malays in Thailand, among others, are faced with considerable difficulties when they begin school. The Rungus and the Iban have to learn two new languages when they enter primary school, Malay and English. Similarly, the Lahu and Patani Malay have to learn Thai and English. These language demands risk loosening children's attachments to their home language and culture. The dangers of neglecting local languages are emphasized by UNESCO (2009):

> Most countries introduce an international language in the upper primary grades, but few countries allocate time to local languages. These policies not only undermine the preservation of linguistic diversity, but also

reduce the impact of multilingualism, which can improve intellectual functioning and intercultural dialogue. (UNESCO, 2009: 104)

Hence, the arguments for including more local languages in primary school curricula are evident, both for speakers of a language who see the increased value in its domain of use expanding from the home to an official setting as well as children from other groups who are exposed to the diversity of languages in their local environments.

The persistence of inherited teaching traditions

A focus on diverse languages, especially those more readily available in the local or regional environment, might also reduce or even eliminate the possibility of complaints about teachers using 'old' or 'traditional' methods to teach English in the primary school classroom. These complaints, alongside those about teachers failing to adopt the communicative approach which is mandated by the curriculum, are legion across many contexts. Educational policymakers rarely, however, stop to consider why these 'old' methods persist. As we noted in Chapter 2, in Thailand the 'inherited tradition' of a grammar-translation approach is a response to a hierarchical context in which school administrators are not questioned by teachers and teachers are not questioned by students and where knowledge is in the gift of teachers to pass on to their students. If primary school teachers are themselves not particularly proficient in a language, as is common with English in many countries and especially in rural areas, then they will inevitably find it difficult to use the prescribed communicative approach and are unlikely to risk losing face in front of their students by attempting to speak the language in situations that are unpredictable. With a grammar-translation approach, the teacher is in control of language use, which remains predictable. Hence, from the perspective of teachers, the method endures because it is useful, a logical response to circumstances in which they are required to teach a language with which they have insufficient familiarity.

The history of educational innovation in Thailand, as elsewhere, provides ample evidence that this situation cannot be changed overnight, despite policymakers' constant exhortations. Irrespective of policy mandates, what happens in the classroom will always be an instantiation of teachers' beliefs about appropriate practice and determined by their skillset: they may accept new policies in theory while maintaining old ways of teaching in practice. Once again, if teachers are not required to focus on unattainable standards in a language with which they have insufficient proficiency, but are instead asked to help children to become familiar with a different way of viewing the world through a language that is closer to their experience, the outcomes for both teachers and children may be more beneficial: teachers will not be labelled as continually incompetent and 'failing', while children will develop positive attitudes towards learning other languages.

The younger the better argument and time for language learning in schools

Yet another reason for a reconsideration of approaches to early language learning is that policymakers appear not to understand the conditions under which languages are learnt in schools, continually falling back on the 'children learn languages easily when they are young, so we should start as early as possible in schools' misconception. This argument is found across the contexts reviewed in this book. We have seen, for example, a former Thai Minister of Education illustrate this with his desire to 'focus his initial reform efforts [for English language teaching] on young Thai children as he felt that it was here that Thailand could reap the greatest benefit' (O'Connor, 2020: np). To understand how inappropriate it is to apply 'the younger the better' view to language learning in schools, we need only consider the amount of time available for learning. Myles (2017) highlights the amount of input children receive as they learn their first language, as well as the nature of learning for young children.

> It seems that young children learn mainly by doing rather than by conscious learning, that is, they learn more implicitly than older children. As a result, they need abundant input and rich interaction to allow their implicit mechanisms to work. After all, it is estimated that children learning their native language are exposed to 17,000 hours of input by age 4. (Myles, 2017: 2)

In contrast to the 17,000 hours of input in their first four years of life, children in school in South Korea, as an example, receive 204 hours of instruction from Grade 3 to Grade 6 for English. Even if they attend private tuition classes, as we have noted that many children do, their total hours of input will still be insufficient to promote the quality of learning that policymakers expect of them simply because they are young. Furthermore, arguments for lowering the starting age for language learning to provide additional input often fail to take account of the fact that time needs to be made available in the curriculum for these added classes. Is it to be taken from other subjects (potentially generating resistance from their teachers) or will the school day be extended to accommodate the extra learning hours? Even if more classroom time is found, experience in countries where early language learning is more successful, as we have observed for Finland, indicates that it is not just a question of time to learn *inside* the classroom, but also one of exposure to the language *outside* the classroom to enhance learning (Mustaparta, 2008; Ringbom, 2012) without which there is little to no reinforcement of what children learn in school.

Resourcing, teachers and early language learning

A key theme of this book has been that mandating the teaching of a foreign language, principally English, to young learners in primary schools is, at best, inherently problematic and, at worst, doomed to failure if the basic requirements of a child-centred curriculum with realistic learning objectives, implemented by linguistically competent, well-trained teachers who use appropriate young learner pedagogy are not met. (It is also worth emphasising that the experience of the Canadian province of Ontario with mandatory French as a second language that we reviewed in Chapter 6 indicates that the problems are not confined to English as a foreign language alone.) This standpoint is hardly radical, as Graddol (2006) summed up the 'hazards' of introducing English to young learners (EYL) more than 15 years ago.

> There are many hazards attached to EYL, not least of which is that it requires teachers who are proficient in English, have wider training in child development, and who are able to motivate young children. Such teachers are in short supply in most countries, but failure at this stage may be difficult to remedy later. (Graddol, 2006: 89)

Moreover, research into effective learning in schools generally, such as that of Vosniadou (2001), which we referred to earlier, highlights the need to consider children's cognitive, physical, social and emotional development in developing a curriculum for teaching the language, factors that are rarely foregrounded in English language curricula, as evidenced by those reviewed in previous chapters.

In an ideal world, education ministries would begin to lay the groundwork for the successful introduction of foreign languages in primary schools well in advance of policy decisions being implemented so that 'failure at this stage' was avoided. Unfortunately, many policymakers continue to insist on mandating the teaching of English without: (a) formulating realistic objectives for language learning given the current proficiency levels of teachers of the language in the system; (b) simultaneously enhancing teachers' proficiency levels through long-term CPD programmes which not only assist them in learning the language and language teaching techniques for young learners but also provide them with in-class support as they use their developing proficiency to teach in new ways; (c) developing new pre-service teacher preparation programmes which provide novice teachers with the requisite language proficiency and teaching skills before they enter the system; and (d) providing long-term, sustained commitment in the implementation of the chosen policies, giving them adequate time to have an impact. Where this is not done, the introduction of foreign languages into the primary curriculum will inevitably promote further inequity between urban areas, which have greater access to resources, and rural areas, where resources are constrained. In Chapter 1 of this book, we saw how the decision to introduce English into primary schools in Vietnam without first ensuring the necessary teachers and resources were available in all schools predictably led to inequality in access to English language education between rural and urban areas (Nguyen *et al.*, 2014). Indeed, the analysis of policy and practice in most of the countries reviewed here indicates that the worldwide march of English into education systems at ever younger ages seems immune either to research or to logic.

With respect to point (d) above, sustained commitment to policies, teachers themselves in many contexts have complained that there is too much change in policy, too often and usually without consultation with them, even though teachers are the group most affected by any changes, a point eloquently made by Hardman and A-Rahman (2014) for Malaysia in Chapter 5 but equally applicable in many other contexts. There is a process of constant adjustment to existing policy or replacement with an entirely new policy whenever there is a change in government and/or minister, which increases teachers' workload but does little to improve classroom practice. The frequent changes at the ministerial level experienced in Thailand and the continual policy change decried by teachers in Malaysia, for example, only worsen the prospects of commitment to long-term processes of change at the school level. Teachers have little incentive to commit to making changes in teaching approaches or any other aspect of school practice if experience tells them that the changes will be rescinded or modified before too long by a new group of administrators. Meanwhile, teachers bear the brunt of public criticism for failures which are not of their own making and are left to cope as best they can with insufficient support in implementing multiple top-down mandates designed to 'improve' their own performance. In many education systems it seems that there is a lack of trust in teachers and their professionalism. How they can be realistically expected to deliver high-quality language education to all children in their classes under these conditions is something of a mystery.

Educational Ecosystems and Early Language Learning

In response to perceived 'failures' in their own systems, education ministries around the world often seek to emulate the practice of countries that are successful in coveted international assessments such as PISA, but tend not to see the education system as a whole. If, for example, other governments truly wished to emulate the Finnish 'success' in education that we discussed in Chapter 6, they would recognise that it has not been an overnight success but is the product of many years of development within a specific sociocultural context, a crucial part of which was teachers' own insistence that they be regarded as equivalent to other professions, and that primary school teachers were not to be treated as less than secondary school teachers. As Simola (2005: 460) explains, 'An essential element in the upward movement of Finnish teachers was their exceptionally persistent striving for professionalism. As early as 1890, primary school teachers were claiming that their extension training should be organized at university level', the start of a decades-long process for professional recognition. The University College of Education was founded in the 1930s in Jyväskylä, and 'Starting in the late 1950s, the teachers' union actively demanded that the training of primary school teachers should be at the same level as that of grammar school teachers, i.e. university level' (Simola, 2005: 460), which culminated in 1979 with their training being raised to Master's degree level.

The 'miracle of education' (Niemi *et al.*, 2012) in Finland was far from an overnight success but was a long struggle, the result of which is that teaching in Finland is now a high-status profession and teachers are respected at all levels of society. Teacher preparation programmes are extremely competitive to enter and all Finnish teachers are educated to Master's level. Teachers are also trusted to implement the foundational goals of a core curriculum in accordance with the needs of the children in their classes, are not subject to constant classroom inspection, and are not continually preoccupied with preparing children for national-level standardised tests (which only occur at the very end of upper secondary education). At the subject level, Finnish teachers of English do not have to conform to expectations that they should use a certain percentage of English in their language classes and, indeed, they have no qualms about using the first language judiciously for classroom management, for discipline, for marking activity boundaries and even for talking about English grammar (Hautamäki, 2008; Miettinen, 2009). In English classes there is a focus on 'cultural skills', which includes knowing about the target culture and comparing it to Finnish culture. Teachers are expected to assess the learning outcomes of the children in their classes and adjust teaching accordingly. Alongside their own autonomy, teachers also help children to develop good language learning habits, including self-motivation and self-evaluation which are central to the educational ethos in Finnish schools at all levels and for all subjects.

Understanding what happens in any education system requires an appreciation of the context of the classroom, the school, and the local and national communities in which it is situated. Although there are similarities across systems and among schools, there are also many differences and each school is as unique as the children who attend it. When teachers are trained to a high level, given autonomy to interpret core curriculum goals according to the needs of the children in their classes and trusted to develop the educational potential of all the children in their classrooms, as in Finland, the unique nature of every child can be catered for appropriately.

Responding to the needs of individual children is, in contrast, much more difficult when top-down mandates dictate to teachers exactly what and how they should teach and when constant evaluation of both teachers and children impedes actual learning within a framework of the '21st century' transferable skills of, *inter alia*, critical thinking, creativity, problem solving, appreciation of diversity and global awareness (Chalkiadaki, 2018) that education systems proclaim are so important for society as a whole in the future. Every teacher in every classroom in every education system responds to the ecosystem around them but it is hard not to wonder whether some education systems are genuinely intent on developing independent, critical and creative learners or whether they would prefer to see most children develop into adults who conform to pre-existing social structures in which decisions are made by those who have long held power. Early language learning can, indeed, contribute to critical thinking, creativity, problem solving, appreciation of diversity and global awareness, but the experience explored in this book indicates that the potential inherent in introducing children to the numerous benefits of learning other languages is not at present being realised for the majority of children in school, whether the language is English in Malaysia, Sri Lanka, South Korea and Thailand, or Tamil as a second national language in Sri Lanka or French in Ontario, Canada. The contrasting experience of learning English in Finland reveals that, if language learning is to be successful, as much depends on language exposure being available in the context outside the classroom as what happens within it. Even then, the Finnish experience indicates that an exclusive focus on English is unlikely to be able to meet all future needs and that developing a multilingual 'national language reserve' is better able to meet needs in society at large, which are likely to be unpredictable.

Concluding Thoughts

International evidence indicates that there is too much failure and demotivation in early language learning experiences in many contexts around the world, which are caused by focusing exclusively in school systems on languages, primarily English, which have little place in society beyond the classroom. Language curricula often set unrealistic goals which fail to take account of local socioeducational realities and the specifics of language use in the context as well as being divorced from other areas of the school curriculum. Western-derived pedagogies are also too often mandated in classroom language teaching, focused exclusively on supposed direct communicative needs and rarely linked to other areas of children's school experience. In primary schools, rather than having a foreign language as a separate subject, it would seem to be more conducive to learning if the language was included as an element of a theme or topic-based approach to the curriculum. In this way, children could recognise the value of other languages – especially if they are present in the local or regional environment – in a direct relationship with other subject learning, discovering that different languages can organise the world in different ways. Similarly, they could learn to represent aspects of their own culture to others through another language, validating their own cultural experiences as equal to but different from others. An approach like this could potentially lead to greater intercultural understanding, an appreciation of other cultures and how they see the world, in addition to learning language relevant to children's educational experience. As Byram (1989: 22) notes, 'There is and has always been in foreign language teaching a contribution to the personal education of learners in terms both of individuals learning about themselves and of social beings learning about others'.

Furthermore, the exclusive focus in many education systems on English as the first foreign language from the early primary years reinforces inequality and is not the key to enhanced life chances for the majority of children that its proponents claim, but instead remains the preserve of elites who use it as one more way to maintain their privilege. Hence, it is my contention that many education systems would benefit from policies that reconceptualise early language learning away from an exclusive focus on English, beginning with languages with which teachers already have some familiarity and which are available locally (such as other Indigenous languages or immigrant languages) or regionally (such as the languages of neighbouring countries), while also fostering an affinity for other languages and cultures rather than focusing on specific proficiency targets. It is in the interest of all children that education systems worldwide stop perpetuating the myth of English as a panacea for economic development at the national level and social advancement at the personal level and instead focus on the benefit that is to be had for young learners in studying a multiplicity of languages – which could still include English alongside other languages – as windows on different ways of looking at the world. If governments really do have the best interests of all children in their education systems at heart, then there is no reason for persisting for so long with approaches that have clearly failed. Children deserve better from their education.

Notes

(1) As of July 2022, only the US has failed to ratify the UN Convention on the Rights of the Child, although it signed it in 1995. See https://tbinternet.ohchr.org/_layouts/15/TreatyBodyExternal/Treaty.aspx?Treaty=CRC&Lang=en
(2) In many countries a number of ancillary fees for children in schools means that education is not always completely free.
(3) Available at https://www.globalgoals.org/goals/4-quality-education/
(4) See https://tradingeconomics.com/south-korea/exports-by-country
(5) See https://tradingeconomics.com/thailand/exports-by-country
(6) See https://tradingeconomics.com/malaysia/exports-by-country
(7) 'Ajarn' is used as an honorific and means 'teacher' in Thai.

References

ADB (Asian Development Bank) (2019) *Asian Development Outlook 2019: Strengthening Disaster Resilience*. Manila: Asian Development Bank. See https://www.adb.org/sites/default/files/publication/492711/ado2019.pdf

Adesope, O.O., Lavin, T., Thompson, T. and Ungerleider, C. (2010) A systematic review and meta-analysis of the cognitive correlates of bilingualism. *Review of Educational Research* 80 (2), 207–245. doi:10.3102/0034654310368803

Agirdag, O. (2014) The long-term effects of bilingualism on children of immigration: Student bilingualism and future earnings. *International Journal of Bilingual Education and Bilingualism* 17 (4), 449–464. doi:10.1080/13670050.2013.816264

Ali, M.S. (2003) English language teaching in primary schools: Policy and implementation concerns. *IPBA E-Journal* 1–14.

Ali, N.L., Hamid, M.O. and Moni, K. (2011) English in primary education in Malaysia: Policies, outcomes and stakeholders' lived experiences. *Current Issues in Language Planning* 12 (2), 147–166. doi:10.1080/14664208.2011.584371

Alladi, S., Bak, T.H., Duggirala, V., Surampudi, B., Shailaja, M., Shukla, A.K., Chaudhuri, J.R. and Kaul, S. (2013) Bilingualism delays age at onset of dementia, independent of education and immigration status. *Neurology* 81 (22), 1938–1944. doi:10.1212/01.wnl.0000436620.33155.a4

Amnesty International (2019) *Sri Lanka 2019*. London: Amnesty International. See https://www.amnesty.org/en/countries/asia-and-the-pacific/sri-lanka/report-sri-lanka/

Amnesty International (2020) Amid pandemic, Sri Lanka pardons soldier convicted of massacre. *Amnesty International Research Report*, 30 April. London: Amnesty International. See https://www.amnesty.org/download/Documents/ASA3722472020ENGLISH.pdf

Amnesty International (2021) *Indigenous Peoples in Canada*. London: Amnesty International. See https://www.amnesty.ca/our-work/issues/indigenous-peoples/indigenous-peoples-in-canada

Appell, G.N. (2000) The Rungus Dusun of Sabah, Malaysia. In L.E. Sponsel (ed.) *Endangered Peoples of Southeast and East Asia: Struggles to Survive and Thrive* (pp. 194–208). Westport, CT: Greenwood Press.

Arcand, J.-L. and Grin, F. (2013) Language in economic development: Is English special and is linguistic fragmentation bad? In E.J. Erling and P. Seargeant (eds) *English and Development: Policy, Pedagogy and Globalization* (pp. 243–266). Bristol: Multilingual Matters.

Arda, S. and Doyran, F. (2017) Analysis of young learners' and teenagers' attitudes to English language learning. *International Journal of Curriculum and Instruction* 9 (2), 179–197.

Arnott, S. (2017) Second language education and micro-policy implementation in Canada: The meaning of pedagogical change. *Language Teaching Research* 21 (2), 258–254. doi:10.1177/1362168815619953

Arnott, S. (2019) Giving voice to our Core French students: Implications for attrition and the discourse on the benefits of learning FSL in Ontario. *McGill Journal of Education/Revue des sciences de l'éducation de McGill* 54 (3), 519–541. doi:10.7202/1069768ar

Aturupane, H. and Wickramanayake, D. (2011) *The Promotion of Social Cohesion through Education in Sri Lanka.* Washington, DC: World Bank.

Aturupane, H., Glewwe, P. and Wisniewski, S. (2013) The impact of school quality, socioeconomic factors, and child health on students' academic performance: Evidence from Sri Lankan primary schools. *Education Economics* 21 (1), 2–37. doi:10.1080/09645292.2010.511852

Azam, M., Chin, A. and Prakash, N. (2010) The returns to English language skills in India. Discussion Paper Series CPD No. 02/10. London: Centre for Research and Analysis of Migration, Department of Economics, University of London.

Azman, H. (2016) Implementation and challenges of English language education reform in Malaysian primary schools. *3L: The Southeast Asian Journal of English Language Studies* 22 (3), 65–78.

Baldauf, R.B., Kaplan, R.B., Kamwangamalu, N. and Bryant, P. (2011) Success or failure of primary second/foreign language programmes in Asia: What do the data tell us? *Current Issues in Language Planning* 12 (2), 309–323. doi:10.1080/14664208.2011.609715

Baltus, R. and Belhiah, H. (2013) Teaching practices of ESL teachers in Ontario. *International Journal of Language Studies* 7 (3), 89–118.

Bangkok Post (2016) Rid English of rote-learning. *Bangkok Post*, 6 June. See https://www.bangkokpost.com/opinion/opinion/1004593/rid-english-of-rote-learning

Bangkok Post (2019) Education needs reform. *Bangkok Post*, 19 July. See https://www.bangkokpost.com/opinion/opinion/1712476/education-needs-reform

Bar-Tal, D. and Rosen, Y. (2009) Peace education in societies involved in intractable conflicts: Direct and indirect models. *Review of Educational Research* 79 (2), 557–575. doi:10.3102/0034654308330969

Bekerman, Z. (2005) Complex contexts and ideologies: Bilingual education in conflict-ridden areas. *Journal of Language, Identity & Education* 4 (1), 1–20. doi:10.1207/s15327701jlie0401_1

Bialystok, E. (2011) Reshaping the mind: The benefits of bilingualism. *Canadian Journal of Experimental Psychology/Revue canadienne de psychologie expérimentale* 65 (4), 229–235. doi:10.1037/a0025406

Bialystok, E. (2018) Bilingual education for young children: Review of the effects and consequences. *International Journal of Bilingual Education and Bilingualism* 21 (6), 666–679. doi:10.1080/13670050.2016.1203859

Bourdieu, P. (2001) *Contre-feux 2: Pour un Mouvement Social Européen [Counter-fire 2: For a European Social Movement].* Paris: Raisons d'agir.

Bradford, A. (2007) Motivational orientations in under-researched FLL contexts: Findings from Indonesia. *RELC Journal* 38 (3), 302–323. doi:10.1177/0033688207085849

Braun, A. (2017) Education policy and the intensification of teachers' work: The changing professional culture of teaching in England and implications for social justice. In S. Parker, K. Gulson and T. Gale (eds) *Policy and Inequality in Education* (pp. 169–185). Singapore: Springer.

Brown, G.K. (2007) Making ethnic citizens: The politics and practice of education in Malaysia. *International Journal of Educational Development* 27, 318–330. doi:10.1016/j.ijedudev.2006.12.002

Brubacher, K. (2013) Teachers' discourses on teaching students of elementary school English literacy development in Ontario. *TESL Canada Journal* 30 (2), 18–35. doi:10.18806/tesl.v30i2.1139

Brunfaut, T. and Green, R. (2019) TRANSFORM project: English language assessment in Sri Lanka. OUTPUT 1 Research paper on English and employability in Sri Lanka. Lancaster: University of Lancaster.

Bruthiaux, P. (2002) Hold your courses: Language education, language choice, and economic development. *TESOL Quarterly* 36 (3), 275–296. doi:10.2307/3588414

Brutt-Griffler, J. (2002) Class, ethnicity, and language rights: An analysis of British colonial policy in Lesotho and Sri Lanka and some implications for language policy. *Journal of Language, Identity & Education* 1 (3), 207–234. doi:10.1207/S15327701JLIE0103_3

Burridge, T. (2010) Why do Finland's schools get the best results? *BBC World News America*, 7 April. See http://news.bbc.co.uk/2/hi/programmes/world_news_america/8601207.stm

Bush, K. and Saltarelli, D. (2000) *The Two Faces of Education in Ethnic Conflict: Towards a Peacebuilding Education for Children*. Florence: Innocenti Research Centre, UN Children's Fund.

Butler, Y.G. (2005) Comparative perspectives towards communicative activities among elementary school teachers in South Korea, Japan and Taiwan. *Language Teaching Research* 9 (4), 423–446.

Butler, Y.G. (2015) English language education among young learners in East Asia: A review of current research (2004–2014). *Language Teaching* 48 (3), 303–342. doi:10.1017/S0261444815000105

Byram, M. (1989) *Cultural Studies in Foreign Language Education*. Clevedon: Multilingual Matters.

Byram, M. and Wagner, M. (2018) Making a difference: Language teaching for intercultural and international dialogue. *Foreign Language Annals* 51 (1), 140–151. doi:10.1111/flan.12319

Cameron, D. (2002) Globalization and the teaching of 'communication skills'. In D. Block and D. Cameron (eds) *Globalization and Language Teaching* (pp. 67–82). London: Routledge.

Carless, D. and Walker, E. (2006) Effective team teaching between local and native-speaking English teachers. *Language and Education* 20 (6), 463–477. doi:10.2167/le627.0

Cha, Y.-K. and Ham, S.-H. (2008) The impact of English on the school curriculum. In B. Spolsky and F. Hult (eds) *The Handbook of Educational Linguistics* (pp. 313–327). London: Wiley-Blackwell.

Chalkiadaki, A. (2018) A systematic literature review of 21st century skills and competencies in primary education. *International Journal of Instruction* 11 (3), 1–16. doi:10.12973/iji.2018.1131a

Chan, K. (2021) The time I was told my daughter needed to speak English in order to do well. *CBC Parents*, 18 May. See https://www.cbc.ca/parents/learning/view/the-time-i-was-told-my-daughter-needed-to-speak-english-in-order-to-do-well

Chang, E.S. (2016) Kirogi women's psychological well-being: The relative contributions of marital quality, mother–child relationship quality, and youth's educational adjustment. *Journal of Family Issues* 39 (1), 209–229. doi:10.1177/0192513X16632265

Chang, K. (2015) Pedagogical approaches in the Republic of Korea. In E.H.-F. Law and U. Miura (eds) *Transforming Teaching and Learning in Asia and the Pacific: Case Studies from Seven Countries* (pp. 67–89). Paris and Bangkok: UNESCO.

Chang, K., Kim, M. and Hayes, D. (2006) Curriculum and materials development for teaching English as a subsequent language to young learners: Research and systemic change. Research Report RRC 2006-14. Seoul: Korea Institute of Curriculum and Evaluation.

Childs, K. (2017) The last Veddas of Sri Lanka. *New Internationalist*, 10 January. See https://newint.org/features/web-exclusive/2017/01/10/the-last-veddas-of-sri-lanka

Cho, J. (2014) Understanding the importance of English education in South Korea and exploring the reasons why South Korean students come to a university in the Midwest. Unpublished thesis, Graduate College, University of Nebraska.

Cho, J. and Huh, J. (2017) New education policies and practices in South Korea. *UNESCO Bangkok*, 20 December. See https://bangkok.unesco.org/content/new-education-policies-and-practices-south-korea

Choe, S., Ku, J., Kim, J., Park, S., Oh, E., Kim, J. and Baek, H. (2013) Strategies for improving the affective characteristics of Korean students based on the results of PISA and TIMSS. Research Report RRE 2013-8. Seoul: Korea Institute for Curriculum and Evaluation.

Choi, T.-H. (2015) The impact of the 'Teaching English through English' policy on teachers and teaching in South Korea. *Current Issues in Language Planning* 16 (3), 201–220. doi:10.1080/14664208.2015.970727

Choi, Y.-H. (2006) Impact of politico-economic situations on English language education in Korea. *English Teaching* 61 (4), 3–26.

Chukhlantseva, E. (2020) 'I learn languages. What's your superpower?', says 5-year-old Julius from Finland. *Learning Scoop*, 30 March. See https://learningscoop.fi/i-learn-languages-whats-your-superpower-says-a-5-year-old-julius-from-finland-2-2/

Chumak-Horbatsch, R. (2008) Early bilingualism: Children of immigrants in an English-language childcare center. *Psychology of Language and Communication* 12 (1), 3–27. doi:10.2478/v10057-008-0001-2

Chung, J. and Choi, T. (2016) English education policies in South Korea: Planned and enacted. In R. Kirkpatrick (ed.) *English Language Education Policy in Asia* (pp. 281–299). New York: Springer.

Colclough, C. (1982) The impact of primary schooling on economic development: A review of the evidence. *World Development* 10 (3), 167–185.

Colenso, P. (2005) Education and social cohesion: Developing a framework for education sector reform in Sri Lanka. *Compare* 35 (4), 411–428. doi:10.1080/03057920500331470

Cook, V. (2001) Using the first language in the classroom. *Canadian Modern Language Review* 57 (3), 402–423. doi:10.3138/cmlr.57.3.402

COPA (Centre Ontarien de Prévention des Agressions) (2018) *Elementary School Guide for Newcomers to Ontario*. See https://settlement.org/downloads/SWIS/Elementary.pdf

Coperahewa, S. (2009) The language planning situation in Sri Lanka. *Current Issues in Language Planning* 10 (1), 69–150. doi:10.1080/14664200902894660

Copland, F., Garton, S. and Burns, A. (2014) Challenges in teaching English to young learners: Global perspectives and local realities. *TESOL Quarterly* 48 (4), 738–762.

Cornell University, INSEAD and WIPO (2019) *The Global Innovation Index 2019: Creating Healthy Lives – the Future of Medical Innovation*. Ithaca, NY, Fontainebleau and Geneva: Cornell University, INSEAD and WIPO.

Council of Europe (n.d.) Plurilingual and intercultural education. European Centre for Modern Languages of the Council of Europe. See https://https://www.ecml.at/Thematicareas/PlurilingualEducation/tabid/1631/language/en-GB/Default.aspx

Council of Europe (2020) *Common European Framework of Reference for Languages: Learning, Teaching, Assessment – Companion Volume*. Strasbourg: Council of Europe. See https://rm.coe.int/common-european-framework-of-reference-for-languages-learning-teaching/16809ea0d4

Coyne, G. (2015) Language education policies and inequality in Africa: Cross-national empirical evidence. *Comparative Education Review* 59, 619–637.

CPF (Canadian Parents for French) (2020) *The State of French Second Language Education in Ontario*. See https://on.cpf.ca/files/2021/02/State-of-FSL-Education-in-Ontario-November-2020.pdf

Cummins, J. (2014) To what extent are Canadian second language policies evidence-based? Reflections on the intersections of research and policy. *Frontiers in Psychology* 5 (358), 1–10. doi:10.3389/fpsyg.2014.00358

Davis, C.P. (2018) Muslims in Sri Lankan language politics: A study of Tamil- and English-medium education. *International Journal of the Sociology of Language* 253, 125–147.

Davis, S.C., Leman, P.J. and Barrett, M. (2007) Children's implicit and explicit ethnic group attitudes, ethnic group identification and self-esteem. *International Journal of Behavioural Development* 31 (5), 514–525. doi:10.1177/0165025407081461

Dearden, J. (2014) *English as a Medium of Instruction: A Growing Global Phenomenon*. London: British Council.

DeKeyser, R. (2013) Age effects in second language learning: Stepping stones toward better understanding. *Language Learning* 63 (Supplement 1), 52–67. doi:10.1111/j.1467-9922.2012.00737.x

Department of Census and Statistics (1952) *Census of Ceylon, 1946*. Colombo: Government Printer.

Department of Census and Statistics (2017) *Sri Lanka Labour Demand Survey – 2017*. Battaramulla: Department of Census and Statistics, Ministry of National Policies and Economic Affairs.

Department of Culture and Heritage (n.d.) *Official Languages*. Nunavut: Government of Nunavut. See https://www.gov.nu.ca/culture-and-heritage/information/official-languages

DFID and World Bank (2000) Towards social harmony in education. Unpublished report. Colombo: Department for International Development (DFID) and World Bank.

Don, Z.H. and Abdullah, M.H. (2019) The reform of English education in Malaysia. *MOE*, 22 May. See https://www.moe.gov.my/en/menumedia/printed-media/newspaper-clippings/the-reform-of-english-language-education-in-malaysia-free-malaysia-today-22-mei-2019

Draper, J. (2015) Towards a curriculum for the Thai Lao of northeast Thailand? *Current Issues in Language Planning* 16 (3), 238–258. doi:10.1080./14664208.2015.1023420

Draper, J. (2019) Language education policy in Thailand. In R. Kirkpatrick and A.J. Liddicoat (eds) *The Routledge International Handbook of Language Education Policy in Asia* (pp. 229–242). London: Routledge.

DSBN (District School Board of Niagara) (2020) *Indigenous Education Report, September 2019–June 2020*. St Catherines, Ontario: District School Board of Niagara. See https://www.dsbn.org/docs/default-source/indigenous-education/indigenous-ed-report-june2020.pdf?sfvrsn=6030461f_4

Dundar, H., Millot, B., Riboud, M., Shojo, M., Aturupane, H., Goyal, S. and Raju, D. (2017) *Sri Lanka Education Sector Assessment: Achievements, Challenges, and Policy Options*. Directions in Development, Washington, DC: World Bank. doi:10.1596/978-1-4648-1052-7. License: Creative Commons Attribution CC BY 3.0 IGO

EF (Education First) (2020) *EF English Proficiency Index: A Ranking of 100 Countries and Regions by English Skills*. Lucerne: Education First. See https://www.ef.com/assetscdn/WIBIwq6RdJvcD9bc8RMd/legacy/__/~/media/centralefcom/epi/downloads/full-reports/v10/ef-epi-2020-english.pdf

Eliadis, P. (2021) Pearl Eliadis on the overreach of Bill 96. *MAX Policy*, 6 December. See https://www.mcgill.ca/maxbellschool/article/the-overreach-of-bill-96

ELSQC (English Language Standards and Quality Council) (2015) *English Language Education Reform in Malaysia: The Roadmap 2015–2025*. Kuala Lumpur: Ministry of Education Malaysia.

Enever, J. (2011) Policy. In J. Enever (ed.) *ELLiE, Early Language Learning in Europe* (pp. 23–42). London: British Council.

Enever, J. (2018) *Policy and Politics in Global Primary English*. Oxford: Oxford University Press.

Erling, E.J. (2015) *The Relationship between English and Employability in the Middle East and North Africa*. Manchester: British Council.

Erling, E.J. and Seargeant, P. (eds) (2013) *English and Development: Policy, Pedagogy and Globalization*. Bristol: Multilingual Matters.

Euromonitor International (2012) *The Benefits of the English Language for Individuals and Societies: Quantitative Indicators from Algeria, Egypt, Iraq, Jordan, Lebanon, Morocco, Tunisia and Yemen*. London: Euromonitor International.

Fenyvesi, K. (2020) English learning motivation of young learners in Danish primary schools. *Language Teaching Research* 24 (5), 690–713. doi:10.1177/1362168818804835

Fitzgerald, S., McGrath-Stamp, S. and Tracey, S. (2019) Intensification of teachers' work under devolution: A 'tsunami' of paperwork. *Journal of Industrial Relations* 61 (5), 613–636. doi:10.1177/0022185618801396

Fitzpatrick, D. (2011) Making sense of the English language policy in Thailand: An exploration of teachers' practices and dispositions. Doctoral thesis, University of Exeter. See https://ore.exeter.ac.uk/repository/handle/10036/3314

FNAE (Finnish National Agency for Education) (2017) *Finland Invests in Early Language Learning*. Helsinki: FNAE. See https://www.oph.fi/sites/default/files/documents/finland_invests_in_early_language_learning.pdf

FNAE (Finnish National Agency for Education) (2018) *Finnish Education in a Nutshell*. Helsinki: FNAE. See https://www.oph.fi/sites/default/files/documents/finnish_education_in_a_nutshell.pdf

FNAE (Finnish National Agency for Education) (2019) *What Languages Do Pupils Study in Basic Education? Statistics on Language Learning and Teaching in Finland*. Helsinki: FNAE. See https://www.oph.fi/sites/default/files/documents/factsexpress1c_2019.pdf

FNAE (Finnish National Agency for Education) (2020) *Funding in Pre-Primary and Basic Education Supports Equity and Equality*. Helsinki: FNAE. See https://www.oph.fi/sites/default/files/documents/funding-pre-primary-and-basic-education-2020_0.pdf

FNBE (Finnish National Board of Education) (2016) *National Core Curriculum for Basic Education 2014*. Helsinki: FNBE.

Foreman-Pack, J. and Wang, Y. (2014) *The Costs to the UK of Language Deficiencies as a Barrier to UK Engagement in Exporting: A Report to UK Trade & Investment*. London: UK Trade and Investment (UKTI) Research.

Franco, A. and Roach, S. (2018) An assessment of the English proficiency of the Thai workforce and its implication for the ASEAN Economic Community: An empirical enquiry. *Open Journal of Business and Management* 6, 658–677. doi:10.4236/ojbm.2018.63050

Franz, J. and Teo, A. (2017) 'A2 is normal' – Thai secondary school teachers' encounters with the CEFR. *RELC Journal* 49 (3), 322–328. doi:10.1177/0033688217738816

Friedrich, D. (2021) Controversies around endangered Indigenous languages in the Canadian Arctic (Part I). *The Arctic Institute*, 4 February. See https://www.thearcticinstitute.org/controversies-endangered-indigenous-languages-canadian-arctic-part-i/

Fry, G.W. (2018) Synthesis, rethinking Thai education: Paradoxes, trends, challenges and opportunities. In G.W. Fry (ed.) *Education in Thailand: An Old Elephant in Search of a New Mahout* (pp. 677–709). Singapore: Springer.

Fry, G.W. and Bi, H. (2013) The evolution of educational reform in Thailand: The Thai educational paradox. *Journal of Educational Administration* 51 (3), 290–319. doi:10.1108/09578231311311483

Gall, L.G. (2015) Québec referendum (1995). *The Canadian Encyclopedia*. See https://www.thecanadianencyclopedia.ca/en/article/quebec-referendum-1995

Garton, S. (2014) Unresolved issues and new challenges in teaching English to young learners: The case of South Korea. *Current Issues in Language Planning* 15 (2), 201–219. doi:10.1080/14664208.2014.858657

Genesee, F. (2007) French immersion and at-risk students: A review of research evidence. *Canadian Modern Language Review* 63 (5), 655–687. doi:10.3138/cmlr.63.5.655

Gill, S.K. (2012) The complexities of re-reversal of language-in-education policy in Malaysia. In A. Kirkpatrick and R. Sussex (eds) *English as an International Language in Asia: Implications for Language Education* (pp. 45–61). Dordrecht: Springer.

Gill, S.K. and Shaari, A.H. (2019) Malaysia's complex language policy journey via Bahasa Melayu and English. In A. Kirkpatrick and A.J. Liddicoat (eds) *The Routledge International Handbook of Language Education Policy in Asia* (pp. 257–271). London: Routledge.

Government of Canada (2019) Government of Canada introduces historic legislation on Indigenous languages. *News Release*, 5 February. See https://www.canada.ca/en/cana dian-heritage/news/2019/02/government-of-canadaintroduces-historiclegislationonin digenous-languages.html

Government of Canada (2021) *Provinces and Territories*. See https://www.canada.ca/en/ intergovernmental-affairs/services/provinces-territories.html

Graddol, D. (2006) *English Next: Why Global English May Mean the End of 'English as a Foreign Language'*. London: British Council. See https://www.teachingenglish.org. uk/sites/teacheng/files/pub_english_next.pdf

Grant, C. (2017) *The Contribution of Education to Economic Growth*. K4D Helpdesk Report. Brighton: Institute of Development Studies.

Gunesekera, M. (2005) *The Postcolonial Identity of Sri Lankan English*. Colombo: Katha Publishers.

Gustavsson, B. (1997) Life-long learning reconsidered. In S. Walters (ed.) *Globalization, Adult Education and Training – Impacts and Issues* (pp. 237–249). London and New York: ZED Books.

Halinen, I. (2018) The new educational curriculum in Finland. In M. Matthes, L. Pulkkinen, C. Clouder and B. Heys (eds) *Improving the Quality of Childhood in Europe, Vol. 7* (pp. 75–89). Brussels: Alliance for Childhood European Network Foundation.

Hallinger, P. (2004) Meeting the challenges of cultural leadership: The changing roles of principals in Thailand. *Discourse: Studies in the Cultural Politics of Education* 25 (1), 61–73. doi:10.1080/0159630042000178482

Hallinger, P. and Bryant, D.A. (2013) Synthesis of findings from 15 years of educational reform in Thailand: Lessons on leading educational change in East Asia. *International Journal of Leadership in Education* 16 (4), 399–418. doi:10.1080/13603124.2013.77 0076

Hallinger, P. and Lee, M. (2011) A decade of education reform in Thailand: Broken prom ise or impossible dream? *Cambridge Journal of Education* 41 (2), 139–158. doi:10.10 80/0305764X.2011.572868

Hanewald, R. (2016) The impact of English on educational policies and practices in Malaysia. In R. Kirkpatrick (ed.) *English Language Education Policy in Asia* (pp. 181–198). New York: Springer.

Hannibal Jensen, S. (2017) Gaming as an English language learning resource among young children in Denmark. *CALICO Journal* 34 (1), 1–19. doi:10.1558/cj.29519

Hardman, J. and A-Rahman, N. (2014) Teachers and the implementation of a new English curriculum in Malaysia. *Language, Culture and Curriculum* 27 (3), 260–277. doi:10 .1080/07908318.2014.980826

Hargreaves, L., Cunningham, M., Hansen, A., MacIntyre, D., Oliver, C. and Pell, T. (2007) *The Status of Teachers and the Teaching Profession in England: Views from Inside and Outside the Profession. Final Report of the Teacher Status Project*. London: Department for Education and Skills.

Harris, I.M. (2004) Peace education theory. *Journal of Peace Education* 1 (1), 5–20. doi:10.1080/1740020032000178276

Harris, S. and Lewer, N. (2008) Peace education in conflict zones – experience from northern Sri Lanka. *Journal of Peace Education* 5 (2), 127–140. doi:10.1080/17400200802264321

Hashim, A. (2009) Not plain sailing: Malaysia's language choice in policy and education. *AILA Review* 22, 36–51. doi:10.1075/aila.22.04has

Hattie, J. (2003) Teachers make a difference. What is the research evidence? Paper pre sented at the Building Teacher Quality: What Does the Research Tell Us? ACER Research Conference, Melbourne, Australia. See http://research.acer.edu.au/ research_conference_2003/4

Hautamäki, T. (2008) Teachers' linguistic choices during language instruction – a com parative study between special needs and basic education. Unpublished BA thesis, University of Jyväskylä.

Havelock, R.G. and Huberman, A.M. (1977) *Solving Educational Problems: The Planning and Reality of Education in Developing Countries.* Paris: UNESCO.

Hayes, D. (1995) In-service teacher development: Some basic principles. *ELT Journal* 49, 252–261. doi:10.1093/elt/49.3.252

Hayes, D. (2000) Cascade training and teachers' professional development. *ELT Journal* 54 (2), 135–145. doi:10.1093/elt/54.2.135

Hayes, D. (2002) Language, textbooks and perspectives on social harmony in Sri Lanka. In J. Lo Bianco (ed.) *Development and Language: Global Influences and Local Effects* (pp. 181–204). Melbourne: Language Australia.

Hayes, D. (2006) Developing teachers in the developing world of Sri Lanka. In M. McCloskey, J. Orr and M. Dolitsky (eds) *Teaching English as a Foreign Language in Primary School* (pp. 141–155). Alexandria, VA: TESOL Publications.

Hayes, D. (2008a) Becoming a teacher of English in Thailand. *Language Teaching Research* 12 (4), 471–494.

Hayes, D. (2008b) *Primary English Language Teaching in Vietnam: A Research Study.* Hanoi: Ministry of Education and Training.

Hayes, D. (2010) 'Education is all about opportunities, isn't it?' A biographical perspective on learning and teaching English in Sri Lanka. *Harvard Educational Review* 80, 517–540.

Hayes, D. (2011) Primary English language teaching: Another obstacle to achievement for the world's oor?/La enseñanza del inglés en la Educación Primaria: ¿otro obstáculo para el logro educativo de los más desfavorecidos? In P. Powell-Davies (ed.) *Word for Word: The Social, Economic and Political Impact of Spanish and English/Palabra por Palabra: El Impactico Social, Económico y Político del Español y del Inglés* (pp. 329–344). Madrid: British Council, Instituto Cervantes & Santillana.

Hayes, D. (2012) Mismatched perspectives: In-service teacher education policy and practice in South Korea. In C. Tribble (ed.) *Managing Change in English Language Teaching: Lessons from Experience* (pp. 99–104). London: British Council.

Hayes, D. (2013) Narratives of experience: Teaching English in Sri Lanka and Thailand. In G. Barkhuizen (ed.) *Narrative Research in Applied Linguistics* (pp. 62–82). Cambridge: Cambridge University Press.

Hayes, D. (2016) The value of learning English in Thailand and its impact on Thai: Perspectives from university students. *Asia Pacific Journal of Education* 36 (1), 73–91. doi:10.1080/02188791.2014.924390

Hayes, D. (2017a) Evaluation of the 'Boot Camp' in-service teacher-training programme for the Office of the Basic Education Commission, Ministry of Education, and the British Council, Thailand. Unpublished report.

Hayes, D. (2017b) Fallacies affecting policy and practice in the teaching of English as a foreign language in state primary schools in Asia. *Asia-Pacific Journal of Education* 37 (2), 179–192. doi:10.1080/02188791.2016.1240660

Hayes, D. (2019) Continuing professional development/continuous professional learning for English language teachers. In S. Walsh and S. Mann (eds) *Routledge Handbook of English Language Teacher Education* (pp. 155–168). London: Routledge.

Hayes, D. (2020) Language education policy and practice in state education systems: Promoting effective practice in foreign language education for young learners. *Language Teaching for Young Learners* 2 (2), 240–261. doi:10.1075/lytl.19017.hay

Hayes, D. and Chang, K. (2014) The politics of comparison: The global and the local in English language teaching and teacher education. In S. Ben Said and L.J. Zhang (eds) *Language Teachers and Teaching: Global Perspectives, Local Initiatives* (pp. 11–25). London: Routledge.

Hayes, D., Perera, M. and Williams, K. (2016) Second national language education, inter-ethnic attitudes and 'positive peace' in Sri Lanka. Unpublished report.

Heinzmann, S. (2013) *Young Language Learners' Motivation and Attitudes: Longitudinal, Comparative and Explanatory Perspectives.* London: A & C Black.

Heo, J. (2013) A case study of team teaching and team teachers in Korean primary schools. Unpublished PhD thesis, Centre for Applied Linguistics, University of Warwick. See http://wrap.warwick.ac.uk/58689/1/WRAP_THESIS_Heo_2013.pdf

Hettiarachchi, S. (2013) English language teacher motivation in Sri Lankan public schools. *Journal of Language Teaching and Research* 4 (1), 1–11. doi:10.4304/jltr.4.1.1-11

Hiew, W. (2016) English language teachers' perceptions and the impact of a standardised professional development programme in Sabah, Malaysia: A mixed methods study. Unpublished PhD thesis, Macquarie University.

Hildén, R. and Kantelinen, R. (2012) Language education – foreign languages. In H. Niemi, A. Toom and A. Kallioniemi (eds) *Miracle of Education: The Principles and Practices of Teaching and Learning in Finnish Schools* (pp. 161–176). Rotterdam: Sense.

Hildén, R., Härmälä, M., Rautopuro, J., Huhtanen, M., Puukko, M. and Silverström, C. (2015) *Outcomes of Language Learning at the End of Basic Education in 2013*. Helsinki: Finnish Education Evaluation Centre. See https://helda.helsinki.fi//bitstream/handle/10138/230315/summary.pdf?sequence=1

Hiver, P. (2013) The interplay of possible language teacher selves in professional development choices. *Language Teaching Research* 17 (2), 210–227. doi:10.1177/1362168813475944

Holliday, A. (1994) *Appropriate Methodology and Social Context*. Cambridge: Cambridge University Press.

Huebner, T. (2019) Language policy and bilingual education in Thailand: Reconciling the past, anticipating the future. *LEARN Journal: Language Education and Acquisition Research Network Journal* 1 (2), 19–29.

Hultberg, P., Santandreu Calonge, D. and Kim, S.-H. (2017) Education policy in South Korea: A contemporary model of human capital accumulation? *Cogent Economics & Finance* 5 (1), 1–16. doi:10.1080/23322039.2017.1389804

Ibrahim, N.A. (1991) In-service training in Malaysia for the New Primary School Curriculum (KBSR). In K.M. Lewin with J.S. Stuart (eds) *Educational Innovation in Developing Countries: Case Studies of Change Makers* (pp. 95–126). London: Macmillan.

ICG (International Crisis Group) (2011) *Reconciliation in Sri Lanka: Harder Than Ever*. Asia Report No. 209, 18 July. Colombo and Brussels: ICG.

Indigenous Languages and Education Secretariat (n.d.) *Languages Overview*. See https://www.ece.gov.nt.ca/en/services/le-secretariat-de-leducation-et-des-langues-autochtones/languages-overview

Irshad, F. (2018) Trilingualism, national integration, and social coexistence in postwar Sri Lanka. In I. Liyanage (ed.) *Multilingual Education Yearbook*. New York: Springer International.

Jayawickrema, E., Jayawickrema, N. and Miller, L. (2010) Triumphalism, fear and humiliation: The psychological legacy of Sri Lanka's civil war. *Dynamics of Asymmetric Conflict* 3 (3), 208–222. doi:10.1080/17467586.2010.531031

Jeon, M. (2020) Native-English speaking teachers' experiences in East-Asian language programs. *System* 88 (1), 1–11. doi:10.1016/j.system.2019.102178

Ji-hye, S. (2021) English education should start at earlier age: Lawmaker. *Korea Herald*, 18 February. See http://www.koreaherald.com/view.php?ud=20210218000810&ACE_SEARCH=1

Jo, S. (2008) English education and teacher education in South Korea. *Journal of Education for Teaching* 34 (4), 371–381. doi:10.1080/02607470802401594

Johnson, D., Umeda, K. and Oh, K. (2017) Teaching English through English: An analysis of a sample of Japanese and South Korean textbooks. *The Language Teacher* 41 (6), 15–19.

Kabilan, M.K. and Veratharaju, K. (2013) Professional development needs of primary school English-language teachers in Malaysia. *Professional Development in Education* 39 (3), 330–351. doi:10.1080/19415257.2012.762418

Kana, G. (2017) Yong: English is key for M'sia to remain competitive. *The Star*, 6 March. See https://www.pressreader.com/malaysia/the-star-malaysia-starbiz/20170306/281539405747394

Kang, D.-M. (2013) EFL teachers' language use for classroom discipline: A look at complex interplay of variables. *System* 41 (1), 149–163. doi:10.1016/j.system.2013.01.002

Kang, H.D. (2012) Primary school English education in Korea: From policy to practice. In B. Spolsky and Y.-I. Moon (eds) *Primary School English-language Education in Asia: From Policy to Practice* (pp. 59–82). New York: Routledge.

Kang, H.-S. (2017) Is English being challenged by Mandarin in South Korea? *English Today* 33 (4), 40–46. doi:10.1017/S0266078417000220

Kapur, R. (2019) Post-election Sri Lanka: Inter-communal relations in Gotabaya Rajapakse's presidency. *Middle East Institute*, 23 December. See https://www.mei.edu/publications/post-election-sri-lanka-inter-communal-relations-gotabaya-rajapaksas-presidency#_ftn7

Katsuno, M. (2012) Teachers' professional identities in an era of testing accountability in Japan: The case of teachers in low-performing schools. *Education Research International* 2, 1–8. doi:10.1155/2012/930279

Kaur, A., Young, D. and Kirkpatrick, R. (2016) English education policy in Thailand: Why the poor results? In R. Kirkpatrick (ed.) *English Language Education Policy in Asia* (pp. 345–361). New York: Springer International.

Khoman, S. (2018) The financing of Thai education. In G.W. Fry (ed.) *Education in Thailand: An Old Elephant in Search of a New Mahout* (pp. 579–596). Singapore: Springer.

Kim, B.-R. (2015) The English fever in South Korea: Focusing on the problem of early English education. *Journal of Education and Social Policy* 2 (2), 117–124.

Kim, G.-J. (2002) Education policies and reform in South Korea. In World Bank (ed.) *Secondary Education in Africa: Strategies for Renewal* (pp. 29–40). Washington, DC: Human Development Sector, Africa Region, World Bank.

Kim, J.-W. (2004) Education reform policies and classroom teaching in South Korea. *International Studies in Sociology of Education* 14 (2), 125–145.

Kim, J., Cho, W., Moon, M., Park, H., Cho, J.-M., Park, J.-H., Choi, Y. and Song, J. (2015) *Education for All 2015. National Review Report: Republic of Korea.* Prepared for the World Education Forum, Incheon, Republic of Korea, 19–22 May.

Kim, N.-Y. (2019) Teachers' administrative workload crowding out instructional activities. *Asia Pacific Journal of Education* 39 (1), 31–49. doi:10.1080/02188791.2019.1572592

Kim, T.-Y. (2011) Korean elementary school students' English learning demotivation: A comparative survey study. *Asia Pacific Education Review* 12, 1–11. doi:10.1007/s12564-010-9113-1

Kim, T.-Y. and Seo, H.-S. (2012) Elementary school students' foreign language learning demotivation: A mixed methods study of Korean EFL context. *Asia-Pacific Education Researcher* 21 (1), 160–171.

Kim, S. and Lee, J.-H. (2010) Private tutoring and demand for education in South Korea. *Economic Development and Cultural Change* 58 (2), 259–296. doi:10.1086/648186

KMOE (Korea Ministry of Education) (2016) *Happy Education for All: Creative Talent Shapes the Future. 2016 Education Policy Plans.* Sejong: Ministry of Education.

KMOE (Korea Ministry of Education) (2017) *Education in Korea 2017.* Sejong: Ministry of Education.

KMOE (Korea Ministry of Education) (2018a) New textbooks for the 2015 National Curriculum. *Press Release*, 9 March. See http://english.moe.go.kr/boardCnts/view.do?boardID=265&boardSeq=73479&lev=0&searchType=null&statusYN=C&page=4&s=english&m=0301&opType=N

KMOE (Korea Ministry of Education) (2018b) Ministry of Education allows English education in kindergartens. *Press* Release, 12 October. See http://english.moe.go.kr/boardCnts/view.do?boardID=265&boardSeq=75491&lev=0&searchType=null&statusYN=C&page=3&s=english&m=0301&opType=N

Knouzi, I. and Mady, C. (2014) Voices of resilience from the bottom rungs: The stories of three elementary Core French teachers in Ontario. *Alberta Journal of Educational Research* 60 (1), 62–80. See https://cdm.ucalgary.ca/index.php/ajer/article/view/55764

Korea Times (2014) English learning fervor. *Korea Times*, 14 February. See http://www.koreatimes.co.kr/www/opinion/2014/02/137_151626.html

Korea Times (2019) S. Korea holds national college entrance exam. *Korea Times*, 14 November. See http://www.koreatimes.co.kr/www/nation/2019/11/181_278688.html?utm_source=dable

Kosonen, K. (2008) Literacy in local languages in Thailand: Language maintenance in a globalised world. *International Journal of Bilingual Education and Bilingualism* 11 (2), 170–188. doi:10.2167/beb492.0

KPM (Kementarian Pendidikan Malaysia) (2001) *Sukatan Pelajaran Kurikulum Bersepadu Sekolah Rendah: Bahasa Inggeris*. Kuala Lumpur: KPM.

Kulsiri, S. (2006) A critical analysis of the 2001 national foreign language standards-based curriculum in the Thai school system. Unpublished PhD thesis, University of Canberra.

Kumashiro, K.K. (2012) *Bad Teacher! How Blaming Teachers Distorts the Bigger Picture*. New York: Teachers College Press.

Kyu-wook, O. (2013) English proficiency in Korea unimproved. *Korea Herald*, 6 November. See http://www.koreaherald.com/view.php?ud=20131106000844

Lapkin, S., Mady, C. and Arnott, S. (2009) Research perspectives on Core French: A literature review. *Canadian Journal of Applied Linguistics* 12 (2), 6–30. See https://journals.lib.unb.ca/index.php/CJAL/article/view/19936

Lathapipat, D. (2018) Inequalities in educational attainment. In G.W. Fry (ed.) *Education in Thailand: An Old Elephant in Search of a New Mahout* (pp. 345–372). Singapore: Springer.

Lathapipat, D. and Sondergand, L. (2016) Thailand's small school challenge and options for quality education. *World Bank Blogs*, 4 October. See https://blogs.worldbank.org/eastasiapacific/thailand-s-small-school-challenge-and-options-quality-education

Lee, C. (2019) Boosting English standards. *The Star*, 9 June. See https://www.thestar.com.my/news/education/2019/06/09/boosting-english-standards/#cxrecs_s

Lee, J.-A. (2009) Teachers' sense of efficacy in teaching English, perceived English language proficiency, and attitudes toward the English language: A case of Korean public elementary school teachers. Doctoral dissertation, Ohio State University. OhioLINK Electronic Theses and Dissertations Center. http://rave.ohiolink.edu/etdc/view?acc_num=osu1233648070

Lee, K. (2014) The politics of teaching English in South Korean schools: Language ideologies and language policy. PhD dissertation, University of Pennsylvania. See http://repository.upenn.edu/edissertations/1339

Lee, J.-H., Han, M.W. and McKerrow, R.E. (2010) English or perish: How contemporary South Korea received, accommodated, and internalized English and American modernity. *Language and Intercultural Communication* 10 (4), 337–357. doi:10.1080/14708477.2010.497555

Leesa-Nguansuk, S. (2021) Nation rises one spot to 28th on IMD Index. *Bangkok Post*, 18 June. See https://www.bangkokpost.com/business/2134215/nation-rises-one-spot-to-28th-on-imd-index

Lenneberg, E. (1967) *Biological Foundations of Language*. New York: John Wiley.

Leppänen, S., Pitkänen-Huhta, A., Nikula, T., *et al.* (2011) National survey on the English language in Finland: Uses, meanings and attitudes. *Studies in Variation, Contacts and Change in English* 5. See https://varieng.helsinki.fi/series/volumes/05/evarieng-vol5.pdf

Li, D. (1998) 'It's always more difficult than you imagine.' Teachers' perceived difficulties in introducing the communicative approach in South Korea. *TESOL Quarterly* 32 (4), 677–703.

Lightbown, P.M. (2000) Anniversary article. Classroom SLA research and second language teaching. *Applied Linguistics* 21 (4), 431–462. doi:10.1093/applin/21.4.431

Linse, C. (2005) English language study in Belarus within the changing sociopolitical context. In F. Salili and R. Hoosain (eds) *Language in Multicultural Education* (pp. 363–378). Greenwich, CT: Information Age.

Little, A.W., Shojo, S., Sonnadara, U. and Aturupane, H. (2019) Teaching English as a second language in Sri Lanka primary schools: Opportunity and pedagogy. *Language, Culture and Curriculum* 32 (2), 113–127. doi:10.1080/07908318.2018.1532437

Littlewood, W. (2007) Communicative and task-based language teaching in East Asian classrooms. *Language Teaching* 40 (3), 243–249. doi:10.1017/S0261444807004363

Liyanage, I. and Canagarajah, A.S. (2014) Interethnic understanding and the teaching of local languages in Sri Lanka. In V.Z.D. Gorter and J. Cenoz (eds) *Minority Languages and Multilingual Education* (pp. 119–135). Dordrecht: Springer.

LLRC (Lessons Learnt and Reconciliation Commission) (2011) *Report of the Commission of Inquiry on Lessons Learnt and Reconciliation.* Colombo: Lakshman Kadirgamar Institute of International Relations and Strategic Studies.

Lo Bianco, J. (1999) A syntax of peace? Pragmatic constraints of language teaching and pragmatics in language learning. In J. Lo Bianco, A.J. Liddicoat and C. Crozet (eds) *Striving for the Third Place: Intercultural Competence through Language Education* (pp. 51–63). Melbourne: Language Australia.

Long, M.H. (1990) Maturational constraints on language development. *Studies in Second Language Acquisition* 12 (3), 251–285. doi:10.1017/S0272263100009165

MacIntyre, A. (1985) *After Virtue: A Study in Moral Theory.* London: Duckworth.

Mady, C.J. (2010) Motivation to study Core French: Comparing recent immigrants and Canadian-born secondary school students. *Canadian Journal of Education* 33 (3), 564–587.

Mady, C., Arnott, S. and Lapkin, S. (2009) Assessing AIM: A study of grade 8 students in an Ontario school board. *Canadian Modern Language Review* 65 (5), 703–729. doi:10.3138/cmlr.65.5.703

Mala, D. (2015) Golds add up to Olympic win. *Bangkok Post,* 8 November. See https://www.bangkokpost.com/thailand/general/757452/golds-add-up-to-olympic-win

Mala, D. (2016) Thai pupils win haul of 36 maths medals. *Bangkok Post,* 28 October. See https://www.bangkokpost.com/thailand/general/1120873/thai-pupils-win-haul-of-36-maths-medals

Mala, D. (2017) Easy lessons to learn in the classroom. *Bangkok Post,* 17 December. See https://www.bangkokpost.com/thailand/special-reports/1380455/easy-lessons-to-learn-in-the-classroom

Mala, D. (2018) Thai English proficiency drops. *Bangkok Post,* 5 November. See https://www.bangkokpost.com/news/general/1570042/thai-english-proficiency-drops

Malalasekera, N.S. (2019) Postwar reconciliation: Parental attitudes towards Sri Lanka's trilingual education policy. MA thesis, University of Alaska Fairbanks.

Marinova-Todd, S.H., Marshall, D.B. and Snow, C.E. (2000) Three misconceptions about age and L2 learning. *TESOL Quarterly* 34 (1), 9–34. doi:10.2307/3588095

Maxwell, W. (2001) Evaluating the effectiveness of the accelerative integrated method for teaching French as a second language. Unpublished Master's thesis, Ontario Institute for Studies in Education, University of Toronto.

McKenna, K. (2021) Quebec seeks to change Canadian Constitution, make sweeping changes to language laws with new bill. *CBC News,* 13 May. See https://www.cbc.ca/news/canada/montreal/quebec-bill-101-language-revamp-1.6023532

MELTA (Malaysian English Language Teaching Association) (2010) A report on the forum 'To go or not to go native: The role of native speaker teachers and trainers in second and foreign language teaching. See https://www.yumpu.com/en/document/read/1163 2598/a-report-on-the-forum-to-go-or-not-to-go-native-the-role-of

Methitham, P. (2009) An exploration of culturally-based assumptions guiding ELT practice in Thailand, a non-colonized nation. Doctoral dissertation, Indiana University of Pennsylvania.

Miettinen, E. (2009) As much English as possible: A study on two secondary school English teachers' language use and the motives behind their language choices. Unpublished BA thesis, University of Jyväskylä.

Mihat, W. (2015) The English language curriculum in Malaysian indigenous primary classrooms: The reality and the ideal. *3L: The Southeast Asian Journal of English Language Studies* 21 (3), 1–12.

Ministry of Education and Culture (2017) *Multilingualism as a Strength: Procedural Recommendations for Developing Finland's National Language Reserve*. Helsinki: Ministry of Education and Culture. See https://minedu.fi/documents/1410845/5875747/Multilingualism_tiivistelmä.pdf/be86bffa-d55f-4935-bff4-2fd150c82067/Multilingualism_tiivistelmä.pdf

Minority Rights Group (2018) *Indigenous Peoples and Ethnic Minorities in Sarawak*. See https://minorityrights.org/minorities/indigenous-peoples-and-ethnic-minorities-in-sarawak/

Mitchell, R., Myles, F. and Marsden, E. (2013) *Second Language Learning Theories* (3rd edn). New York: Routledge.

Mittal, A. (2015) *The Long Shadow of War: The Struggle for Justice in Postwar Sri Lanka*. Oakland, CA: Oakland Institute.

MOE (Ministry of Education) (2008) *The Basic Education Core Curriculum B.E. 2551/A.D. 2008*. Bangkok: Ministry of Education.

MOE (Ministry of Education) (2017) *2016 Educational Statistics*. Bangkok: Office of the Permanent Secretary, Ministry of Education.

MOEM (Ministry of Education Malaysia) (2013a) *Executive Summary: Malaysia Education Blueprint 2013–2025 (Pre-School to Post-Secondary Education)*. Kuala Lumpur: Kementerian Pendidikan (Ministry of Education) Malaysia.

MOEM (Ministry of Education Malaysia) (2013b) *Malaysia Education Blueprint 2013–2025 (Pre-School to Post-Secondary Education)*. Kuala Lumpur: Kementerian Pendidikan (Ministry of Education) Malaysia.

MOEM (Ministry of Education Malaysia) (2014) *Malaysia Education Blueprint: Annual Report 2014*. Putrajaya: Ministry of Education Malaysia.

MOEM (Ministry of Education Malaysia) (2015) *Kurikulum Standard Sekolah Rendah: Dokumen Standard Kurikulum dan Pentaksiran. Bahasa Inggeris SK. Tahun Enam*. Kuala Lumpur: Kementerian Pendidikan (Ministry of Education) Malaysia.

MOEM (Ministry of Education Malaysia) (2019) *Malaysia Education Blueprint 2013–2025. Annual Report 2018*. Putrajaya: Ministry of Education Malaysia.

MOEM (Ministry of Education Malaysia) (2020) *Quick Facts 2020: Malaysia Educational Statistics*. Kuala Lumpur: Educational Planning and Research Division, Ministry of Education Malaysia.

MOEO (Ministry of Education Ontario) (2001) *The Ontario Curriculum Grades 1–8: Native Languages*. Toronto: Queen's Printer for Ontario. See http://www.edu.gov.on.ca/eng/curriculum/elementary/nativelang18curr.pdf

MOEO (Ministry of Education Ontario) (2008) *Supporting English Language Learners: A Practical Guide for Ontario Educators, Grades 1 to 8*. Toronto: Queen's Printer for Ontario. See http://www.edu.gov.on.ca/eng/document/esleldprograms/guide.pdf

MOEO (Ministry of Education Ontario) (2013) *The Ontario Curriculum: French as a Second Language*. Toronto: Queen's Printer for Ontario. See http://www.edu.gov.on.ca/eng/curriculum/elementary/fsl18-2013curr.pdf

MOESL (Ministry of Education Sri Lanka) (2008) *National Policy and a Comprehensive Framework of Actions on Education for Social Cohesion and Peace (ESCP)*. Battaramulla: Social Cohesion and Peace Education Unit, Ministry of Education, Sri Lanka.

MOESL (Ministry of Education Sri Lanka) (2020) *Annual School Census of Sri Lanka. Final Report – 2020*. Battaramulla: Statistics Branch, Ministry of Education, Sri Lanka. See http://www.statistics.gov.lk/Education/StaticalInformation/SchoolCensus/2020

MOESL (Ministry of Education Sri Lanka) and NEREC (National Education Research and Evaluation Centre) (2016) *National Report. National Assessment of Achievement of Students Completing Grade 4 in Year 2015 in Sri Lanka*. Battaramulla: Ministry of Education, Sri Lanka and National Education Research and Evaluation Centre, Faculty of Education, University of Colombo, Sri Lanka. See https://edu.cmb.ac.lk/nerec/?page_id=63

Mohanty, A. (2017) Multilingualism, education, English and development: Whose development? In H. Coleman (ed.) *Multilingualisms and Development: Selected Proceedings of the 11th Language & Development Conference, New Delhi, India, 2015* (pp. 261–280). London: British Council.

Moodie, I. and Feryok, A. (2015) Beyond cognition to commitment in South Korean primary schools. *The Modern Language Journal* 99 (3), 450–469. doi:10.1111/modl.12238

Moodie, I. and Nam, H. (2016) English language teaching research in South Korea: A review of recent studies (2009–2014). *Language Teaching* 49 (1), 63–98. doi:10.1017/S026144481500035X

Moon, J.I. (2014) Groping for a new English teaching strategy. *Pacific Science Review* 16, 207–211. See https://www.sciencedirect.com/science/article/pii/S1229545014000163

Moon, Y.I. (2013) Opportunities for English learning in Korea. Paper presented at the 11th Asia TEFL International Conference, Manila, Philippines, 26–28 October.

Mudugamuwa, I. (2019) Number of national schools to be increased to 1000. *Daily News*, 12 December. See http://www.dailynews.lk/2019/12/12/local/205494/number-national-schools-be-increased-1000

Muhonen, S. (2017) In Finland it's easier to become a doctor or lawyer than a teacher – here's why. *The Hechinger Report*, 16 October. See https://hechingerreport.org/teacher-voice-in-finland-its-easier-to-become-a-doctor-or-lawyer-than-a-teacher-heres-why/

Muñoz, C. (ed.) (2006a) *Age and the Rate of Foreign Language Learning*. Clevedon: Multilingual Matters.

Muñoz, C. (2006b) The effects of age on foreign language learning: The BAF project. In C. Muñoz (ed.) *Age and the Rate of Foreign Language Learning* (pp. 1–40). Clevedon: Multilingual Matters.

Mustaparta, A.K. (2008) Finland country note: Globalisation and linguistic competencies in the Finnish education system. Paper presented at the 12th OECD-Japan Seminar on Globalisation and Linguistic Competencies: Responding to Diversity in Language Environments, 22–24 October, Tokyo. See https://www.oecd.org/education/ceri/41486518.pdf

Myles, F. (2017) Learning foreign languages in primary schools: Is younger better? *Languages, Society & Policy*. doi:10.17863/CAM.9806

NCERT (National Council of Educational Research and Training) (2005) *National Curriculum Framework 2005*. New Delhi: NCERT.

NEC (National Education Commission) (1992) *First Report of the National Education Commission*. Colombo: NEC.

NEC (National Education Commission) (2003) *Proposals for a National Policy Framework on General Education*. Nugegoda: NEC.

NEC (National Education Commission) (2016) *Raising the Quality of Education: Proposals for a National Policy on General Education in Sri Lanka*. Nugegoda: NEC. See http://nec.gov.lk/wp-content/uploads/2017/02/NEC-GEP-final-English.pdf

NEC (National Education Commission) (2017) *New Education Act for General Education in Sri Lanka: Context, Issues and Proposals. Final Report*. Nugegoda: NEC. See http://nec.gov.lk/wp-content/uploads/2017/12/Towards-a-New-Education-Act.pdf

Nesdale, D., Durkin, K., Maass, A. and Griffiths, J. (2004) Group status, outgroup ethnicity and children's ethnic attitudes. *Applied Developmental Psychology* 25 (2), 237–251. doi:10.1016/j.appdev.2004.02.005

Nguyen, D.C., Le, T.L., Tran, H.Q. and Nguyen, T.H. (2014) Inequality of access to English language learning in primary education in Vietnam: A case study. In H. Zhang, P.W.K. Chan and C. Boyle (eds) *Equality in Education: Fairness and Inclusion* (pp. 139–153). Rotterdam: Sense Publishers.

NIE (National Institute of Education) (2017) *English Language. Teacher's Guide: Grade 03*. Maharagama: NIE. See www.nie.lk/pdffiles/tg/eGr03TG%20English.pdf

NIE (National Institute of Education) (2018) *Proposed New Educational Reforms and Related Opinion Survey*. Maharagama: NIE. See https://nie.lk/pdffiles/other/eOM%20 Curriculum%20Reserach%20Report.pdf

NIE (National Institute of Education) and MEHE (Ministry of Education and Higher Education) (2000) *National Curriculum Policy Sri Lanka*. Maharagama: NIE and MEHE.

Niemi, H., Toom, A. and Kallioniemi, A. (eds) (2012) *Miracle of Education: The Principles and Practices of Teaching and Learning in Finnish Schools*. Rotterdam: Sense Publishers.

Nunan, D. (2003) The impact of English as a global language on educational policies and practices in the Asia-Pacific region. *TESOL Quarterly* 37 (4), 589–613. doi:10.2307/3588214

OCOL (Office of the Commissioner of Official Languages) (2016) *What Canadians Think about Learning English and French*. See https://www.clo-ocol.gc.ca/en/statistics/infographics/what-canadians-think-english-french

OCOL (Office of the Commissioner of Official Languages) (2019) *Accessing Opportunity: A Study on Challenges in French-as-a-Second-Language Education Teacher Supply and Demand in Canada*. See https://www.clo-ocol.gc.ca/sites/default/files/accessing-opportunity-fsl.pdf

OCOL (Office of the Commissioner of Official Languages) (2021) *Understanding Your Language Rights*. See https://www.clo-ocol.gc.ca/en/language_rights/act

O'Connor, J. (2020) Government seeks 10,000 fluent English speakers to teach in Thai schools in major policy reversal. *Thai Examiner.com*, 13 September. See https://www.thaiexaminer.com/thai-news-foreigners/2020/09/13/government-seeks-10000-fluent-english-speakers-to-teach/

OECD (Organization for Economic Cooperation and Development) (2005) *Teachers Matter: Attracting, Retaining and Developing Effective Teachers. Overview*. Paris: OECD Publishing.

OECD (Organization for Economic Cooperation and Development) (2011) *How's Life?: Measuring Well-Being*. Paris: OECD Publishing.

OECD (Organization for Economic Cooperation and Development) (2016) *Economic Outlook for Southeast Asia, China and India, 2016: Enhancing Regional Ties*. Paris: OECD Publishing.

OECD (Organization for Economic Cooperation and Development) (2017) *Korea. Country Note – Results from PISA 2015 Students' Well-Being*. See https://www.oecd.org/pisa/PISA2015-Students-Well-being-Country-note-Korea.pdf

OECD (Organisation for Economic Cooperation and Development) (2019) *Country Note: Finland*. See https://www.oecd.org/pisa/publications/PISA2018_CN_FIN.pdf

OECD (Organization for Economic Cooperation and Development)/UNESCO (United Nations Educational, Scientific and Cultural Organization) (2016) *Education in Thailand: An OECD-UNESCO Perspective*. Reviews of National Policies for Education. Paris: OECD. doi:10.1787/9789264259119-en

OHCHR (Office of the High Commissioner for Human Rights) (2016) Statement of the United Nations Special Rapporteur on minority issues, Rita Izsák-Ndiaye, on the conclusion of her official visit to Sri Lanka, 10–20 October 2016. *Media Release*, 20 October. See https://www.ohchr.org/en/2016/10/statement-united-nations-special-rapporteur-minority-issues-rita-izsak-ndiaye-conclusion

ONEC (Office of the National Education Commission) (1999) *National Education Act of B.E. 2542 (1999)*. Bangkok: Office of the Prime Minister.

ONESCD (Office of the National Economic and Social Development Board) (2017) *The Twelfth National Economic and Social Development Plan (2017–2021)*. Bangkok: Office of the Prime Minister.

Othman, J. and Kiely, R. (2016) Pre-service teachers' beliefs and practices in teaching English to young learners. *Indonesian Journal of Applied Linguistics* 6 (1), 50–59. doi:10.17509/ijal.v6i1.2661

Othman, J. and Muijs, D. (2013) Educational quality differences in a middle-income country: The urban-rural gap in Malaysian primary schools. *School Effectiveness and School Improvement* 24 (1), 1–18. doi:10.1080/09243453.2012.691425

Park, J.-K. (2009) 'English fever' in South Korea: Its history and symptoms. *English Today* 25 (1), 50–57. doi:10.1017/S026607840900008X

Park, J.S.-Y. (2009) *The Local Construction of a Global Language: Ideologies of English in South Korea*. Berlin: Mouton de Gruyter.

Park, J.S.-Y. (2011) The promise of English: Linguistic capital and the neoliberal worker in the South Korean job market. *International Journal of Bilingual Education and Bilingualism* 14 (4), 443–455. doi:10.1080/13670050.2011.573067

Park, S. (2010) Teacher policies in Korea. Presentation at the 'Benchmarking Education Systems for Results' East Asia Regional Conference, 21–23 June, Singapore.

Parkin, A. (2019) *PISA 2018: Summary of Results for Canada*. Toronto: Environics Institute for Survey Research. See https://www.environicsinstitute.org/docs/default-source/default-document-library/pisa-2018-results-overview71de830d03554fcab65ab6447291f13a.pdf?sfvrsn=cba7f840_0

Paronen, P. and Lappi, O. (2018) *Finnish Teachers and Principals in Figures*. Helsinki: Finnish National Agency for Education. See https://www.oph.fi/sites/default/files/documents/finnish_teachers_and_principals_in_figures.pdf

Perera, S. (2001) *The Ethnic Conflict in Sri Lanka: A Historical and Sociopolitical Outline*. Washington, DC: World Bank.

Perera, M. (2006) 'Why not? But I can't' – influence of a 'culture of poverty' on learning: A case study. *Sabaragamuwa University Journal* 6 (1), 23–34.

Peters, E., Noreillie, A.-S., Heylen, K., Bulté, B. and Desmet, P. (2019) The impact of instruction and out-of-school exposure to foreign language input on learners' vocabulary knowledge in two languages. *Language Learning* 69 (3), 747–782. doi:10.1111/lang.12351

Phillipson, R. (2009) *Linguistic Imperialism Continued*. New York: Routledge.

Piyaman, P., Hallinger, P. and Viseshsiri, P. (2017) Addressing the achievement gap: Exploring principal leadership and teacher professional learning in urban and rural primary schools in Thailand. *Journal of Educational Administration* 55 (6), 717–734. doi:10.1108/JEA-12-2016-0142

Pomson, A. (2002) The *rebbe* reworked: An inquiry into the persistence of inherited traditions of teaching. *Teaching and Teacher Education* 18 (1), 23–34.

Powell, R. (2002) Language planning and the British empire: Comparing Pakistan, Malaysia and Kenya. *Current Issues in Language Planning* 3 (3), 205–279. doi:10.1080/14664200208668041

Prapaisit de Segovia, L. and Hardison, D.M. (2009) Implementing education reform: EFL teachers' perspectives. *ELT Journal* 63 (2), 154–162. doi:10.1093/elt/ccn024

Premarathna, A., Yogaraja, S.J., Medawattegedara, V., Senarathna, C.D. and Abdullah, R.M. (2016) *Study on Medium of Instruction, National and International Languages in General Education in Sri Lanka*. Nugegoda: National Education Commission. See http://nec.gov.lk/wp-content/uploads/2016/04/9-Final-.pdf

Pugh-Kitingan, J., Miller, M.T., Ling, J.W.K., Atin, V.P., Porodong, P., Lajumin, P. and Kluge, A. (2018) Report of the project 'Review of Ethnologue' descriptions of languages in Sabah. *Borneo Research Bulletin* 49, 221–240.

Punchi, L. (2001) Resistance towards the language of globalization: The case of Sri Lanka. *International Review of Education* 47 (3–4), 361–378.

Punthumasen, P. (2007) International program for teacher education: An approach to tackling problems of English education in Thailand. Paper presented at the 11th

UNESCO-APEID Conference, Bangkok, Thailand, 12–14 December 2007. See http://backoffice.onec.go.th/uploaded/Category/EngBook/ProblemEngEd13dec07-03-03-2011.pdf

Rabbidge, M. and Chappell, P. (2014) Exploring non-native English speaker teachers' classroom language use in South Korean elementary schools. *TESL-EJ* 17 (4), 1–18. See www.tesl-ej.org/wordpress/issues//volume17/ej68/ej68a2/

Rajadurai, J. (2010) 'Malays are expected to speak Malay': Community ideologies, language use and the negotiation of identities. *Journal of Language, Identity & Education* 9 (2), 91–106. doi:10.1080/15348451003704776

Rajala, R. (2019) Digital gaming preferences among Finnish primary school students and their connection to English language learning. Bachelor's thesis, University of Jyväskylä. See https://jyx.jyu.fi/handle/123456789/64905

Rashid, R.A.B., Rahman, S.B.A. and Yunus, K. (2017) Reforms in the policy of English language teaching in Malaysia. *Policy Futures in Education* 15 (1), 100–112. doi:10.1177/1478210316679069

Rassool, N. (2013) The political economy of English language and development: English vs. national and local languages in developing countries. In E.J. Erling and P. Seargeant (eds) (2013) *English and Development: Policy, Pedagogy and Globalization* (pp. 45–67). Bristol: Multilingual Matters.

Reardon, B.A. (2000) Peace education: A review and projection. In B. Moon, M. Ben-Peretz and S. Brown (eds) *Routledge International Companion to Education* (pp. 397–425). London: Routledge.

Research Team (2013) *Reforming National Education: Analyses and Recommendations on Malaysia Education Blueprint.* Kuala Lumpur: LLG Cultural Development Centre.

Ricento, T. (2018) Globalization, language policy and the role of English. In J.W. Tollefson and M. Pérez-Milans (eds) *The Oxford Handbook of Language Policy and Planning* (pp. 221–235). Oxford: Oxford University Press.

Ringbom, H. (2012) Review of recent applied linguistics research in Finland and Sweden, with specific reference to foreign language learning and teaching. *Language Teaching* 45 (4), 490–514. doi:10.1017/S0261444812000225

RSK (Raja Shiksha Kendra) (2007) *State Curriculum Framework 2007 Madhya Pradesh: English.* Bhopal: RSK.

Ryu, D. and Kang, C. (2013) Do private tutoring expenditures raise academic performance? Evidence from middle-school students in South Korea. *Asian Economic Journal* 27 (1), 59–83. doi:10.1111/asej.12002

Saengpassa, C. (2018) Rajabhat teacher degree to be cut back to 4 years. *The Nation,* 18 October. See http://www.nationmultimedia.com/detail/national/30356649

Schleicher, A. (2019) *PISA 2018: Insights and Interpretations.* Paris: OECD. See https://www.oecd.org/pisa/PISA%202018%20Insights%20and%20Interpretations%20FINAL%20PDF.pdf

SchoolAdvisor (2021) Dual language programme in national and private schools and the second language integration in international schools. *SchoolAdvisor,* 23 February. See https://schooladvisor.my/articles/dual-language-programme-in-national-and-private-schools-and-the-second-language-integration-in-international-schools

Schweisfurth, M. (2011) Learner-centred education in developing country contexts: From solution to problem? *International Journal of Educational Development* 31 (5), 425–432. doi:10.1016/ijedudev.2011.03.005

SEAMEO, Teachers' Council of Thailand & SEAMEO INNOTECH (2018) *Southeast Asia Teachers' Competency Framework (SEA-TCF).* Bangkok: Teachers' Council of Thailand.

Seargeant, P. and Erling, E.J. (2011) The discourse of 'English as a language for international development': Policy assumptions and practical challenges. In H. Coleman (ed.)

Dreams and Realities: Developing Countries and the English Language (pp. 248–267). London: British Council.

Sen, A. (2007) *Civil Paths to Peace: Report of the Commonwealth Commission on Respect and Understanding*. London: Commonwealth Secretariat.

Sethunga, P., Wijesundera, S., Kalamany, T. and Karunanayake, S. (2016) *Study on the Professional Development of Teachers and Teacher Educators in Sri Lanka*. Nugegoda: National Education Commission.

Shaeffer, S. (2018) Pre-school and primary education: Thailand's progress in achieving education for all. In G.W. Fry (ed.) *Education in Thailand: An Old Elephant in Search of a New Mahout* (pp. 93–124). Singapore: Springer.

Shiga, M. (2008) Development of primary English education and teacher training in Korea. *Journal of Education for Teaching* 34 (4), 383-396. doi:10.1080/02607470802401651

Shin, H. (2007) English language teaching in Korea: Toward globalization or *glocalization*? In J. Cummins and C. Davison (eds) *International Handbook of English Language Teaching* (pp. 75–86). Boston, MA: Springer.

Silva, N.C.R. (2018) Failure of reconciliation in Sri Lanka and risk of reproduction of war? Paper presented at the 7th International Conference on Building Resilience: Using Scientific Knowledge to Inform Policy and Practice in Disaster Risk Reduction, 27–29 November 2017, Bangkok, Thailand. *Procedia Engineering* 212, 1075–1082. doi:10.1016/j.proeng.2018.01.139

Simola, H. (2005) The Finnish miracle of PISA: Historical and sociological remarks on teaching and teacher education. *Comparative Education* 41 (4), 455–470. doi:10.1080/0305006500317810

Singhadechakul, C. (2015) Current Thai education policies and reform. Paper submitted to APEC Human Resources Development Working Group Education Network Meeting, 15 May 2015, Boracay, the Philippines.

Sjöholm, K. (2004) Swedish, Finnish, English? Finland's Swedes in a changing world. *Journal of Curriculum Studies* 36 (5), 637–644. doi:10.1080/0022027042000186600

Smith, E. (2018) *Key Issues in Education and Social Justice* (2nd edn). Thousand Oaks, CA: Sage.

Smith, K.J. (2003) Minority language education in Malaysia: Four ethnic communities' experiences. *International Journal of Bilingual Education and Bilingualism* 6 (1), 52–65. doi:10.1080.13670050308667772

So, K. and Kang, Y. (2014) Curriculum reform in Korea: Issues and challenges for twenty-first century learning. *Asia-Pacific Education Researcher* 23 (4), 795–803. doi:10.1007/s40299-013-0161-2

Song, J.J. (2011) English as an official language in South Korea: Global English or social malady? *Language Problems & Language Planning* 35 (1), 35–55. doi:10.1075/lplp.35.1.03son

Song, J.J. (2012) South Korea: Language policy and planning in the making. *Current Issues in Language Planning* 13 (1), 1–68. doi:10.1080/14664208.2012.650322

Sørensen, B.R. (2008) The politics of citizenship and difference in Sri Lankan schools. *Anthropology and Education Quarterly* 39 (4), 423–443. doi:10.1111/j.1548-1492.2008.00031.x.

Statistics Canada (2017a) *Census in Brief: The Aboriginal Languages of First Nations People, Métis and Inuit*. See https://www12.statcan.gc.ca/census-recensement/2016/as-sa/98-200-x/2016022/98-200-x2016022-eng.pdf

Statistics Canada (2017b) *Census in Brief: English-French Bilingualism Reaches New Heights*. See https://www12.statcan.gc.ca/census-recensement/2016/as-sa/98-200-x/2016009/98-200-x2016009-eng.pdf

Statistics Canada (2018) *Language Highlight Tables: 2016 Census*. See https://www12.statcan.gc.ca/census-recensement/2016/dp-pd/hlt-fst/lang/Table.cfm?Lang=E&T=11&Geo=00

References 183

Statistics Canada (2021) *Table 17-10-0009-01 Population Estimates, Quarterly.* doi:10.25318 /1710000901-eng

Statistics Finland (2020) *Statistical Yearbook of Finland 2020.* Helsinki: Statistics Finland. See https://www.stat.fi/tup/julkaisut/tiedostot/julkaisuluettelo/yyti_stv_ 202000_2020_23211_net.pdf

Statistics Finland (2021) *Population Structure 2020.* Helsinki: Statistics Finland. See https://www.stat.fi/til/vaerak/2020/vaerak_2020_2021-03-31_en.pdf

Staudinger, U.M. (2001) Theory of lifespan development. In N.J. Smelser and P.B. Baltes (eds) *International Encyclopedia of the Social and Behavioral Sciences* (pp. 8844–8848). Oxford: Pergamon.

Stephen, J. (2013) English in Malaysia: A case of the past that never really went away? *English Today* 29 (2), 3–8. doi:10.1017/S0266078413000084

Sukamolson, S. (1998) English language education policy in Thailand. *Asian Englishes* 1 (1), 68–91. doi:10.1080/13488678.1998.10800995

Sundqvist, P. and Wikström, P. (2015) Out-of-school digital gameplay and in-school L2 English vocabulary outcomes. *System* 51, 65–76. doi:10.1016/j.system.2015.04.001

Sylvén, L. and Sundqvist, P. (2012) Gaming as extramural English L2 learning and L2 proficiency among young learners. *ReCALL* 24 (3), 302–321. doi:10.1017/S0958344 01200016X

Takahashi, K. (2012) The great English-language deficiency hype. *Bangkok Post*, 12 February. See https://www.bangkokpost.com/opinion/opinion/279415/the-great-english-language-deficiency-hype

Tangkitvanich, S. and Sasiwuttiwat, S. (2012) Revamping the Thai education system: Quality for all. *TDRI Quarterly Review* 27 (2), 3–12. See https://tdri.or.th/ en/2012/09/tdri-quarterly-review-june-2012

Taylor, A. (2013) Finland used to have the best education system in the world – What happened? *Business Insider,* 3 December. See https://www.businessinsider.com/ why-finland-fell-in-the-pisa-rankings-2013-12

Taylor, C. and Lafayette, R. (2010) Academic achievement through FLES: A case study for promoting greater access to foreign language study among young learners. *The Modern Language Journal* 94 (1), 22–42. doi:10.1111/j.1540-4781.2009.00981.x

Teichman, Y. and Bar-Tal, D. (2008) Acquisition and development of a shared psychological intergroup repertoire in a context of an intractable conflict. In S.M. Quintana and C. McKown (eds) *Handbook of Race, Racism and the Developing Child* (pp. 452–482). Hoboken, NJ: John Wiley.

Thanthong-Knight, S. (2015) Thais' poor English to hurt job prospects in Asean community. *Bangkok Post*, 19 March. See https://www.bangkokpost.com/news/special-reports/501904/thais-poor-english-to-hurt-job-prospects-in-asean-community

The Star (2013) 70% of English Teachers Not Fit to Teach. *The Star*, 11 September. See https://www.thestar.com.my/news/nation/2013/09/11/idris-many-teachers-not-fit-to-tea ch-70-of-english-instructors-found-to-be-incapable-says-education/

Ting, S.-H. (2003) Impact of language planning on language attitudes: A case study in Sarawak. *Journal of Multilingual and Multicultural Development* 24 (3), 195–210. doi:10.1080/01434630308666498

Trakulkasemsuk, W. (2018) English in Thailand: Looking back to the past, at the present and towards the future. *Asian Englishes* 20 (2), 96–105. doi:10.1080/13488678.2-17. 1421602

Tran, M.P. (2017) Exploring young learners' informal learning of English language: A comparative study on the perspectives of 11–13-year-old pupils in Finland and Vietnam. Master's thesis, University of Eastern Finland. See https://erepo.uef.fi/ bitstream/handle/123456789/17918/urn_nbn_fi_uef-20170480.pdf

Trudell, B. (2005) Language choice, education and community identity. *International Journal of Educational Development* 25 (3), 237–251. doi:10.1016/j.ijedudev.2004. 08.004

Trudell, B., Young, C. and Nyaga, S. (2015) Language, education and development: Implications of language choice for learning. In S. McGrath and Q. Yu (eds) *Routledge Handbook of International Education and Development* (pp. 133–149). London: Routledge.

UN (United Nations) (1989) *Convention on the Rights of the Child*. New York: UN. See https://treaties.un.org/doc/Treaties/1990/09/19900902%2003-14%20AM/Ch_IV_11p.pdf

UNDP (United Nations Development Programme) (2018) *Human Development Indices and Indicators: 2018 Statistical Update. Korea (Republic of)*. New York: UNDP. See http://hdr.undp.org/sites/all/themes/hdr_theme/country-notes/KOR.pdf

UNESCO (United Nations Educational, Scientific and Cultural Organization) (2009) *Investing in Cultural Diversity and Intercultural Dialogue: UNESCO World Report*. Paris: UNESCO. See https://unesdoc.unesco.org/ark:/48223/pf0000185202

UNESCO (United Nations Educational, Scientific and Cultural Organization) (2017) *2017/2018 Global Education Monitoring Report: Thailand Highlights*. Bangkok: UNESCO. See https://bangkok.unesco.org/content/20172018-global-education-monitoring-report-thailand-highlights

UNICEF (United Nations Children's Fund) (2018) *Bridge to a Brighter Tomorrow: The Patani Malay-Thai Multilingual Education Programme*. Bangkok: UNICEF.

Vosniadou, S. (2001) *How Children Learn*. Geneva: International Bureau of Education.

Werker, J.F. and Byers-Heinlein, K. (2008) Bilingualism in infancy: First steps in perception and comprehension. *Trends in Cognitive Science* 12 (4), 144–151. doi:10.1016/j.tics.2008.01.008

Wijesekera, H.D., Alford, J. and Mu, M.G. (2019) Forging inclusive practice in ethnically-segregated school systems: Lessons from one multiethnic, bilingual education classroom in Sri Lanka. *International Journal of Inclusive Education* 23 (1), 23–41. doi:1 0.1080/13603116.2018.1514730

Williams, G. (2010) *The Knowledge Economy, Language and Culture*. Bristol: Multilingual Matters.

Witte, J. (2000) Education in Thailand after the crisis: A balancing act between globalization and national self-contemplation. *International Journal of Educational Development* 20 (3), 223–245. doi:10.1016/S0738-0593(99)00059-0

Workopolis (2015) Is it still worth learning a second language in Canada in 2015? *Workopolis*, 19 May. See https://careers.workopolis.com/advice/is-it-still-worth-learning-a-second-language-in-canada-in-2015/

World Bank (2015) *Thailand: Wanted, a Quality Education for All*. Bangkok: World Bank. See https://openknowledge.worldbank.org/handle/10986/22355

World Bank (2018) Sri Lanka and World Bank sign $100 million to modernize the education system. *Press Release*, 25 July. Colombo: World Bank.

Yoon, L. (2022a) Total expenditure on private education in South Korea in 2021, by subject (in trillion South Korean won). *Statista*. See https://www.statista.com/statistics/1042882/south-korea-total-spending-for-private-education-y-subject/

Yoon, L. (2022b) Total expenditure on private education in South Korea in 2021, by school level (in trillion South Korean won). *Statista*. See https://www.statista.com/statistics/1042875/south-korea-total-spending-for-private-education-by-school-level

Young, M.Y.C. (2006) Macao students' attitudes toward English: A post-1999 survey. *World Englishes* 25 (3/4), 479–490. https://doi.org.10.1111/j.1467-971X.2006.00468.x

Zaman, E.T. (2019) The representation of English language in the Malaysia Education Blueprint 2013–2025: A CDA perspective. PhD thesis, Lancaster University. See https://eprints.lancs.ac.uk/id/eprint/138292/1/2019TengkuEnalizaphd.pdf

Index

Abdullah, M.H. 95
Accelerated Integrative Method (AIM) 122
activity-based learning 35, 77, 133–134
Activity-Based Oral English (ABOE) 77
additive bilingualism 94
Adesope, O.O. 2, 16
after-school classes 60
age of learner 9–11 *see also* 'younger the better'
Agenda 2030 142–143
Agirdag, O. 2
Ali, N.L. 108, 110–111
Alladi, S. 2
Amnesty International 72, 116
Appell, G.N. 94
Arabic 111, 118, 139
A-Rahman, N. 102, 103, 108, 110, 161
Arcand, J.-L. 4
Arda, S. 15–16
Arnott, S. 119, 120, 121, 122, 138
ASEAN 4, 26, 146
aspirations to learn English 148–149
assimilationist policies 46, 124
attitudes to learning *see also* motivation to learn languages
   bilingualism 149
   Canada 119, 121, 138–139
   Finland 129, 132
   general educational value of early language learning 150–151
   impact on outcomes 15–16
   negative attitudes to learning English 16
   positive attitudes as goal of education 148–149
   Sri Lanka 78, 80
Aturupane, H. 79, 86
authenticity 37, 38, 49, 58
autonomy 37, 50, 108, 162

'Awakening to languages' approach 20
Azam, M. 6, 146
Azman, H. 100, 109, 110, 111, 112, 147

Bahasa Malaysia 93, 94, 95, 96, 97, 109, 147
Baldauf, R.B. 9
Baltus, R. 123–124
Barcelona Age Factor (BAF) project 10–11
Bar-Tal, D. 73, 79
behaviour 55–57
Bekerman, Z. 71
Belhiah, H. 123–124
benefits of learning additional languages in primary schools 2–3, 152–164
Bi, H. 28
Bialystok, E. 3, 16
bilingual education 25, 74, 87–88
bilingualism *see also* linguistic diversity; multilingualism; plurilingualism
   attitudes to learning 149
   benefits of 2
   Canada 113–114, 115, 119, 123, 138
   Finland 114, 126
   Malaysia 97, 109–110
   as norm 20
   South Korea 46
Bisu 24
Bourdieu, P. 13–14
Bradford, A. 15
Brown, G.K. 93
Brubacher, K. 124
Brunfaut, T. 81
Bruthiaux, P. 148
Brutt-Griffler, J. 70
Bryant, D.A. 41
Buddhism 34
Burridge, T. 128

Bush, K. 72
Butler, Y.G. 3, 51, 52
Byers-Heinlein, K. 124
Byram, M. 2, 150, 164

Cameron, D. 19
Canada 113–125, 137–139, 160
Carless, D. 58
Cha, Y.-K. 6–7, 14
Chalkiadaki, A. 162
Chan, K. 124
Chang, E.S. 59
Chang, K. 47, 53, 56, 143, 146
Chappell, P. 51, 155
checking for understanding 36
China 8, 15, 29, 65, 144
Chinese (Mandarin) 4, 65, 94, 97, 109, 111, 117, 139, 144
Cho, J. 47, 49, 144
Choi, T. 54, 56
Choi, T.-H. 50
Choi, Y.-H. 64–65
Chukhlantseva, E. 134, 135, 152
Chumak-Horbatsch, R. 124
Chung, J. 54, 56
class sizes 36
classroom discipline 51, 55
classroom practices
 Finland 131
 inherited teaching traditions 158
 Malaysia 102, 106–107, 110
 South Korea 48–54, 56–57
 Thailand 34–37
Colclough, C. 145
Colenso, P. 72
College Scholastic Ability Test (CSAT) 48, 52, 59, 61, 64, 65, 144
colonialism
 Canada 115, 116
 Malaysia 91, 92, 145, 147
 Sri Lanka 67, 69, 70, 89, 147
Commission of Inquiry on Lessons Learnt and Reconciliation (LLRC, 2011) 73–74
Common European Framework of Reference (CEFR) 20, 38–39, 99, 105, 122, 131, 153–154
communicative language teaching
 Canada 121
 conclusions on 149–151, 154–156
 language teaching methods 18–19

versus locally appropriate curricula 65
 Malaysia 100, 110
 South Korea 49, 50–51
 Thailand 32, 37, 40
context of learning *see also* out-of-school exposure to English
 Canada 119, 124
 as important factor 10, 149–151
 Malaysia 110–111
 South Korea 65
 Sri Lanka 86–87
continuing professional development (CPD) 18, 43, 103–108
Copland, F. 52
Council of Europe 20, 154
course books 34–35, 104, 106
Covid-19 22, 156
Coyne, G. 12
Critical Period Hypothesis 9–10
cultural norms 37, 143
cultural skills 162 *see also* intercultural understanding
Cummins, J. 119, 123, 138
curriculum
 Canada 124, 138
 conclusions on 152–161, 163–164
 developmental sensitivity of curriculum 52
 Finland 130, 131
 French as a Second Language in Canada 120–122
 gap between curriculum and classroom practice 40, 49–50
 languages in primary education generally 17–18, 19
 locally appropriate curricula 65, 156–158
 Malaysia 98–103, 108, 109–111
 South Korea 48–54, 56
 Sri Lanka 76–77, 82–83
 Thailand 23, 30–34, 40
 topic-based approaches 164
 Western influences 33

Davis, C.P. 69, 76
Davis, S.C. 73
Dearden, J. 12
declining standards discourse 91, 103, 150
DeKeyser, R. 10

demotivation 51, 52, 106–107, 121–122, 138, 163
DFID 72
dialects 24
diversity *see* linguistic diversity
Don, Z.H. 95
Doyran, F. 15–16
Draper, J. 24
Dual Language Programmes 103
Dundar, H. 8, 145

'earlier is better' 3–4, 9–11, 150, 159
economic benefits of multilingualism 149
economic growth and general improvements in education 8, 45, 47
economic rationales for English
  conclusions on 143–152
  generally 4–9
  Malaysia 91, 95, 96, 97, 109
  South Korea 47
  Sri Lanka 80–81
  Thailand 25–30
ecosystems 135–138, 161–163
educational bureaucracy 29
educational funding
  conclusions on 159–161
  Malaysia 94–95, 99, 103
  South Korea 45
  Sri Lanka 76, 88
  Thailand 28
educational reform
  conclusions on 141–164
  'earlier is better' 3–4, 9–11, 150, 159
  Malaysia 97–98, 100 103, 107, 109–110, 111
  neoliberal education reform 56
  South Korea 45–46
  Thailand 29–30
EF English Proficiency Index 139, 150
egalitarian ideal (South Korea) 46
Eliadis, P. 116
elites
  beneficiaries of English education 146, 147
  English proficiency 26
  Malaysia 96, 103
  private schools 31
  South Korea 63
  Sri Lanka 80, 82
ELTDP 104, 155

employability
  conclusions on 145–146, 148–149
  Malaysia 95
  and proficiency levels 5–6, 148
  and quality of education 145–146
  returns from all languages 149
  South Korea 47, 54, 61, 64, 144
  Sri Lanka 81
  Thailand 26
endangered languages 24, 69, 109, 116, 117
Endangered Languages Project 69
Enever, J. 38, 60, 148
English
  attitudes to learning 15–16
  Canada 115, 123
  economic value of 3, 4–9
  and educational opportunity 15–16
  Finland 114, 131, 132, 133, 134, 136, 137, 152, 163
  and globalisation 13–14
  impact of learning English on children in school 15–17
  instrumental value of English 15, 47, 96, 151
  as an international language 13, 26, 47, 52, 97, 141
  language of international competitiveness 4–5, 11, 143, 145, 146
  as a lingua franca (ELF) 32, 47
  as link language (Sri Lanka) 71, 80–88, 147
  Malaysia 145
  official status in Sri Lanka 70
  policy rationales for English learning 3–15
  and power 14
  South Korea 47, 146
  Sri Lankan curriculum 76–77, 78
  Thailand 25–30, 146
  as third language in Sri Lanka 67
  for tourism 26
  as working language of ASEAN 26
  world events and the choice of second language 7
English First 5
'English is enough' 134
English Proficiency Index (EPI) 5
English Programme in Korea (EPIK) 57–59

English-medium education
  Malaysia 96, 103
  policy rationales for 3–4, 12–13, 155
  South Korea 50
  Sri Lanka 70, 74, 87–88, 89
  Thailand 23
Environment Related Activities 77
environmental factors in learning 11
  see also context of learning; out-
  of-school exposure to English
equity 22, 46, 61, 66, 120, 142–143,
  156–158
Erling, E.J. 6, 146, 148, 149
ethnic differences
  Malaysia 93, 94, 95–96, 101, 103, 109
  Sri Lanka 78–80, 87–88, 89, 147–148
Euromonitor International 6
European Centre for Modern
  Languages of the Council of
  Europe 20
European Union 20
extra-curricular provision 138–139

Fenyvesi, K. 16
Feryok, A. 55
Finland 114, 125–140, 149, 152, 154, 159
Finnish 114, 126–127, 131–132, 133, 136
first language as resource 12, 35, 51, 60,
  102, 111, 121, 124, 162
first language literacy *see also* mother
  tongue-medium education
  Canada 123
  importance of 3
  Malaysia 97, 101
  South Korea 60, 65
  Sri Lanka 74, 88, 89
  Thailand 27
Fitzpatrick, D. 40
Foreman-Peck, J. 8
Franco, A. 26
Franz, J. 39, 40
Freidrich, D. 117
French
  Canada 113–125, 138–139, 148, 160
  Finland 132, 133, 134
  history of French as a foreign
  language 7, 13
Fry, G.W. 28, 29, 33, 34, 145

Gall, L.G. 116
gaming 136–137

Garton, S. 49, 50, 51, 52, 53
gatekeeping requirement, English as
  48, 144
gender and choice of second
  language 133
gender and English proficiency 85, 100
gender of teachers 48, 78, 98, 133
general educational achievement, benefits
  of language learning for 2
general educational quality,
  improvements in 26–27
general educational value of early
  language learning 150–151
generalist versus specialist teachers 54,
  55, 87
German 7, 114, 132, 133, 134, 137, 139
Gill, S.K. 95, 96, 147
Global Innovation Index (2019) 26
globalisation 2–3, 13–14, 64, 65, 95,
  134, 151
Graddol, D. 160
grammar-translation method 36, 37, 158
Grant, C. 8
Green, R. 81
Grin, F. 4
group working 35, 110
Gunesekera, M. 82, 147, 148

Halinen, I. 135
Hallinger, P. 23, 36–37, 41
Ham, S.-H. 6–7, 14
Hannibal Jensen, S. 136
happiness 43, 61, 129
Hardison, D.M. 40
Hardman, J. 102, 103, 108, 110, 161
Hargreaves, L. 130
Harris, I.M. 72
Harris, S. 73
Hashim, A. 94, 96
Hattie, J. 41
Havelock, R.G. 102
Hayes, D. 3, 9, 14, 15, 24, 25, 26, 48, 53,
  71, 79, 81, 84, 108, 146
Heo, J. 57
heteroglossic language practices 88
Hettiarachchi, S. 81–82
hierarchical societies 37
Hiew, W. 106, 107
high-stakes tests 16, 48, 51, 144
Hildén, R. 131, 132, 137
Holliday, A. 19

homeroom teachers 55
hours per week for foreign language
    instruction
  conclusions on 159
  Finland 129
  Malaysia 98–99, 110, 111
  South Korea 48–49, 64
  Sri Lanka 77, 86
  Thailand 32–33, 42
Huberman, A.M. 102
Huebner, T. 24
Huh, J. 49
Hultberg, P. 45, 47

Iban 93, 111, 157
Ibrahim, N.A. 108
identity markers
  Canada 124
  English in Malaysia 91
  Finland 136
  Malaysia 96
  teachers' 120
  Thai in Thailand 24
immersion education 47, 119, 121,
    122, 139
immigrant languages 10, 117–118,
    124, 127
implicit messaging in textbooks 83–85
India 6, 12, 149
Indigenous languages
  Canada 116–117, 124–125, 138
  Finland 126
  Malaysia 93, 101, 111
  Sri Lanka 69
  valuing of 142–143, 157
inequality 15, 156–158, 164 see also
    elites; poverty; socioeconomic
    status
  and English 146–148
  Finland 134
  Malaysia 100, 101, 103
  South Korea 45, 52–53, 62–63
  Thailand 27, 29
informal learning 137
institutional theory 6–7
instructional contexts compared to
    naturalistic 10–11
instrumental value of English 15, 47,
    96, 151
Intensive English Teacher Training
    Programme (IETTP) 53

intercultural understanding 2, 73, 141,
    157, 163–164
interethnic attitudes 78–80, 87–89,
    147–148
international business, English as
    language of 6–7
international competitiveness
  English as language of 4–5, 11, 143,
    145, 146
  Finland 134
  Malaysia 91
  South Korea 47
  Thailand 32
internet, English on the 134, 136
Irshad, F. 69, 70

Japanese 46, 134, 139, 144
Jayawickrema, E. 71
Jeon, M. 58
Ji-hye, S. 5
Jo, S. 47
Johnson, D. 50

Kabilan, M.K. 107
Kadazandusun 93, 111
Kana, G. 4
Kang, C. 61
Kang, D.-M. 55, 56
Kang, H.D. 49, 64
Kang, H.-S. 54
Kang, Y. 50, 61, 63
Kantelinen, R. 137
Kapur, R. 72
Kaur, A. 26
Khoman, S. 28
Kim, B.-R. 44, 59
Kim, G.-J. 46
Kim, J.-W. 56
Kim, S. 60–61
Kim, T.-Y. 51, 52
Knouzi, I. 119, 120
knowledge economy 146
Korean 46
Kosonen, K. 24
Kulsiri, S. 33
Kumashiro, K.K. 56
Kyu-wook, O. 5

L1 see first language as resource;
    first language literacy
Lafayette, R. 2

Lahu 24, 157
language audits 65
'language ignorance' 7–8
language rights 115
'language showers' 133–134, 152
language socialisation 11, 143
Lapkin, S. 119, 120
Lappi, O. 130
Lathapipat, D. 27
'learned helplessness' 87
learner-centred education (LCE)
    Malaysia 100, 108, 110
    pedagogy 19
    South Korea 56
    Sri Lanka 87
    Thailand 23, 31, 33–37
Lee, J.-A. 53, 55
Lee, J.-H. 4, 60–61
Lee, K. 50, 53
Lee, M. 23, 36–37
Lee, Myung-Bak 47
Leesa-Nguansuk, S. 146
Lenneberg, E. 9
Leppänen, S. 136
Let's Learn English 83, 87
Lewer, N. 73
Li, D. 47
lifespan cognition theories 10
Lightbown, P.M. 77
linguistic diversity
    Canada 115–116, 117–118, 123–125,
        137–140
    Finland 114, 127, 132–135
    focus on trading partners 144–145
    generally 19–20
    Malaysia 92–98, 157–158
    plurilingualism 20
    South Korea 46–48, 65–66
    Sri Lanka 67, 69
    Thailand 24–25, 157–158
Linse, C. 48
literacy in first language
    Canada 123
    importance of 3
    Malaysia 97, 101
    South Korea 60, 65
    Sri Lanka 74, 88, 89
    Thailand 27
Little, A.W. 86, 87, 89
Littlewood, W. 19
Lo Bianco, J. 73

locally appropriate curricula 65,
    156–158
Long, M.H. 10
'losing face, avoiding 37
low-level students 55–56

Mady, C. 119, 120, 122, 124
Mala, D. 11, 23, 41
Malalasekera, N.S. 80
Malay 93, 94, 95, 96, 97, 109, 147
Malaysia 4, 91–112, 143–144, 146–147,
    155, 161
Mandarin Chinese 65, 94, 97, 109, 111,
    117, 139, 144
Marinova-Todd, S.H. 10
Maxwell, W. 122
medium of instruction see also English-
    medium education; mother
    tongue-medium education
    Canada 139
    Malaysia 93, 96, 97, 111, 147
    South Korea 50
    Sri Lanka 74–76, 78–80, 82, 89
    Thailand 25
metacognitive awareness 2
metalinguistic awareness 2
Methitham, P. 33
migration 20, 115–116, 117–118,
    123, 127
Mihat, W. 101, 102, 103, 111
Minority Rights Group, Malaysia 93–94
Mitchell, R. 11
Mohanty, A. 12–13, 14
Moodie, I. 49, 54, 55
Moon, J.I. 52, 151
Moon, Y.I. 16
mother tongue proficiency 13
mother tongue-medium education
    see also first language literacy
    generally 12–13
    Malaysia 94
    Sri Lanka 70, 74, 75–76
    Thailand 25, 43
motivation to learn languages 41,
    51–52, 80, 121 see also
    demotivation
Mudugamuwa, I. 76
Muhonen, S. 130
Muijs, D. 99
multilingualism
    attitudes to learning 149

Canada 115–116, 123–125, 137–139
Finland 132–138
Malaysia 92, 109–112, 144–145, 157–158
Sri Lanka 67, 69
Thailand 24, 25, 157–158
multinational corporations, as driver for English 6
Muñoz, C. 10–11
Mustaparta, A.K. 127, 134, 136, 137, 159
Myles, F. 151, 159

Nam, H. 49, 54
'national language reserve' 114, 134, 137, 151–152
nation-building 24, 68
'native speaker' ideology 59
native speaker teachers 57–59, 154–156
'native-like' standards, as goal 9, 32, 53, 154–156
native-speaker teaching assistants 53, 57
naturalistic contexts 10, 11
neoliberal education reform 56
Nesdale, D. 79, 80
Nguyen, D.C. 9, 160
Niemi, H. 129, 162
Nunan, D. 12

O'Connor, J. 156, 159
OECD 26, 44, 45, 61, 62, 118, 128–129
OECD/UNESCO 22, 28, 42
'Official English' movement in South Korea 46–47
official languages
Canada 113–114, 115, 116–117
Finland 114
Malaysia 93, 94, 95
Sri Lanka 67–68, 70–71
older learners 10, 11
ONCHR 80
O-NET (Thailand) 22, 23
Othman, J. 99
out-of-school exposure to English 18, 36, 65–66, 137, 141, 149–150, 159, 163

'parentocracy' 60, 148
parents 3, 9, 134, 148–149
Park, J,-K. 63
Park, J.S.-Y. 14, 58

Park, S. 48
Park Gueun-hye 64
Paronen, P. 130
partial competencies, developing 20
Patani Malay 24, 25, 157
peace-building 72, 73, 84
pedagogy
Canada 120–122
conclusions on 154–156
language teaching methods 18–19
Malaysia 99, 103–107
South Korea 48–54
Thailand 23, 34–37, 43
Perera, S. 67, 86–87
performance gap 45, 63
personal meaning, learning English for 52
Peters, E. 137
PISA
Canada 118, 120
Finland 127–128, 129, 161
South Korea 44, 45, 60, 62, 63
Thailand 27, 43
Piyaman, P. 41
play-based learning 133–134
plurilingualism 19–20, 24, 94, 154 see also bilingualism; multilingualism
Pomson, A. 37
'positive peace' 72–74
poverty 3, 27, 60, 84, 86–87, 141–142, 148
Powell, R. 92
power 13–14, 71
Prapaisit de Segovia, L. 40
Premarathna, A. 79
pre-primary education 30–31, 60, 118, 124, 126, 152
private schools 30, 31
private tuition 46, 52–53, 59–62
ProELT 104, 105, 106, 155
proficiency levels
basic English proficiency as goal 64, 100
and employability 148
expansion of notions of 134–135
Finland 131
French in Canada 119–120, 138–140
low-level students 55–56
Malaysia 95, 96, 97–99, 101, 102, 110, 111–112, 146–147
Sri Lanka 85–86

proficiency levels (*Continued*)
    teachers' 38, 52–53, 80, 99, 103–107,
      122, 158, 160
    'Teaching English through English'
      (TETE) 50
Pugh-Kitingan, J. 93
Punchi, L. 82
Punthumasen, P. 32
purpose of education 151

quality of education in general,
      improving 8, 142–143, 145–146
    South Korea 44, 47–48
    Thailand 26–30, 42
Québec 114–118

Rabbidge, M. 51, 155
Rajadurai, J. 96
Rajala, R. 137
Rashid, R.A.B. 96, 97, 102, 107, 110
Rassool, N. 6
Reardon, B.A. 72
reconciliation/peace-building 72
regional languages, adding to
    curriculum 43
Ricento, T. 6, 146
right to education 141–142
Ringbom, H. 126, 132, 133, 140, 159
Roach, S. 26
Rosen, Y. 73
rote learning 23, 31, 49, 110
Rungus 94, 157
rural areas
    conclusions on 160–161
    Finland 134
    Malaysia 97, 98, 99, 101, 103
    quality of education in Thailand
      27, 28
    Sri Lanka 76, 84, 85, 86, 87, 89
    Thailand 36, 41
Russian 7, 132, 134, 137
Ryu, D. 61

Saengpassa, C. 39
Saltarelli, D. 72
Sámi 126
Schleicher, A. 118, 128–129
Schweisfurth, M. 19
SEAMEO 42
Seargeant, P. 6
second language acquisition

Critical Period Hypothesis 9
    importance of context 10
second national language (2NL)
    education 67, 72–74, 76–80, 88–89,
      94, 127, 133, 148
Semai 111
Sen, A. 88
Seo, H.-S. 51
Sethunga, P. 78, 80
Shaari, A.H. 96
Shaeffer, S. 28, 30, 34–35
Shiga, M. 54, 57
Shin, H. 55
Silva, N.C.R. 72
Simola, H. 129, 135, 161, 162
Sinhala 67, 69, 70, 75, 76, 80, 88–89,
    147–148
Sjoholm, K. 126
Smith, E. 15
Smith, K.J. 93
So, K. 50, 61, 63
social capital 3, 149
social cohesion 67–68, 72, 88–90,
    94, 111
social harmony 1, 55, 68, 72, 82, 84
social justice 15, 17, 68
social status attached to speaking
    English 81–82, 95–96
social stratification 62–63
sociocultural aspects 37, 135
socioeconomic status
    access to private tuition 59–60
    and the benefits of English 3, 146–148
    English as an international
      language 141
    Finland 128
    Malaysia 100, 101, 109–112
    South Korea 44–45, 62–63
    Sri Lanka 86, 89, 147–148
    Thailand 27
Song, J.J. 46, 47, 61, 62, 63
Sørensen, B.R. 88
South Korea 4–5, 16, 44–66, 143–144,
    146, 148, 150, 151, 159
Southeast Asia Teachers Competency
    Framework 42
Spanish 7, 118, 134, 137, 139
specialist primary language teachers 54,
    55, 87
Sri Lanka 1, 8, 15, 67–90, 143, 145, 146,
    147–148, 155

standardised curricula versus local
needs 156–158
standardised tests 47, 53, 56, 85, 86, 98,
129, 131
Staudinger, U.M. 10
Stephen, J. 147
subtractive bilingualism 94
Sukamolson, S. 40, 41
Sundqvist, P. 136
supplementary materials 35, 83
Sustainable Development Goals
142–143
Swedish 114, 126–127, 131–132, 133,
134, 136, 137

Takahashi, K. 26
Tamil
Malaysia 94, 97, 109, 111
Sri Lanka 67, 69, 70, 75, 76, 80,
88–89, 147–148
Task-Based Language Teaching (TBLT)
18–19, 154–156
Taylor, A. 128
Taylor, C. 2
teacher training
cascade models 108
CPD (continuing professional
development) 18, 43, 103–108
Finland 130, 162
initial teacher training 53, 54–57, 58,
77, 87
Malaysia 98, 103–107
native speaker trainers 104, 155
in-service training 40, 43, 53, 104
Sri Lanka 77–78, 87
Thailand 35, 41, 43
teacher-centered pedagogy
continuance of 158
Malaysia 99
Thailand 23, 31, 33, 34, 37
teachers
accountability 130
autonomy 37, 50, 108, 162
Canada 120–122
consultation of 102–103
English as requirement for entry to
the profession 54
Finland 129–130, 140, 161–162
gender of 48, 78, 98, 133
generalist versus specialist teachers
54, 55, 87

as key change agents 66, 102, 161
Malaysia 103–108, 155
measures of teacher effectiveness 56
modelling language use 35, 53
native speaker models 32
persistence of inherited teaching
traditions 158
proficiency levels 38, 52–53, 80, 99,
103–107, 122, 158, 160
resources for language learning 18
second national language (2NL)
education 79
shortages of 3, 41, 80, 89, 103, 122
social status attached to speaking
English 81–82
South Korea 48, 56
specialist primary language teachers
54, 55, 87
stress and burnout 56
subject knowledge 38–40
Thailand 36, 38–40, 41, 156
teacher-student relationships 35, 37, 130
teaching assistants (native-speaker)
53, 57
'Teaching English through English'
(TETE) 50–51, 155
teaching methodologies 18–19
Teo, A. 39, 40
textbooks
Malaysia 101
South Korea 49
Sri Lanka 82–85
teacher training 104, 106
Thailand 34–35, 36
Thai 24
Thailand 4–6, 8, 11, 12, 22–43, 143–146,
150, 151, 155, 156, 158–159
Thanthong-Knight, S. 4
time allotted for foreign language
instruction
conclusions on 159
Finland 129
Malaysia 98–99, 110, 111
South Korea 48–49, 64
Sri Lanka 77, 86
Thailand 32–33, 42
TIMSS (Trends in International
Mathematics and Science Study)
44, 45
Ting, S.-H. 95–96
tourism 26

trading partners 6–7, 144–145
trait attribution tasks 79
Trakulkasemsuk, W. 26, 32
Tran, M.P. 137
translanguaging 88
trilingualism in Sri Lanka 73–74, 80, 88
Trudell, B. 12, 13, 25, 43
Turkey 16
TV 134, 136, 137

UK 8
UN Convention on the Rights of the
    Child 141–142, 145
UN Human Development Index (HDI) 4
UN Special Rapporteur 79–80
UN Sustainable Development Goals
    142–143
UNDP 5
UNESCO 24, 27, 116, 156–157
UNESCO 2017/18 Global Education
    Monitoring Report 25
United States 7, 13, 14
universalisation 13–14
university entrance tests 47–48, 61, 87
utilitarian approaches to language
    learning 65, 145, 151

Veratharaju, K. 107
Vietnam 9, 160

Vietnamese 144
vocabulary learning objectives 33
Vosniadou, S. 153, 160

Wagner, M. 2
Walker, E. 58
Wang, Y. 8
Wanniyalaeto 69
washback from high-stakes exams 40,
    51, 52, 64, 65, 91
well-being 43, 61–62, 63, 129
Werker, J.F. 124
Western influences
    CLT as 65
    course books 34–35
    English Programme in Korea (EPIK) 57
    generally 18, 19
    Thailand 33–34
Wickramanayake, D. 79
Wijesekera, H.D. 76, 78, 87–88, 89, 147
Williams, G. 143
Witte, J. 151
Workopolis 138
World Bank 8, 27, 28, 29, 72, 80, 81,
    145, 146

Yoon, L. 59
Young, M.Y.C. 15
'younger the better' 3–4, 9–11, 150, 159